Interpreting and Implementing the TRIPS Agreement

Interpreting and Implementing the TRIPS Agreement

Is it Fair?

Edited by

Justin Malbon

Professor, Law School, Monash University, Australia

and

Charles Lawson

Senior Lecturer, Law School, Griffith University, Australia

Edward Elgar

Cheltenham, UK • Northampton, MA, USA

Published by
Edward Elgar Publishing Limited
Glensanda House
Montpellier Parade
Cheltenham
Glos GL50 1UA
UK

Edward Elgar Publishing, Inc.
William Pratt House
9 Dewey Court
Northampton
Massachusetts 01060
USA

A catalogue record for this book
is available from the British Library

Library of Congress Control Number: 2008927696

ISBN 978 1 84720 144 7

Printed and bound in Great Britain by MPG Books Ltd, Bodmin, Cornwall

Contents

Contributors

Christopher Arup – Professor, Monash University, Melbourne, Australia

Ermias Tekeste Biadgleng – Programme Officer, Programme on Innovation and Access to Knowledge, the South Centre, Geneva, Switzerland

Graham Dutfield – Professor, Law School, Leeds University, Leeds, United Kingdom

Jakkrit Kuanpoth – Senior Lecturer, Faculty of Law, University of Wollongong, Australia

Charles Lawson – Senior Lecturer, Law School, Griffith University, Australia

Justin Malbon – Professor, Law School, Monash University, Australia

Jay Sanderson – Senior Research Fellow, Australian Centre for Intellectual Property in Agriculture, Brisbane, Australia

Xu Yi-chong – Professor, St Francis Xavier University, Canada

Abbreviations

AB: (WTO) Appellate Body
ACP: African, Caribbean and Pacific Nations
ASEAN: Association of Southeast Asian Nations
AUSFTA: Australia-United States Free Trade Agreement
BGB: German Civil Code *Bürgerliches Gesetzbuch*
CBD: Convention on Biological Diversity
Cipro: Ciprofloxacin, a drug produced by Bayer
CISG: (UN) Convention on the International Sale of Goods
COP: Conference of the Parties to the CBD
CTE: (WTO) Committee on Trade and Environment
DSB: (WTO) Disputes Settlement Body
DSU: (WTO) Dispute Settlement Understanding
EC: European Commission
EPC: European Patent Convention
EPO: European Patent Office or Organisation
EU: European Union
FAO: (UN) Food and Agriculture Organization
FTA: Free Trade Area or Agreement
GATS: (WTO) General Agreement on Trade in Services
GATT: (WTO) General Agreement on Tariffs and Trade
GSP: Generalised System of Preferences
ICTSD: International Centre for Trade and Sustainable Development
IP: Intellectual Property
IPR: Intellectual Property Rights
ISOC: (CBD) Inter-Sessional Meeting on the Operations of the Convention
ISP: Internet Service Provider
ITU: International Telecommunications Union
LDC: Less or Least Developed Country
MFN: Most-Favoured Nation
MTN: Multilateral Trade Negotiations
NAFTA: North American Free Trade Agreement
NGO: Non-Governmental Organisation
OECD: Organisation for Economic Co-operation and Development
PCT: Patent Cooperation Treaty

RAM: Random Access Memory
RTA: Regional Trade Agreement(s)
SACU: Southern African Customs Union
SUSFTA: Singapore-United States Free Trade Agreement
TBT: Technical Barriers to Trade
TIFA: Trade and Investment Framework Agreement
TK: Traditional Knowledge
TPM: Technological Protection Measures
TRIMS: (WTO) Trade-Related Investment Measures agreement
TRIPS: (WTO) Trade-Related Aspects of Intellectual Property Rights agreement
TRIPS-plus: Provisions in free trade agreements relating to intellectual property rights that exceed TRIPS requirements
TUSFTA: proposed Thailand-United States Free Trade Agreement
UN: United Nations
UNCTAD: United Nations Conference on Trade and Development
UNDP: United Nations Development Program
UNIDROIT Principles: UNIDROIT Principles of International Commercial Contracts
UPOV: International Union for the Protection of New Varieties of Plants
USTR: United States Trade Representative
VUSBTA: Vietnam-United States Free Trade Agreement
WCT: WIPO Copyright Treaty
WHO: World Health Organization
WIPO: World Intellectual Property Organization
WPPT: WIPO Performances and Phonogram Treaty
WTO: World Trade Organization

1. Introduction

The European Patent Office recently released its report *Scenarios for the Future* addressing how intellectual property regimes might evolve by 2025 (European Patent Office 2007). While there seems little doubt that intellectual property is now entrenched as a policy instrument intended to promote creativity, invention and innovations that contribute to economic development, the form and content of how this should be attained remains contested. This edited collection enjoins the global intellectual property debate by offering a range of perspectives about how the World Trade Organization's Agreement on Trade-Related Aspects of Intellectual Property Rights (TRIPS) is and should be interpreted and implemented. Like the *Scenarios for the Future* report, the collection takes a broader view of TRIPS' interpretation, recognising that to attain legitimacy and public trust and support TRIPS implementation must accommodate a broad spectrum of views and deliver real and meaningful economic developments to a wider global community.

According to the European Patent Office Report, the patent system must accommodate multiple players and stakeholders from different cultures and 'with different worldviews and aspirations who are working towards different goals within a global environment' (European Patent Office 2007, p. 11). The challenge, the Report notes, is to find ways of meeting the specific developmental requirements of disparate nations at a global level, 'because a system that blocks the access of poor people to essential drugs or food will eventually lose its credibility' (European Patent Office 2007, p. 11). The Report also asks whether TRIPS is adaptable enough in the face of changing global priorities in areas such as health and development, and how TRIPS will cope as the balance of power creates antagonisms around natural resources and energy as consumption rockets. It is evident that the TRIPS debate is central to determining the way in which global intellectual property rights are to be given effect. The agreement offers potential as a means for promoting greater international equity and engagement with the world economy or as a tool for wealthy nations to extract excessive rents from poorer countries. This book engages in the debate by examining the interpretive possibilities of the TRIPS' text as well as the external threats it faces, particularly the threat of relative irrelevancy due to free trade agreements containing TRIPS-plus terms.

Professor Arup adopts a contextual and socio-legal approach to viewing the way in which institutions approach the interpretation of key documents such as TRIPS. In doing so he avoids the temptation to ignore the complexity and fluidity of law making, and presents a way of thinking about TRIPS' interpretation that focuses on the continuing competitive and cooperative efforts to structure interpretation selectively and steer a path through the criss-cross of regulation. Although TRIPS is the most emphatic of the WTO agreements, it has, as he notes, its share of gaps, generalities, ambiguities, allowances, irresolutions and postponements.

With the negotiations about amending TRIPS having stalled, the grey areas are becoming even more contested. Some have argued there are flexibilities in the TRIPS' text that allows for a more 'equitable' interpretation of its provisions, although as Arup observes, the outcomes of this argument will be more in keeping with some members' legal cultures than others, with common law rather than civil law countries for instance. The negotiation stasis is not only shifting the action to treaty interpretation, it is also prompting an outbreak of TRIPS-plus terms in bilateral free trade agreements, which in turn is placing increased pressure upon the interpretation debate. Arup makes the apt observation that it is becoming increasingly difficult to find a straight line through the field:

> Those wanting more stringent and more relaxed interpretations compete actively. They experiment with a variety of strategies to influence interpretation inside the WTO and outside.

Arup asks why interpretation has been so unruly. After fulfilling his commitment to a contextualised examination, he claims that the increasing complexity and volatility of the political environment is clearly a reason. TRIPS was an extraordinary moment in international intellectual property law making, but such unifying law leads to new divergences that are never resolved conclusively. Importantly, he identifies the increasing complexity of creativity, invention and innovation and the volatility of the political environment as factors influencing interpretations, and calls for consideration about how best to channel these divergences.

Professor Dutfield is concerned about what he terms the new intellectual property fundamentalism, which in its most extreme form labels copying as piracy as if the two words are synonyms, and even links piracy to terrorism. The rhetoric has sharp jagged edges and is often aimed at demonising developing countries. The rhetoric appears to be designed to justify strategies adopted by principally the United States and the European Union to impose higher standards than TRIPS itself requires (TRIPS-plus). Looking to the problems that TRIPS was intended to solve about copyright piracy, unauthorised use of trade marks, and unwelcome competition from generic drug firms able to take advantage of patent regimes excluding drugs from protection, Dutfield asserts that TRIPS-plus strategies are being driven because TRIPS is inadequate as far as the demanders of ever higher intellectual property (IP) protection levels are concerned. He predicts, with a measure of irony, that the push by the US and the EC for unprecedentedly strong IP protection may be short-lived due to a reassessment of self-interest after the proportion of domestic patents granted to Indian and Chinese inventors increases dramatically, which may well occur over the next decade or so.

Professor Xu reminds us that making rules for the protection of intellectual property rights (IPRs) involves finding a balance between the interests of right-holders and right-users. The balance is presently skewed unduly in favour of right-holders. She sees that there are three institutions available for redressing the imbalance and advancing the multilateral agenda: the TRIPS Council, the WTO's Disputes Settlements Body and the WTO Ministerial Conferences. She sees that the enforcement of TRIPS inevitably involves political and diplomatic processes within which both active and passive instruments are utilised. Her discussion is mapped against the realpolitik of developing countries being vulnerable to aid withdrawal and trade sanctions for not complying with developed country demands, which reinforces their unequal bargaining power leading to excessive IP rent extractions and the significant transfer of resources from developing to developed countries. All this is causing an alarming disparity between the rich and poor. The legitimacy of the international trade system, at least insofar as it concerns intellectual property, will increasingly be undermined unless there is improved access to effective and affordable medicines and the technologies necessary for reversing the rising trend of high mortality and morbidity from infectious and non-communicable diseases.

Xu ultimately places faith in the WTO institutions as offering better opportunities for promoting the interests of developing countries than operating outside those institutions. She admits that the availability of the institutionalised setting through which collective actions can be taken does not by itself guarantee the rebalance of the interests of right-holders and right-users, but it does offer the best way for restraining the strong and protecting the weak.

Dr Kuanpoth raises concerns about the constraints TRIPS places upon developing countries on instituting domestic policies and laws that minimise socio-economic costs and maximise national benefits. He raises additional concerns about those countries being compelled into free trade agreements with TRIPS-plus terms. Developing countries enter a Faustian pact in which they are enticed by the possibility of tariff reductions on agricultural, clothing and other products in return for closing down opportunities to put forward issues of concern in the WTO forums. These issues include the harmonisation of TRIPS and the United Nations *Convention on Biological Diversity*, access to medicines, the protection of genetic resources, Farmers' Rights and the recognition and protection of traditional knowledge.

Kuanpoth is in essence offering a cautionary tale, in which he describes the ways in which bilateral free trade agreements lead to trade-offs that seriously damage the medium- and long-term interests of developing countries. His particular focus is on the impact of the TRIPS-plus standards on Asian countries, including Singapore, Vietnam and potentially Thailand. More generally, he raises concerns about TRIPS and TRIPS-plus impacts upon domestic laws and policies relating to living organisms, access to medicines and the protection of test data, trademarks and digital technologies.

Mr Biadgleng reminds us that TRIPS was promoted as an instrument that would balance the aims of advancing and protecting innovation with national public welfare interests. Developing nations' interests were to be accommodated, and possibly advanced. He notes, however, that with limited exceptions developing nations have yet to see the promised better days under TRIPS. They are primarily concerned about gaining IP benefits from learning, reverse engineering and the acquisition of existing technologies. Gaining meaningful outcomes from the enforcement of TRIPS will require, in Biadgleng's view, an assessment of the level of adjustment expected of developing countries, the degree that TRIPS facilitates technology transfers and the extent of the rewards for the contribution of developing countries in terms of biological resources, traditional knowledge and cultural expression.

TRIPS, as has been mentioned in other chapters, claims to be about balancing competing interests, balancing the interests of creators and users and balancing international and national policy objectives. The interests to be balanced in the creator-user scales must include the users in the developed countries, including generic pharmaceutical manufacturers. National policy-making that responds to domestic competing interests should be placed on the international-domestic balancing scales. In Biadgleng's assessment, a one-size-fits-all set of international standards is unsustainable. The required standards should be calibrated according to a nation's level of development. That is, the development balance should be brought into the mix. This would require a calibration of TRIPS and FTA implementation obligations at a level appropriate to a country's degree of development, without the expectation that they will implement obligations to developed nation standards. The task of achieving balance amongst these competing interests and objectives is, of course, somewhat complex.

Lawson and Sanderson centre their discussion upon the inherent conflicts between TRIPS and the United Nations' Convention on Biological

Diversity (CBD). TRIPS requires genetic materials to be protected by patents or a *sui generis* plant variety regime that privately appropriates genetic resources. TRIPS allows for patent or *sui generis* protection without requiring prior informed consent, mutually agreed terms and benefit-sharing. The CBD, on the other hand, sets those requirements. The way in which this apparent conflict is resolved has consequences for both the CBD and TRIPS. Lawson and Sanderson consider the likely effects various interpretation possibilities will have on the CBD and on TRIPS. They believe the CBD provides some insight into the failure to negotiate a satisfactory balance between access and benefit-sharing, as well as providing some indication of future developments that are likely to affect the interpretation and development of TRIPS.

Professor Malbon picks up on concerns expressed in a number of chapters in this book about the impact on developing nations of TRIPS-plus provisions in bilateral free trade agreements. Critics claim that the provisions are unfair or exploitative and serve the self-interest of a strong state at the expense of the interests of a weak state. He asks how it might be decided within a legal framework whether TRIPS-plus terms are unfair or exploitative. He proposes a plausible set of reforms of treaty law, which align with developments in domestic laws of contract, to deal with a party that abuses its dominant position by extracting unfair treaty terms. He then speculates on the impact such reform measures would have upon the interpretation and enforcement of the TRIPS agreement and TRIPS-plus terms in free trade agreements.

This book has its genesis in a forum that was held in Brisbane in late 2004 which was attended by a number of the authors of chapters in this book. The attendees presented early drafts of the chapters that appear in this book, which were discussed and debated during the forum. The forum was funded by a grant from the Australian Research Council, for which we are truly grateful. Professor Malbon also thanks Professor Lionel Bentley for kindly facilitating his stay for six months at the Centre for Intellectual Property and Information Law, University of Cambridge, which he heads. The book was compiled and edited in Cambridge and Brisbane. The editors thank for their assistance with this publication Catherine Elgar, Luke Adams and Nep Elverd at Edward Elgar.

REFERENCE

European Patent Office (2007), *Scenarios for the Future*, Munich, www.epo.org, visited July 2007.

2. TRIPS as competitive and cooperative interpretation

Christopher Arup

1. INTRODUCTION

This chapter offers a way of thinking about the field of TRIPS interpretation – not so much the record of interpretive practices as the continuing competitive and cooperative efforts to structure interpretation selectively and steer a path through the criss-cross of regulation. Interpretation is not a mechanical task, it depends on who is deciding and the styles and sources of law for deciding.

This chapter first lays out features of the law making field, characterises the mix of competitive and cooperative strategies, and asks whether this process of interpretation will ever be closed off. It then tests these propositions against the experience with interpretation in two places – inside the WTO as dispute settlement and outside within bilateral treaty making. Throughout, the experience is illustrated by the interpretations given to pharmaceutical patent protection.

2. THE DYNAMICS OF THE FIELD

Where should we look for insights into international intellectual property law making? Those from socio-legal studies would recommend that we do not start by looking for formal hierarchies of legal authority and settled, static rules for conduct. Globalisation blurs the boundaries between jurisdictions of law and multiplies the encounters between divergent legalities. It is better now to track the currents, circuits and communities of interpretation. For this task, organising principles like regulatory networks, global governance and legal pluralism will provide greater assistance.

As a force for convergence of law, the impact of TRIPS should not be underestimated. It provides a strong pro-rights framework for any consideration of intellectual property policy. TRIPS is by no means the first international intellectual property convention, but we can say it has truly projected intellectual property rights (IPRs) on a global scale. It is remarkable that we feel as if we are sharing the 'same' regulatory conversation about intellectual property.[1] Given the range to the World Trade Organization (WTO) membership and the substance of its prescriptions, almost every measure can now be read as a response to TRIPS.

In the early days of the WTO, the common contention was that law would replace power-based political relations and diplomatic deals made within closed circles with a transparent rule-based multilateral regime. The WTO would give security and predictability to the conduct of trade relations and within this rubric to the protection of intellectual property rights. In the most expansive view, the WTO agreements would become the constitution for a world economy. Legal constitutions constrain while authorising the operation of politics. So WTO law would be at the harder end of the spectrum of law. The agreements would produce rules and the task for the dispute settlement system would be to apply those rules, adjudicating on complaints of non-compliance.

2.1 Legal Pluralism

It is clear that an institution like the WTO gives politics and culture another space in which to play, as much as it produces legal rules to be applied. If the 1995 agreements are the key reference point for the members, broadly this potential lies in what Drahos (2002) characterises as a shift from coercion to dialogue.

On this understanding, we do not expect WTO law to operate in an autonomous space. It interacts with the economic, political and cultural currents that run through the WTO. The legal provisions have an impact on the calculations of the parties, they encourage cooperation and compliance, and they stimulate further discourse over norms. Nonetheless, interpretive practices are influenced, not just by internal legal considerations such as rule-conformity, but also by economic rationalities, political sensitivities, cultural mores – and indeed the divergent legal approaches the parties bring to interpretation. This means there is competition as well as cooperation.

In this vein, while TRIPS is the most emphatic of the WTO agreements, it has its share of gaps, generalities, ambiguities, allowances, irresolutions and postponements (Arup 2000). Such indeterminacy provides an opportunity to argue for competing interpretations of the text, especially regarding its 'flexibilities' (Lawson 2004). While there is a natural interest in any move in the direction of international legalisation, this looser fit finds resonance in much contemporary international relations and international law scholarship too (Finnemore and Toope 2001). This scholarship employs a more relaxed sense of where law is to be found as well as what it is. It lets in 'law making', not just by nation states and international conventions, but also by aid banks, philanthropic foundations, multinational corporations, indigenous peoples, research groups and share networks. WTO implementation has revealed the play in the system. The recent experience is marked by the emergence of fault lines within the developed countries, the increasing assertiveness of some of the larger developing nations, and the articulation of alternative views of intellectual property resources and entitlements by global civil society.

So, while some might strive to ensure that TRIPS is a self-contained source of law, its many soft spots mean that other texts and processes will enjoy a sphere of operation too. Those other legal sources are to be found both inside and outside the WTO. In the broadest view of the field, they include local custom, informal understandings, marketplace transactions, national constitutions and legislation, state and municipal government laws, administrative and judicial rulings, bilateral and regional agreements between governments, trans-national epistemic,` advocacy and regulatory networks and official international organisations and treaties.

In this criss-crossing of the field, the challenge for all scholars is not just to identify the multiple sources of intellectual property law. The task is to map the interactions between them. Thus, the interest lies in locating the actors, principles and processes that mediate the interaction between them (Braithwaite and Drahos 2000).

2.2 Competitive and Cooperative Interpretation

On this basis, interpretation forms part of an interface between legalities. It reaches out beyond the text of a particular treaty such as TRIPS to interact with other sources of law. As Slaughter (2004) has portrayed international law making, the links extend out both vertically and horizontally.

In a vertical relationship between the international and national levels, we expect public international law to limit the nation state's choice of intellectual property regulation. International standardisation or harmonisation can be understood as an effort to overcome the uncertainty of conflict of laws and regulatory competition. But such law does not simply direct national law. It might indeed coordinate national regulation, so that countries can be confident that other, possibly more powerful, countries will need to respect the same standards. But it might consciously leave gaps for national legislation and lower levels of law to operate. It might set minimum protections on which they can advance unilaterally or bilaterally. Or it might allow countries to take exceptions or attach qualifications to protections.

In horizontal relations, international sources of law will not simply be in competition for supremacy. The multi-polar pattern to international agreements provides scope for forum shopping and new issue linkages. There is movement back and forth between international organisations in search of the most sympathetic rules and resources (Helfer 2004). Such a situation suggests a rivalry between organisations and at times a clash of norms. But it also points to the interconnectedness, the complex interdependencies, which increase the chances of hybrid regimes being formed.

The strongest move is in search of a new agreement that will trump those existing agreements regarded as unsatisfactory. Yet such a move does not necessarily achieve this conclusion. It may instead increase the complexity of law in the field; it may produce alternative views of the same issue. These views provide further options or at the least they add to the symbolic capital to be deployed in the competition over interpretations.

Interaction occurs not just when new treaties are being aligned against existing treaties, domestic law and other sources of law. It is often an ongoing process. For instance, interaction is built into the implementation of a treaty. Thus, some treaties lay out their own provisions for interpretation in order to manage the interaction with other treaties. They might seek to control the sources that can be considered or even to be self-contained. They might fall back on the Vienna Convention on the Law of Treaties, which offers guidance not only for reading agreements but also for choosing between agreements where they overlap. Such a conscious design of relationships with other sources of law often gives rise to its own questions of interpretation. Certainly, all this proves relevant to the way in which the WTO dispute settlement bodies make interpretations of agreements such as TRIPS.

More interactively again, the treaties find spaces in which to defer to each other's view or draw on each other's resources. Compliance might be shown, for example, by adherence to the standards of another international convention or to customary law. Increasingly, treaties contain 'cohabitation clauses' and an interpretation might be sought that reconciles an agreement with other international law – the Vienna Convention specifies this approach. Operative here is a sense of the respective jurisdictions of the international organisations, or the capacity at least to let in consideration of sources external to the organisation and the texts of its own agreements, when shaping the interpretation of these agreements (Trachtman 1999).

How is all this done? Organisations develop a repertoire of processes by which to reach interpretations. We see this now at the WTO in the implementation of TRIPS. Dispute settlement rulings are one important avenue, but the members have other options. They include: the opportunity to exercise restraint in questioning compliance, the provision of alternative paths to compliance, negotiation, compromise and settlement of disputes, and the opportunity for the members to come together consensually to declare interpretations or grant waivers of obligations.

Given the weight of the WTO, much of this mediation of interpretations is occurring within and around the WTO itself. But it also occurs out on the broad terrain of international intellectual property. While the legal processes of the WTO present opportunities to channel the issues of interpretation in a variety of ways, the members are also prepared to go outside the WTO to resolve issues if need be. Fashioning new links, they shift to other multilateral forums or descend to bilateral or regional agreements. Eventually, those external solutions might affect the opportunities to take up the WTO's own TRIPS options, indeed they might enter into the conversation within the WTO itself over TRIPS.[2]

2.3 Constitutional Closure?

At this point, it is necessary to enter a caution. Perhaps there is a temptation to overstate the complexity and fluidity of law making. As lawyers, we remain interested in how clashes are resolved, at least for the time being, and how rulings are obtained in a particular case (see, for example, Pauwelyn 2003). Neither is this dogged inquiry out of keeping with the inquiries made in other international relations disciplines. They may still stress the part that power plays (persuasive, economic, coercive or hegemonic) in determining relationships between sources of law.

We might still expect certain countries to be striving, in coalition with producer interests, to see that their own distinctive models of intellectual property law are adopted as the international norm. Some such models are exported directly to other countries; others are inserted into the workings of the international networks and institutions. New ideas gain dominance; the power of particular countries returns. Once again, coercion may take the place of dialogue (Sands 2005).

In recent developments, some see signs of a new jurisprudence, at its strongest a new constitutionalism, which would entrench trans-national rights of commerce and property over national public regulation. They see legalisation returning in a very hard form. This new 'constitutionalism' has both a substantive programme and a legal approach to interpretation (Schneiderman 2000). In substance, global producers, traders and investors will enjoy commercial freedoms and property protections worldwide. Legally, there will be careful specifications, not just of the content of those rights, but also the means by which their interpretation will be determined. These specifications concern the tribunals which rule on disputes and the sources of law on which they draw for interpretations.

For now, constitutionalism is not an adequate way to characterise the WTO and the TRIPS agreement (von Bogdandy 2003). However, we should maintain a watching brief. It is fair to say that the moderating views have really only managed to keep the agreement open in certain respects. They have not resulted in any rewriting of the rules, whether to make intellectual property work harder for independent and alternative producers, or to guarantee access for essential uses outside the forces of the market. If the current round of negotiations comes to nothing, we may see a return to the dispute settlement system and an insistence on the current TRIPS legalities (McRae 2004).

Furthermore, the pressure to secure intellectual property interpretations is being applied at other points. Most notable are the bilateral FTAs, which promote detailed substantive requirements and seek to control relationships with other sources of law. Their intellectual property provisions mainly add to TRIPS protection (TRIPS-plus) but they do also seek to restate TRIPS provisions in terms favourable to one party's producers or to establish an alternative system to settle disputes. So, those wishing to limit the flexibilities within TRIPS do not let up; they shift their interpretive strategies to another tack.

This pressure could have a cumulative effect, modifying the impact of TRIPS itself. It circumvents the WTO process, perhaps building models to be taken back to it at a later date as evidence of a new regulatory consensus, while dividing countries that might have coalesced around an alternative policy.

This may be why some countries (as well as some non-government organisations) have reached the view that there is only limited value in exploring the flexibilities of TRIPS. While these spaces should be defended, a more positive approach is to construct a superior framework that elevates to a primary position such public goods as access to knowledge, cultural diversity and biological diversity. Then the guarantee of IPRs, and certainly any extension to IPRs, will be subordinated to these principles, to be supported only where they prove to be consistent.[3]

Can we say how this competition might end up? Attempts to construct new frameworks are an interesting move in the competition for new rules, indeed for interpretations of existing rules. Finally, though, these efforts are no more likely to order the relationships hierarchically than the other strategies we have identified. Instead, they too will add to the richness of the field and the need to mediate between competing legal perspectives. They remind us to remain alert to the diversity in the living law – in this instance the sheer variety of public and private intellectual property law around the world.

For instance, all sorts of countries are now putting FTAs and regional trade agreements (RTAs) together, including developing countries in Latin

America and Africa (Vivas-Ergui 2003). Any variation between the FTAs will stand in the way of saying a new consensus has been formed on international protection. As they produce alternative models for intellectual property, they provide further legal resources to deploy. In support of 'globalisation from below', Rodriguez-Garavito (2005, p. 267) suggests that 'counter-hegemonic trans-national coalitions' are also shifting among the different legal scales (international, national) and types (hard, soft) of law to exploit the tensions and contradictions in this 'kaleidoscopic legal landscape'.

In this chapter, I wish now to look for the evidence for this characterisation in two places. My aim here is not so much to document particular interpretations of TRIPS, which necessarily can be intricate, as to illustrate this competition and cooperation for interpretation.

3. WTO DISPUTE SETTLEMENT

3.1 Negotiated Interpretations

The evidence is found first within the WTO itself with the experience of dispute settlement. WTO dispute settlement starts with the notification of a complaint by a member country and the conduct of consultations to see if a mutually acceptable solution can be achieved. As in domestic civil justice, WTO complaints are often settled 'out of court'. After ten years, the TRIPS agreement has attracted only a few rulings of substance. Therefore, complaints, to the extent they are being made, might largely set up a bargaining relationship; this freedom to settle could produce creative solutions that go beyond mere observance of the legalities of the agreement.

While Art 3.5 of the DSU says all solutions formally raised under the consultation and dispute settlement provisions shall be consistent with the covered agreements, the notifications of mutually acceptable solutions do not appear to be screened rigorously by the Disputes Settlements Body (DSB) for their legality. Indeed, the parties are under no real compulsion to report their settlement to the WTO (Arup 2006). It is for them to determine whether a change to domestic legislation is necessary to bring it into conformity with TRIPS. The force of the complaint might be sufficient, at least for those who are not comfortable with protracted litigation.[4]

What safeguards exist to ensure they are limited to genuine complaints? Only now is a jurisprudence emerging that might place a legal check on the use of the system strategically to place pressure on a party to concede an interpretation. Criteria are being elaborated for the bringing of complaints and the making of requests for consultations and the establishment of panels. Nonetheless, the jurisprudence remains permissive because the system's preference is to encourage the parties to resolve complaints themselves (Arup 2006). Their procedural protection is the right to hold out for a panel ruling.

Nonetheless, a panel ruling that a provision is non-conforming does not necessarily produce compliance. As well as recourse to the Appellate Body, there are opportunities, which again may favour the more powerful countries, to go to arbitration over what constitutes compliance with a ruling. Many developing countries are daunted by this kind of procedural exhaustion, especially when their markets are not big enough to make retaliation much of a threat in the first place.

Thus, the United States Government has enjoyed some leeway in complying with rulings against it. Generally, it has been able to plead the separation between the Administration and Congress to say that it can only make its best efforts to obtain a change in the law.[5] It still has not changed its law to comply with the ruling in the *Copyright Homestyle Exemption* case (a change that would apply to the benefit of all members), preferring to pay the respondent, the European Communities, financial compensation instead (WT/DS160/R). Now in the *Cuban Rum* case (WT/DS176/AB/R), it has been given an indefinite reprieve from the need to comply.[6] So, it seems, interpretations can be resisted as well as promoted.

3.2 Receptive Adjudication

When asked to make a ruling, the WTO panels face choices about interpretation too. If there is space to highlight one aspect of interpretation here, it is the extent to which the panels let in consideration of sources external to the words of the substantive requirement itself. In the WTO context, to place greater weight on external sources is to allow discussion of the politics of meanings. So the panels face choices between open and closed, literal and purposive, insistent and deferential, narrow and broad approaches to interpretation.

One way to open up is to embrace external views, not just the views of the complainant and respondent government parties, but third party governments and non-government organisations. For example, the *amicus curiae* option has itself involved the interpretation of DSU Article 13 affording the panels the right to seek information and technical advice from any individual or body they consider appropriate. It has also attracted a hostile political response from most member governments.

A second is to read the text holistically, giving genuine weight to the preambles and statements of objectives and principles that might capture the important political compromises of the agreement. The DSU says the provisions of the agreements may be clarified in accordance with the customary rules of interpretation of public international law. The Appellate Body has accepted that those customary rules include the Vienna Convention on the Law of Treaties. The Convention in turn provides that a treaty should be interpreted in good faith, in accordance with the ordinary meaning to be given to the terms of the treaty, in their context and in light of its object and purpose (see Lennard 2002). However, in the *Canada–Patent Protection for Pharmaceutical Products* case, the panel stressed that the words of Art 30 represented the political compromise between protection and access; the earlier Arts 7 and 8 could not be enlisted to expand the scope of exceptions (WT/DS114/R).

Both the panels and the Appellate Body have been criticised for a strictly literalist approach, preferring to consult dictionaries for the meaning of words rather than think about the purposes and policies behind the WTO agreements. The Appellate Body does have a narrower brief than the panels; it is charged under DSU Art 17.6 to examine the issues of law covered in the panel reports and the legal interpretations developed there by the panels. Nonetheless, Weiler's characterisation is negative: 'the almost obsessive attempts of the Appellate Body to characterize wherever possible the normal, wide-ranging, sophisticated, multi-faceted and eminently legitimate interpretations of the Agreement as "textual" resulting from the ordinary meaning of words' (2001, p. 206). Picciotto (2005) suggests that this legal formalism stems from its concern about legitimacy.

Of course a key question is the scope to be allowed to national measures before they are ruled non-conforming with TRIPS. Faced with a complaint of inconsistency, a panel is required to interpret both the WTO provision and the national measure in question. It is offered the respondent's own characterisation of the national measure as being consistent with TRIPS, or perhaps an assurance that it will administer the measure in a manner that is consistent (see also TRIPS Art 1.1).

To what extent should the panel defer to that characterisation? Should it, as part of its standard of review, give the national measure a margin of appreciation (Howse 2000; Picciotto 2003)? The Appellate Body says, because the duty of the panel is to uphold the rights and obligations in the agreements, the interpretation must be made objectively.

Instead, we might suggest, the allowance for the national measure, and the means for managing difference, might be found in the liberal way the TRIPS provision itself is interpreted. So, for example, in *Canada – Patent Protection for Pharmaceutical Products*, the panel would not take evidence that the law of another member country, the United States, had contained an exception prior to TRIPS to allow secondary producers to seek regulatory approvals as evidence of the intent behind Art 30. Nor would it take evidence that several other countries (including Australia) had introduced exceptions after TRIPS had commenced, as evidence of subsequent state practice. But it did interpret Art 30 as allowing the exception.

The panels must also manage the relationship with other international treaties and the general (non-convention) international law. Here the tribunal faces a choice whether to insist on the precedence of the TRIPS agreement to the exclusion of other international law, or to find a way to accommodate and thus to promote the standards being set in other international forums.[7]

Only rarely do the WTO agreements make links outside expressly. An exception is the incorporation of selected Paris and Berne articles within TRIPS. TRIPS draws directly on the cognitive work of these established conventions, even their considerable political legitimacy. This debt extends to the interpretive work done with these conventions, for example the panel in the *United States-Homestyle Exemption* case drawing on the *acquis* of Art 9(2) of the Berne Convention to help with the interpretation of the scope of the exceptions to copyright infringement.

Otherwise, the argument is whether that law forms part of the surrounding rules of international law, which, on the strength of Vienna Convention Art 31(3)(c), should be taken into account, at least in interpreting the provisions of the TRIPS agreement itself (Bartels 2001). This capacity to look beyond the words again is vital to the tenor of TRIPS. It encourages respect, not just to the other IP conventions such as the 1996 WIPO treaties, but also to international treaties with an alternative take (somewhat) on the field such as the United Nations Convention on Biological Diversity.

A brake on this is the Art 31(3)(c) requirement that this other international law is applicable in the relations between the parties. The Appellate Body is saying that the panels are not obliged to take such law into account unless the parties to the dispute are bound by that law (WT/DS291/R). Perhaps all members of the WTO need to be bound, given their common interest in how the WTO agreements are interpreted. For the international law that is not binding like this, the panels have a choice whether to give weight to it. In the *United States-Homestyle Exemption* case, the Panel was happy to reconcile TRIPS with the WIPO Treaties, WCT and WPPT, even though they were not operative at the time. The Panel found that there was a considerable overlap in signatories and they were all 'part of the same corpus of international intellectual property protection'.

The panels must decide how ready they are, not just to resolve ambiguities, but also to fill gaps in the agreements where they fail to offer a solution to the dispute. Should they feel free to build a common law of international trade? Some take the view that the gaps and limits are there deliberately; they represent the compromise decisions taken at the negotiation stage over the legitimate reach of TRIPS (Krajewski 2001). In support, DSU Art 3.2 says that the rulings of the panels cannot add to or diminish the rights and obligations provided in the covered agreements.

Some have been advocating recourse to equitable principles to temper the application of the TRIPS agreement. Such WTO rights should be exercised fairly and in good faith, out of consideration for the developing countries, which in the past have enjoyed allowances of special and differential treatment (Footer 2001). Such a willingness to fill gaps could just as well result in stronger protection. If non-violation complaints were made available, the scope for protective interpretations would increase considerably. Again this approach is controversial. Whatever outcomes it might produce substantively, it is more in keeping with some members' legal cultures than others, with common law rather than civil law countries for instance (Weiler 2001).

3.3 Changing Tack

The rulings in *United States-Homestyle Exemption* and *Canada-Patent Protection for Pharmaceutical Products* illustrate the many interpretive choices before the panels. They also hint at the wider strategies to manage interpretation.

Following the disagreements at the 1999 Seattle Ministerial Meeting, we see that the management strategies search wider again, with the members withholding key issues from the dispute settlement bodies. At a delicate moment for relations between the North and the South, the multi-claim disputes, United States-Brazil and United States-Argentina, were settled out of court (Sell 2003; Ghanotakis 2004). Then the members applied a moratorium to bringing complaints under the TRIPS agreement, which has held until today, except for the dispute over Europe's geographical indications and now between the United States and China over enforcement.

At the 2001 Doha Meeting of Ministers, the members fashioned a collective solution to interpretation on the issue of TRIPS and public health. The Doha Declaration can be regarded as an attempt to allow members liberal use of TRIPS flexibilities, free from challenge in the dispute settlement system. Among its provisions, it states that each member has the right to grant compulsory licences and the freedom to determine the grounds on which such licences are granted; following Art 31(b), it says that each member has the right to determine what constitutes a national emergency or other circumstances of extreme urgency, it being understood that public health crises, including those relating to HIV/AIDs, tuberculosis, malaria and other epidemics, can be so. It also reinforces Art 6 in stating that each member is free to establish without challenge its own regime for the exhaustion of rights (WT/MIN(01)/DEC/2).

Despite this breadth, the Declaration left issues to be resolved within the TRIPS Council. As we know, Art 31(f) insists that compulsory licensing should be exercised predominantly for the supply of the domestic market of the member authorising such use. Most developing countries have not enjoyed the capacity to manufacture drugs locally.[8] It took almost two years for the WTO to devise a system that would permit trade in generic drugs made under compulsory licence (Press/350/Rev.1; see also Matthews 2004).

On this occasion, the members chose to waive the condition in Art 31(f). Perhaps a permissive interpretation either of Art 31 or 30 would have been too blatant an abuse of the legalities. The waiver was a temporary one; late in 2006 they amended TRIPS to incorporate the system (IP/C/41). The system is elaborately constructed, placing restrictions on both exporting and importing countries. Paradoxically, it may generate demand for interpretation itself. Braithwaite and Drahos observe that the provisions reveal a familiar pattern: 'Developing countries are drawn into complex juridical webs that they do not have the resources to disentangle and that ultimately do not serve them' (2004, p. 220).

For example, the United States Government has argued for a narrow reading of the concession in the Declaration to 'public health crises including those relating to HIV/AIDS, tuberculosis, malaria and other epidemics'. In another instance, right until the moment that amendment was adopted, the United States was insisting that the Chairman's statement be part of the text. This statement promises an extremely conservative use of compulsory licensing. Instead, it has an uncertain status, being read out again at the time the amendment was adopted.[9] Use of the system is yet to be tested; it looks as if Thailand will be the first to do so.[10]

3.4 Shifting Forum

Other issues have been kept from TRIPS interpretation by pursuing dialogue with a forum outside the WTO. For example, members might have used dispute settlement to test the TRIPS legality of national systems for the recognition and reward of traditional knowledge. These systems might be challenged as inconsistent with TRIPS – as a condition placed on the patentability of plants and animals under Art 30 or an effective *sui generis* system for the protection of plant varieties under Art 27.3(b).

Some countries want TRIPS amended to make such a system a requirement for patentability, rather than a permissible space in which countries try to obtain acceptance of their own system individually. A disclosure requirement has the best chance. The deal would be agreement to patent protection for plant and animals becoming obligatory. The question is whether it would be better to leave traditional knowledge to WIPO or the CBD (Dutfield 2004). WIPO has worked on models for take-up in national legislation, the United States only participating on the basis that there be no treaty (Gibson 2005). Now, WIPO has produced some very useful draft objectives and principles. The CBD too has been concerned largely with model building, though it is moving slowly now towards an access and benefit-sharing regime (Lawson and Sanderson, this volume).

So what role does the output of these other international organisations play in the interpretation of TRIPS Art 27.3(b)? While they are unlikely to override the patents intellectual property framework, they generate alternative symbolic capital (Helfer 2004). Perhaps they slow the move to patentability of plants and animals. More positively, they suggest that recognition and reward for traditional knowledge can be compatible with patentability. Given, however, the Appellate Body's conservatism about recognising other international instruments, the amendment of TRIPS might still be necessary.

4. THE BILATERAL FREE TRADE AGREEMENTS

From outside the WTO again, the new wave of FTAs is providing another source of interpretations. These FTAs bear a complex relation to TRIPS, one that is partly supportive and partly supplementary, but partly competitive too.

The United States has been most active promoting stronger intellectual property provisions bilaterally. For the developing countries, a bilateral intellectual property agreement might have come as a condition for obtaining a bilateral investment agreement from a country that is a major source of much needed capital. These countries were brought on side too with threats of trade sanctions, withdrawal of aid and preferences, and complaints to the WTO (Drahos 2001). Now, the more comprehensive FTAs offer the prospect of improved market access for industrial goods and agricultural produce, proving attractive also to developed countries such as Australia.

Securing commitments from the bilateral partner may form part of a broad strategy to strengthen intellectual property rights. The United States is writing a 'script' for a series of bilateral agreements; the AUSFTA intellectual chapter was very much like the US-Singapore, US-Chile and US-CAA chapters. This script is carefully revised and refined in the light of experience.

Interaction with the TRIPS agreement means that in each case the FTA provisions are adopted on an MFN basis, so that the partner gives the protections to the nationals of the other members of the WTO immediately (Vaver and Basheer 2006).[11] Australia, for example, extends the stronger protections it has given United States nationals, to the nationals of other members of the WTO, such as the countries of the European Union, Japan and China, without the guarantee of reciprocity. Then the protections are included in later FTAs. The United States moves on to other partners and Australia too is inclined to help in disseminating the model when it seeks to conclude FTAs with countries in its region, such as the People's Republic of China.[12]

However, any variation between the FTAs will also stand in the way of saying a new consensus has been formed on international protection. Australia may be a willing enough partner in dissemination; nevertheless it will need to judge whether intellectual property demands prejudice its goals in other sectors and its relations generally with its prospective partners. Ultimately, it might be more politic to confine its demands to the specific problems Australian producers are encountering, rather than to push the maximum agenda on intellectual property.

It is easy to forget that many other FTAs and RTAs are being forged too, some with their own intellectual property provisions. Take, for example, the Andean Community pact on recognition of traditional knowledge (Ruiz 2004). The most likely outcome is that the bilateral agreements add to complexity and diversity. They form part of the process of competitive and cooperative interpretation; the members of the Andean Community for instance are now being split by the United States' demands for FTAs.[13]

5. FTAS-TRIPS

Mostly, these FTA commitments are regarded as supplementing or extending TRIPS protections; they are seen as 'TRIPS-plus'. TRIPS expressly authorises the members to give more extensive protection to intellectual property than its own provisions require. Art 1.1 states that the members are free to institute more extensive protection than is required by the agreement, provided such protection does not contravene the provisions of the agreement.

But do they simply extend protection beyond TRIPS? In issue here is the nature of the TRIPS provisions. For instance, in its bilateral initiatives with developing countries, the United States has been pressing its partners to forego their allowances or flexibilities under TRIPS. These forbearances include the phase-in periods for implementation, the right to except plants and animals from patentability, the right to adopt a *sui generis* system of protection for plant varieties other than the 1991 version of the International Convention for the Protection of Plant Varieties (UPOV), and access to the full set of grounds for compulsory licensing in Art 31 (and beyond) (Vivas-Ergui 2003; Oliva 2003). Is it simply TRIPS-plus to remove these allowances or could they be viewed as part of a balance struck in TRIPS between protection and access, giving member countries assurances that they have some flexibility?

The drive to cut through the troublesome vagaries and allowances of TRIPS can also be seen close at hand in the Australia-United States Free Trade Agreement (AUSFTA; Arup 2004). While much of the content of the intellectual property chapter is clearly TRIPS-plus, it also does away with some of the TRIPS flexibilities. It does not always do so directly. Rather, the text contains its own versions of key TRIPS provisions. Such provisions are being restated or elaborated expressly, 'for the sake of greater certainty'. The effect is to narrow and tighten the TRIPS provisions. Are these restatements simply TRIPS-plus, or do they obtain a more favourable version of a TRIPS provision for one of the partners?[14]

This approach is evident on several fronts. By way of illustration, we focus once again on pharmaceutical patent protection. The backdrop to this AUSFTA interest is the desire to safeguard the rights of pharmaceutical producers, when there is such global concern about access to essential medicines. If access is a concern that must be met, the United States Government wants to ensure that cheap drugs are not re-routed from the developing countries and imported into the more affluent markets like Australia. These cheaper drugs might be either discounted brand-name lines or generic copies.[15] The United States wants also to discourage developed countries from becoming involved in the manufacture of generics, under compulsory licence, either for their domestic market or for export to other countries (Kuhlik 2004).[16]

5.1 The AUSFTA Provisions

The AUSFTA intellectual property rights chapter begins by acknowledging key multilateral agreements. Each party affirms that it has ratified or acceded to a list of such agreements. The list includes the Patent Cooperation Treaty (1970), the Paris Convention (1967) and TRIPS itself (1974). Each party also promises to make its best efforts to comply with the provisions of the Patent Law Treaty (2000).

However, AUSFTA makes express provision for patent rights too. In certain instances, its specifications restate or elaborate on the TRIPS provisions. So, in a truncated version of TRIPS Art 27.1, AUSFTA Art 17.9 opens by requiring each party to make patents available for any invention, whether a product or process, in all fields of technology.

AUSFTA goes on to say that the parties confirm that patents shall be available for any new uses or methods of using a known product. This kind of 'refinement' is significant even in the established jurisdictions like Australia. Not only do competitors apply for their own patents, the first producers attempt to extend the life of their inventions by obtaining further patents (a practice sometimes called 'evergreening').

Like TRIPS, patentability is subject to the requirement that an application satisfy the demands of novelty, inventive step and industrial application. However, AUSFTA reaches further, requiring each party also to provide that the claimed invention is useful if it has a specific, substantial and credible utility. This interpretation of the utility requirement has previously been spread at a lower level through the understandings reached between the patent offices in the Trilateral Cooperation Commission (Davies 2002).

AUSFTA confines the permitted exclusions to patentability to just two of the TRIPS categories, the *ordre public* and morality exception and the methods of treatment exception. With this curtailment, we might say that the FTA partner is choosing to be cut out of the dialogue at the WTO over the exception for plants and animals.

5.2 Import and Export Controls

As we saw above, TRIPS interpretation has faced a difficulty reconciling the Articles laying out the patent holder's rights with those making allowance for exceptions and limitations. Here especially, AUSFTA aims to cut through the uncertainties of TRIPS; it is purposeful, circumscribing Australia's options.

AUSFTA does not actually repeat the TRIPS Art 27.1 requirement for patents to be available and patent rights to be enjoyable without discrimination as to place of invention, field of technology, or whether products are imported or locally produced. Neither does it include the TRIPS Art 28 enumeration of the patent's exclusive rights, which are to prevent third parties from making, using, offering for sale, selling – or importing for those purposes.

AUSFTA does reproduce the wording of TRIPS Art 30. It also contains provision for governments to grant compulsory licences. However, it confines the TRIPS Art 31 grounds to two: non-commercial public use and the case of national emergency or other circumstances of extreme urgency. It includes nothing of the Doha Declaration on TRIPS and Public Health to assist with interpretation of this second ground.[17] Yet it does not include the constraint of Art 31(f).

With that kind of set-up, AUSFTA limits several key rights. One control concerns the importation of patented drugs sold more cheaply in another country. AUSFTA does not adopt TRIPS Art 6. The United States has argued that the Article is not substantive (Abbott 2002). It just keeps issues of exhaustion, and the legality of importing copies for sale in a market overseas, out of WTO dispute settlement. Other countries say it means, despite the wording of Arts 27 and 28, that a member country may authorise parallel importation.

Instead, AUSFTA Art 17.9.4 aims to secure the patent holder's rights to control imports of cheaper drugs. It requires each party to provide that the exclusive right of the patent holder to prevent importation shall not be limited by the sale or distribution outside its territory, at least where the patentee has placed restrictions on import by contract or other means.[18]

Another control concerns the export of generic drugs. Some countries clearly plan to do so, India primarily, but also some developed countries with production capacity, the Canadian Government recently passing legislation to enable its industry to do so. AUSFTA Art 17.9.6 seeks to limit this move, tying down TRIPS Art 30 and the freedoms allowed in the panel ruling in *Canada–Patent Protection for Pharmaceutical Products*. So it provides that if, under the limited exceptions allowed to the exclusive rights, a party permits the use of the subject matter of a subsisting patent to generate the information necessary to support an application for marketing approval of another pharmaceutical product, then that product must not be made, used, sold, or *exported* for any other purpose.

5.3 Marketing Generic Drugs

AUSFTA also seeks to limit the rights of secondary producers (the producers of generic drugs) who seek to rely on the undisclosed test data the patent holder has originally submitted to obtain marketing approval for a new pharmaceutical product.

First, AUSFTA gives the patent holder exclusive use of the data for a minimum of five years. TRIPS Art 61 only requires members to prevent unfair competitive use of such data.

Thereafter, a party may permit a secondary producer to use the data to support an application for marketing approval. However, AUSFTA Art 17.10.4 requires the parties to provide measures to prevent the springboarding, secondary producer from actually marketing a product or a product for an approved use – where that product or use is 'claimed in a patent'.

In the United States and Canada, this kind of protection has drawn the drugs safety administrations into policing patents. It has given further encouragement to evergreening. To implement this requirement, the Australian Government chose instead to place an obligation upon the secondary producer, when it seeks marketing approval, to certify that it will not be doing so. The courts are empowered to apply a penalty if the certificate is false. This places the onus on the secondary producer to gauge the validity and scope of the subsisting patent.

At the time the FTA was being implemented, the opposition parties held a majority in the upper house of the Australian Parliament (the Senate). The Labor Opposition countered the Government requirement with an amendment obliging the patent holders to certify the bona fides of any infringement proceedings they might take against the secondary producer who does go to market. They must certify that the proceedings are commenced in good faith, have reasonable prospects of success and will be conducted without unreasonable delay. A court may apply a penalty if the certificate is false. The amendment also provides for orders if the plaintiff obtains an interlocutory injunction in such circumstances.

The United States Administration first expressed its concern about this course of action by reserving its rights to certify that Australia's implementing legislation was in accordance with the AUSFTA requirements (Australian Financial Review 2004a and 2004b). It queried the Government's own legislation, suggesting it did not go far enough to prevent the marketing of products claimed in a patent. It then charged that the Opposition's amendment undermines the FTA's protection for patents. But it has raised a further point: that the amendment runs contrary to the TRIPS Art 27.1 requirement, omitted from the AUSFTA counterpart, that patents be granted and rights enjoyed without discrimination as to field of technology.[19]

Despite this pressure, the Australian Government did not attempt to have the amendment repealed. In mid-November 2004, the United States Administration exchanged letters with the Australian Government certifying compliance with the FTA. In its letter the Australian Government reassures the United States that the generic producers will have to give notice in advance of their product entering the marketplace. This is to ensure that patent holders will have adequate opportunity to seek injunctive relief against infringers before infringing products reach the market.

The United States remained adamant that the Labor amendment imposes a 'potentially significant, unjustifiable, and discriminatory burden on the enjoyment of patent rights, specifically of owners of pharmaceutical patents'.[20] The Administration signalled it would watch closely how the Australian law is implemented, reserving the right to take action – either bilaterally under the FTA or in the WTO under the DSU – if it believes

United States producers are being treated unfairly (Australian Financial Review 2004c and 2004d).

It may be that another reason for the FTA restatement of TRIPS is to give the parties access to the inter-governmental dispute settlement process of the FTA – where AUSFTA overlaps with TRIPS, not just where the FTA carries TRIPS-plus rights. In any case, as we have seen, the coverage of the two agreements is not always that easy to separate.

Where non-compliance with a WTO agreement is alleged, the WTO DSU presses members to use the WTO itself for redress (DSU Art 23; see WT/DS152/R regarding unilateral national measures of self-help). However, in Art 21.4, AUSFTA purports to give the complaining party a choice between its own dispute settlement and the WTO (John 2004). The choice allows the complainant to forum shop for the more favourable interpretation. Commentators have been counselling FTA countries to exercise caution when agreeing to one-on-one dispute settlement provisions with more powerful countries (Drahos 2006).

The dispute settlement chapter of AUSFTA states that the panels shall 'consider the provisions of the Agreement in accordance with applicable rules of interpretation as reflected in Arts 31 and 32 of the Vienna Convention on the Law of Treaties'. If the complainant chooses the FTA process, will the application of Vienna Convention Arts 31 and 32, and specifically Art 31.3(c), let in consideration of the WTO TRIPS jurisprudence or that of the other multilateral conventions? It is possible the FTA ruling will put a particular bilateral gloss on key TRIPS provisions. This interpretation will apply between the two parties to the FTA. The broader question is whether this interpretation will be given weight, should the same issue be raised at the WTO (Waincymer 2002, pp. 176–189).[21]

6. CONCLUSIONS

The closure that produced the 1994 TRIPS agreement now seems like an extraordinary moment in international intellectual property law making. More treaty making has occurred, notably the WIPO WCT and WPPT, but the field has become more fluid and less certain. Where treaty making has stalled, the action has moved to treaty interpretation. Increasingly it is difficult to find a straight line through the field. Those wanting more stringent and more relaxed interpretations compete actively. They experiment with a variety of strategies to influence interpretation both inside and outside the WTO.

This chapter concentrates on describing or capturing the fluid multipolar field of interpretation. We might begin to ask why interpretation has been unruly. The increasing complexity and volatility of the political environment is clearly a reason. Given the subject matter of intellectual property, the pace of change in research, technology and markets is another factor. Nonetheless, the explanations are also to be found in the nature of international law itself. Teubner (2001) shows how unifying law leads to new divergences. Unifying law, such as the TRIPS agreement, is really a legal irritant that sets off a chain reaction. We might talk about how best to channel that reaction, as scholars of the WTO do so very constructively (see, for example, Pauwelyn 2006), but never, I would submit, conclusively.

NOTES

1. On the nature of such conversations, see Black 2002.
2. 'NGOs say use of bilaterals impairs transparency and access to TRIPS', *World Intellectual Property Report*, volume 19, issue 2, p. 23, 2005.
3. The most current example is the promotion of the development agenda at WIPO. Its supporters insist it be discussed in conjunction with proposals to strengthen intellectual rights within a Substantive Patent Law Treaty or a Broadcasting, Cablecasting and Webcasting Organizations Treaty. Progress has been slow but now WIPO claims some success, see WIPO, 'Member States Make Significant Headway in Work on a WIPO Development Agenda', WIPO Press Release PR/478/2007, Geneva, 26 February 2007; 'WIPO Members Agree on Development Agenda', *Bridges Weekly Trade News Digest*, volume 11, number 22, 20 June 2007.
4. Ghanotakis 2004 reads the United States' disputes with Argentina, South Africa and Guatemala this way. Certainly, the empirical evidence indicates that complainants are generally successful in obtaining concessions from respondents in settlements out of court and this holds true for TRIPS complaints (Busch and Reinhardt 2003).
5. To the chagrin of supporters of India who remember that in *India–Pharmaceutical Patents* the Government was required to obtain legislative change to secure mail-box protection legally, see WT/DS50/AB/R.
6. 'US Given Indefinite Reprieve in Cuban Rum Case', *World Intellectual Property Report*, volume 19, issue 8, p. 18, 2005.
7. This search for context might also draw in the other WTO agreements, not just in their direct application to trade in goods and services with intellectual property content but for the sake of interpreting TRIPS itself. But the panels have encountered problems applying GATT jurisprudence to an agreement as novel as TRIPS, see WT/DS50/AB/R.
8. Those that do are constrained now that the grace period for instituting patent protection is over, e.g. for India, see Matthews 2004.
9. 'International: WTO Deal on TRIPs/Medicine Welcomed by Governments, Industry', *World Intellectual Property Report*, volume 19, issue 8, p. 18, 2005.
10. Thailand might do so, see 'Thailand: Health Ministry Breaks Patents on Heart Drug, HIV Treatment Kaletra', *World Intellectual Property Report*, volume 21, issue 3, p. 23, 2007. Rwanda is the first country to notify its intention to import under the paragraph 6 system, see WTO News, 20 July 2007.
11. At least so far as they fall within the TRIPS definition of the 'protection' of 'intellectual property', see TRIPS Art 3 and WT/DS176/AB/R.
12. The Australian Minister for Trade once said we would be a beachhead for stronger intellectual property protection in Asia; we would use the FTA as a template when we go to negotiate in China; see *The Australian* (2005), 'All Eyes on Asia in Copyright Duel', 1–2 January 2005, Sydney: News Corporation.

13. 'Peru, Columbia Spar with Venezuela on IP, Threatening Andean Accord', *World Intellectual Property Report*, volume 20, issue 3, p. 3, 2006. See further, 'IP Standards in the US – Peru FTA: Health and Environment', *Bridges Monthly Review*, volume 10, number 1, p. 17, January–February 2006.
14. Compare the European experience too: Vaver and Basheer 2006.
15. The producers may practise price differentiation and discount in some markets; the generic copies may be made while a grace period applies under TRIPS to patent protection or where compulsory licensing is allowed.
16. There is also a concern with the 'leakage' of pharmaceuticals which are provided at affordable prices under public pharmaceutical benefits schemes; see Drahos et al. 2004. American senior citizens cross the border into Canada to take advantage of its scheme.
17. The United States Government resisted a request from the Australian Government that it be included.
18. Australia is among 23 developed countries that have ruled themselves out of importing generic drugs made under compulsory licence as part of the TRIPS scheme.
19. Note Canada's complaint against the European Communities, WT/DS153 which has not been prosecuted.
20. Exchange of letters, 17 November 2004. The letters can be inspected at the USTR website, at www.ustr.gov.
21. In WT/DS308/AB/R the Appellate Body upheld the Panel's decision that it had no discretion to decline its jurisdiction in a case properly brought before it. Comity with NAFTA was not a crucial factor in its interpretation of the relevant WTO agreement (the GATT 1994).

REFERENCES

Abbott, F. (2002), 'The TRIPS-legality of Measures Taken to Address Public Health Crises: Responding to USTR State-industry Positions that Undermine the WTO', in D. Kennedy and J. Southwick (eds), *The Political Economy of International Trade Law: Essays in Honour of Robert Hudec*, Cambridge: Cambridge University Press, pp. 311–342.

Arup, C. (2000), *The New World Trade Organization Agreements: Globalizing Law Through Services and Intellectual Property*, Cambridge: Cambridge University Press.

Arup, C. (2003), 'The State of Play of Dispute Settlement "Law" at the WTO', *Journal of World Trade*, 37(5), 897–920.

Arup, C. (2004), 'The United States-Australia Free Trade Agreement: The Intellectual Property Chapter', *Australian Intellectual Property Journal*, 15(4), 205–226.

Arup, C. (2006), 'Perspectives on WTO dispute settlement: the role for negotiated solutions' in Amanda Gore [et al] (eds) *Ten Years of WTO Dispute Settlement: Australian Perspectives*, Barton ACT: Office of Trade Negotiations of the Department of Foreign Affairs and Trade, pp. 72–88.

Bartels, L. (2001), 'Applicable Law in WTO Dispute Settlement Proceedings', *Journal of World Trade*, 35(3), 499–519.

Black, J. (2002), 'Regulatory Conversations', in S. Picciotto and D. Campbell (eds), *New Directions in Regulatory Theory*, Oxford: Blackwell, Oxford, pp. 163–196.

Braithwaite, J. and P. Drahos (2000), *Global Business Regulation*, Cambridge: Cambridge University Press.

Busch, M. and E. Reinhardt (2003), 'Developing Countries and General Agreement on Tariffs and Trade Dispute Settlement', *Journal of World Trade*, 37(4), 719–735.

Davies, L. (2002), 'Technical Cooperation and the International Coordination of Patentability of Biotechnological Inventions', *Journal of Law and Society*, 29(1), 137–162.

Drahos, P. (2001), 'BITS and BIPS – Bilateralism in Intellectual Property', *Journal of World Intellectual Property*, 4(6), 791–808.

Drahos, P. (2002), 'Negotiating Intellectual Property Rights: Between Coercion and Dialogue', in P. Drahos and R. Mayne (eds), *Global Intellectual Property Rights: Knowledge, Access and Development*, Basingstoke: Palgrave Macmillan, pp. 161–182.

Drahos, P. (2007), 'Weaving Webs of Influence; the United States Free Trade Agreements and Dispute Resolution,' *Journal of World Trade*, 41(1), 191–210.

Drahos, P. and J. Braithwaite (2004), 'Hegemony Based on Knowledge: The Role of Intellectual Property', in J. Chen and G. Walker (eds), *Balancing Act: Law, Policy and Politics in Globalisation and Global Trade*, Sydney: Federation Press, pp. 204–223.

Drahos, P., B. Lokuge, T. Faunce, M. Goddard and D. Henry (2004), 'Pharmaceuticals Intellectual Property and Free Trade: The Case of the US-Australia Free Trade Agreement', *Prometheus*, 22(3), 243–257.

Dutfield, G. (2004) 'Introduction', in C. Bellman, G. Dutfield and R. Mendez-Ortiz (eds), *Trading in Knowledge: Development Perspectives on TRIPS, Trade and Sustainability*, London: Earthscan, pp. 1–22.

Finnemore, M. and S. Toope (2001), 'Alternatives to "Legalization": Richer Views of Law and Politics', *International Organization*, 55(3), 743–758.

Footer, M. (2001), 'Developing Country Practice in the Matter of WTO Dispute Settlement', *Journal of World Trade*, 35(1), 55–98.

Ghanotakis, E. (2004), 'How the U.S. Interpretation of Flexibilities Inherent in TRIPS Affects Access to Medicines for Developing Countries', *Journal of World Intellectual Property*, 7(4), 563–591.

Gibson, J. (2005), *Community Resources, Intellectual Property, International Trade and Protection of Traditional Knowledge*, Aldershot: Ashgate.

Helfer, L. (2004), 'Regime Shifting: The TRIPS Agreement and New Dynamics of International Intellectual Property Lawmaking', *Yale Journal of International Law*, 29(1), 1–83.

Howse, R. (2000), 'Adjudicative Legitimacy and Treaty Interpretation in International Trade Law', in J. Weiler (ed.), *The EU, the WTO, and the NAFTA: Towards a Common Law of International Trade?*, Oxford: Oxford University Press, pp. 35–70.

IP/C/41 (2005), Implementation of Paragraph 11 of the General Council Decision of 30 August 2003 on the Implementation of Paragraph 6 of the Doha Declaration on the TRIPS Agreement and Public Health: Proposal for a Decision on an Amendment to the TRIPS Agreement, Geneva: World Trade Organization.

John, T. (2004), *Arguing with a Friend: Dispute Resolution under AUSFTA*, Research Note No. 14, Parliamentary Library: Parliament of Australia.

Krajewski, M. (2001), 'Democratic Legitimacy and Constitutional Perspectives of WTO Law', *Journal of World Trade*, 35(1), 167–186.

Kuhlik, B. (2004), 'The Assault on Pharmaceutical Intellectual Property', *University of Chicago Law Review*, 71(1), 93–109.

Lawson, C. (2004), '"Flexibility" in TRIPS: Using Patented Inventions Without the Authorisation of the Rights Holder', *Australian Intellectual Property Journal*, 15(3), 141–153.

Lennard, M. (2002), 'Navigating By the Stars: Interpreting the WTO Agreements', *Journal of International Economic Law*, 5(1), 17–89.

McRae, D. (2004), 'What is the Future of WTO Dispute Settlement?', *Journal of International Economic Law*, 7(1), 3–21.

Matthews, D. (2004), 'WTO Decision on Implementation of Paragraph 6 of the Doha Declaration on the TRIPS Agreement and Public Health: A Solution to the Access to Essential Medicines Problem?', *Journal of International Economic Law*, 7(1), 73–107.

Oliva, M. (2003), 'Intellectual Property in the FTAA: Little Opportunity and Much Risk', *American University International Law Review*, 19(1), 45–67.

Pauwelyn, J. (2003), *Conflict of Norms in Public International Law: How WTO Law Relates to Other Rules of International Law*, Cambridge: Cambridge University Press.

Pauwelyn, J. (2006), 'The Transformation of World Trade', *Michigan Law Review*, 104(1), 1–65.

Picciotto, S. (2003), 'Private Rights and Public Standards in the WTO', *Review of International Political Economy*, 10(3), 377–405.

Picciotto, S. (2005), 'The WTO's Appellate Body: Legal Formalism as a Legitimation of Global Governance', *Governance*, 18(3), 477–503.

Press/350/Rev.1 (2003), *Decision Removes Final Patent Obstacle to Cheap Drug Imports*, WTO News Press/350, 30 August 2003, Geneva: World Trade Organization.

Rodriguez-Garavito, C. (2005), 'Nike's Law: The Anti-Sweatshop Movement, Transnational Corporations, and the Struggle over International Labor Rights in the Americas', in B. De Sousa Santos and C. Rodriguez-Garavito (eds), *Law and Globalization from Below: Towards a Cosmopolitan Legality*, Cambridge: Cambridge University Press, pp. 64–91.

Ruiz, M. (2004), 'The Andean Community Regimes on Access to Genetic Resources, Intellectual Property, and the Protection of Indigenous Peoples' Knowledge', in C. Bellman, G. Dutfield and R. Mendez-Ortiz (eds), *Trading in Knowledge: Development Perspectives on TRIPS, Trade and Sustainability*, London: Earthscan, pp. 238–245.

Sands, P. (2005), *Lawless World: America and the Making and Breaking of Global Rules*, London: Allen Lane.

Schneiderman, D. (2000) 'Investment Rules and the New Constitutionalism', *Law and Social Inquiry*, 25(3), 757–788.

Sell, S. (2003), *Private Power, Public Law; The Globalization of Intellectual Property Rights*, New York: Cambridge University Press.

Shaffer, G. (2003), *Defending Interests: Public-Private Partnerships in WTO Litigation*, Washington: Brookings Institution Press.

Shanker, D. (2002), 'The Vienna Convention on the Law of Treaties, the Dispute Settlement System of the WTO and the Doha Declaration on the TRIPS Agreement', *Journal of World Trade*, 36(4), 721–772.

Slaughter, A. (2004), *A New World Order*, New Jersey: Princeton University Press.

Teubner, G. (2001), 'Legal Irritants: How Unifying Law Ends Up in New Divergences', in P. Hall and D. Soskice (eds), *Varieties of Capitalism: The*

Institutional Foundations of Comparative Advantage, Oxford: Oxford University Press, pp. 417–441.

Trachtman, J. (1999), 'The Domain of WTO Dispute Resolution', *Harvard International Law Journal*, 40(2), 333–377.

Vaver, D. and S. Basheer (2006), 'Popping Patented Pills: Europe and a Decade's Dose of TRIPS', *European Intellectual Property Review*, 28(5), 282–291.

Vivas-Ergui, D. (2003), *Regional and Bilateral Agreements and a TRIPS-plus World: the Free Trade Area of the Americas (FTAA)*, TRIPS Issues Papers, Geneva: Quaker United Nations Office.

Von Bogdandy, A. (2003), 'Legitimacy of International Economic Governance: Interpretative Approaches to WTO Law and the Prospects of its Proceduralization', in S. Griller (ed.), *International Economic Governance and Non-Economic Concerns: New Challenges for the International Economic Order*, New York: SpringerWien, pp. 103–148.

Waincymer, J. (2002), *WTO Litigation: Procedural Aspects of Formal Dispute Settlement*, London: Cameron and May.

Weiler, J. (2001), 'The Rule of Lawyers and the Ethos of Diplomats – Reflections on the Internal and External Legitimacy of WTO Dispute Settlement', *Journal of World Trade*, 35(2), 191–207.

WT/DS50/AB/R (1997), *India – Patent Protection for Pharmaceuticals and Agricultural Chemical Products*, Geneva: World Trade Organization.

WT/DS114/R (1997), *Canada – Patent Protection for Pharmaceutical Products*, Geneva: World Trade Organization.

WT/DS152/R (1999), *United States – Sections 301–310 of the Trade Act 1974*, Geneva: World Trade Organization.

WT/DS153 (1998), *European Communities – Patent Protection for Pharmaceutical and Agricultural Chemical Products*, Geneva: World Trade Organization.

WT/DS160/R (1999), *United States – s 110(5) of the US Copyright Act*, Geneva: World Trade Organization.

WT/DS176/AB/R (1999), *United States – Section 211 Omnibus Appropriations Act of 1998*, Geneva: World Trade Organization.

WT/DS291/R (2006), *European Communities – Measures Affecting the Approval and Marketing of Biotech Products*, Geneva: World Trade Organization.

WT/DS308/AB/R (2006), *Mexico – Taxes on Soft Drinks*, Geneva: World Trade Organization.

WT/MIN(01)/DEC/2 (2001), *Declaration on the TRIPS Agreement and Public Health*, Geneva: World Trade Organization.

Australian Financial Review (2004a), 'US Raises Doubts as FTA Passes', 13–14 August 2004, Melbourne: Fairfax Business Media.

Australian Financial Review (2004b), 'US Trade Deal in Danger of Collapse', 20–21 August 2004, Melbourne: Fairfax Business Media.

Australian Financial Review (2004c), 'US Wins Legal Pledge on Generic Drugs', 23 November 2004, Melbourne: Fairfax Business Media.

Australian Financial Review (2004d), 'US Wants FTA Toughened Up', 4–5 December 2004, Melbourne: Fairfax Business Media.

The Australian (2005), 'All Eyes on Asia in Copyright Duel', 1 January 2005, Sydney: News Corporation.

'Thailand: Health Ministry Breaks Patents on Heart Drug, HIV Treatment Kaletra', *World Intellectual Property Report*, volume 21, issue 3, p. 23, 2007.

'Peru, Columbia Spar with Venezuela on IP, Threatening Andean Accord', *World Intellectual Property Report*, volume 20, issue 3, p. 3, 2006.
'International: WTO Deal on TRIPs/Medicine Welcomed by Governments, Industry', *World Intellectual Property Report*, volume 20, issue 1, p. 29, 2006.
'NGOs say use of bilaterals impairs transparency and access to TRIPS', *World Intellectual Property Report*, volume 19, issue 2, p. 23, 2005.
'US Given Indefinite Reprieve in Cuban Rum Case', *World Intellectual Property Report*, volume 19, issue 8, p. 18, 2005.
'Brazil Issues Compulsory Licence for AIDS Drug', *Bridges Weekly Trade News Digest*, volume 11, number 16, p. 1, 9 May 2007.
'WIPO Members Agree on Development Agenda', *Bridges Weekly Trade News Digest*, volume 11, number 22, 20 June 2007.
'IP Standards in the US–Peru FTA: Health and Environment', *Bridges Monthly Review*, volume 10, number 1, p. 17, January–February 2006.
WIPO, Press Release 12/478/2007, Geneva, 26 February 2007.

3. Knowledge diplomacy and the new intellectual property fundamentalism

Graham Dutfield

1. INTRODUCTION

In theory, the flexibilities of the World Trade Organization-administered TRIPS Agreement should provide developing countries with ample opportunities for creative interpretations of its provisions. Despite this, developing country freedom to exploit these opportunities is diminishing rapidly. Dispute settlement jurisprudence is one cause, but this is far less significant than that the United States, in particular, and the European Union, have developed successful strategies to hold developing countries to more rigid and higher standards of IP protection than TRIPS compliance requires. In some respects these standards of protection are even higher than those the United States has been willing to accept domestically.

One of the most effective strategies being employed is that of so-called free trade agreements (FTAs) containing highly constraining and protectionist 'TRIPS plus' IP provisions that seem to be aimed to serve the interests of developed world corporations. The FTA negotiations and FTAs themselves seem to be neither wholly free, since the IP provisions in them are inherently protectionist, nor fair to the weaker negotiating parties. Unsurprisingly, business and pro-business interest groups have been very much behind the promotion of TRIPS plus measures. They are popular with the United States government and the European Commission not only because they work, but also because the United States and European economies, along with those of Japan and certain East Asian countries that tend also to favour TRIPS plus IP protection, are the major producers and exporters of patent, copyright and trade mark-protected goods and services and therefore have much to gain from them.

Increasingly, the promoters of TRIPS plus rules are deploying rhetoric that I refer to as the new intellectual property fundamentalism. In its most extreme form, the rhetoric labels copying as piracy as if the two words are synonyms, and even links piracy to terrorism. As this chapter points out, this fundamentalism seems largely to demonise developing countries. It also tends to be expressed in places like Washington to rally developed world foreign and trade ministries and international organisations into leaning more heavily on the poor countries.

It is contended that the new IP fundamentalism is both dishonest and potentially dangerous. Neither the United States nor the European Union would countenance the elimination of well-established limitations to rights that allow copying of patent and copyright-protected goods and works under certain conditions. And yet, some developing countries have been pressured to adopt IP standards that are even stronger than in some developed countries. One example is the extension of the copyright term to life of the author plus 70 years in FTAs, as in the United States and Europe, but without adopting also the fair use doctrine that is integral to American copyright law and that makes the whole system more balanced.

History teaches us that today's rich countries prospered in part by imitating first and innovating later. Korea copied from Japan and the West, Japan imitated the United States and Europe, the United States in its turn copied from the European countries, who copied from each other and – something they rarely acknowledge – from the Middle and Far East. Much of this copying could not have happened under today's rules. If they cannot copy any IP at all, one may reasonably ask, will today's poor nations ever catch up?

In the last part of the chapter, it is suggested that those governments that have been promoting strong international IP standards since the launch of the Uruguay Round and that are now pushing for TRIPS plus standards may eventually have a change of heart. Will the United States government be so pro-patent when the proportion of domestic patents granted to Indian and Chinese inventors increases dramatically, or if more and more United States firms 'reward' their government for so aggressively promoting their interests by shifting their research operations to countries where top scientists are cheap and available and patent rights less enforceable causing, to borrow the words of former United States presidential candidate Ross Perot, a giant sucking sound as research jobs and investment go out of the United States? It is suggested that the present situation, in which unprecedentedly strong IP protection[1] is considered necessary on both utilitarian and moral grounds, may be short-lived. In the coming decades, the United States may even take the role of the leading patent- and copyright-sceptic nation as it was, to some extent, in the past.[2]

2. TRIPS IN CONTEXT

The international law of IP is complex, evolutionary and highly dynamic, never more so than today. Businesses that operate across national boundaries are never satisfied with the current IP rules, at least not for long. Since certain governments are structured in ways that allow the interests of such businesses headquartered within their jurisdictions (or even sometimes outside them) to convert rapidly to national trade policies and negotiating strategies that align closely to these interests, the pressure for change can become irresistible.

Until recently, TRIPS seemed to be the most important element of the effort to pull up developing countries' IP standards of protection and enforcement to the level of the developed countries and to modernise IP protection so as to accommodate rapid advances in emerging fields like biotechnology and the digital technologies. But now, the drivers of change are beginning to see TRIPS and the WTO forum as at least as much a brake as an accelerator. Indeed, TRIPS may be outliving its purpose for those corporations that successfully lobbied for an IP agreement in the Uruguay Round and the governments that took up their demands.

To understand what is going on, it is important to be clear about the problems that TRIPS was intended to solve, leaving to one side, as we should, the pro-development and social welfare language of certain of its articles (such as the Preamble and Arts 7 and 8). These are copyright piracy, unauthorised use of trade marks, and unwelcome competition from generic drug firms able to take advantage of patent regimes excluding drugs from protection. TRIPS has failed to solve these problems completely, and in consequence, other solutions have been employed, which are described in the next section of this chapter.

What does transnational industry actually want? In the area of patents, the priority is global harmonisation pitched at a level such that TRIPS is the floor; the absolute minimum that is acceptable.[3] Initial demands for international harmonisation were directed mainly at procedural matters and aimed to reduce the uncertainty and duplication of effort caused by different patent offices examining applications for the same invention and to reduce costs for the applicants. The United States, European and Japanese patent offices have been in close contact since 1983 and are cooperating in a number of areas to coordinate their approaches to searches, examinations and other procedures.

Moves are afoot at the World Intellectual Property Organization (WIPO) to go much further than TRIPS by intensifying substantive patent law harmonisation in the interests, it appears, of helping well-resourced companies to acquire geographically more extensive and secure protection of their inventions at minimised cost (Musungu and Dutfield 2003). Substantive harmonisation is more than just making the patent systems of countries more like each other in terms of enforcement standards and administrative rules and procedures. It means that the actual substance of the patent standards will be exactly the same to the extent, for example, of having identical definitions of novelty, inventive step and industrial application. Given the rich countries' interests in harmonisation, it is likely to result in common (and tightly drawn) rules governing exceptions to patent rights, and the universal removal of any options to exclude types of subject matter or fields of technology from patentability on grounds of public policy or national interest.

Harmonisation is important with copyright too, especially in such areas as term of protection and subject matter. For example, the developed countries are encouraging the developing countries to extend the term of copyright protection beyond that required by TRIPS to life of the author plus 70 years, as in Europe and the United States. But the situation is a little different. One reason is that the complex array of stakeholders[4] whose economic and moral interests are affected by copyright makes harmonisation much more difficult to achieve. Another is that rapid technological developments have made the transnational copyright industries determined to achieve an international regime that is sufficiently dynamic to respond speedily to the massive opportunities and vulnerabilities afforded by technological advances. These advances: (a) provide new means for copyright owners to disseminate their works to the public; but they also (b) threaten to undermine the control over markets in these works by enabling copiers to flood markets with unauthorised versions of these works and by allowing potential consumers to copy them. Such 'dynamic responsiveness' cannot be achieved at the WTO, since the WTO agreements have proved not to be susceptible to the substantial periodic revisions that would be necessary to satisfy industry.

3. TRIPS AND ITS ALTERNATIVES

As mentioned, TRIPS is inadequate as far as the demanders of ever higher IP protection levels are concerned. Consequently, the TRIPS approach is being supplemented by an expanding menu of alternatives. These include:

(1) '*Missionary work*', including the sending by developed country governments, business associations and WIPO of experts to spread the IP gospel.
(2) *The dissemination of propaganda* extolling the virtues of intellectual

property, and claiming that IP piracy is inimical to development, that it deters investment, that it is immoral or unfair, or that it supports terrorist activities.

(3) *Technical assistance* provided by international organisations, developed countries' governmental agencies and IP offices, and business and law associations. IP technical assistance often seeks to promote standards of IP protection higher than those required by TRIPS in order to protect the interests of providers and funders. Programmes can involve training courses, the dissemination of propaganda extolling the virtues of intellectual property and the harm caused by piracy, and the drafting of legislation.[5]

(4) *Latent or overt trade threats and intimidation* by rich countries towards poor countries they accuse of condoning piracy, of having 'inadequate' IP systems, or even for openly considering issuing a compulsory licence for a patented drug in a health emergency.[6]

(5) *Divide and rule tactics* in multilateral negotiations.[7]

(6) *Forum management*. The idea behind the forum management concept is that *where* negotiations take place can make a big difference to their outcome, and is therefore a strategic matter. Achieving goals relating to certain issues can involve the opening, closing and shifting of negotiating or jurisdictional forums. For example, in the 1980s the United States opened up GATT as another forum to pursue its IP-related interests. At the same time it kept the WIPO forum open to introduce 'TRIPS-plus' standards through new conventions such as the WIPO Copyright Treaty, and the Substantive Patent Law Treaty currently under negotiation. On the other hand, while the United States is seeking to confine traditional knowledge (TK) to WIPO's Intergovernmental Committee on Intellectual Property and Genetic Resources, Traditional Knowledge and Folklore, several developing countries have insisted that TK also be covered by WIPO's Standing Committee on the Law of Patents, and in the TRIPS Council.

Perhaps the most significant new development in the field of IP forum management is the proliferation of bilateral and regional negotiations on trade and investment that have led to many developing countries adopting heightened standards of IP protection through the resulting agreements. These bilateral and regional agreements have proved to be a useful way to get individual, or sometimes groups of, developing countries to introduce so-called 'TRIPS plus' provisions that go beyond what TRIPS requires. The TRIPS plus measures typically involve:

(1) extending patents and copyright to new kinds of subject matter;
(2) eliminating or narrowing permitted exceptions, including those still provided for in United States and European IP laws;
(3) extending protection terms;
(4) introducing new TRIPS-mandated IP rules earlier than the transition periods allowed by TRIPS; and
(5) ratifying new WIPO treaties containing TRIPS plus measures, such as the WIPO Copyright Treaty.

In addition, they appear sometimes to require, at least implicitly, that developing country parties drop certain IP-related demands the same countries are making in multilateral forums.

The United States and the European Community both use the bilateralism strategy, but the United States has been the more aggressive. Nonetheless, as an active and sophisticated IP forum manager, the United States interest in bilateralism and regionalism does not mean abandoning the multilateral approach. In this case forum management entails the proliferation of forums, keeping as many open at the same time as possible. According to the former United States Trade Representative, Robert Zoellick, United States trade strategy is about not putting all of America's eggs in one basket:[8]

> When the Bush Administration set out to revitalize America's trade agenda almost three years ago, we outlined our plans clearly and openly: We would pursue a strategy of 'competitive liberalization' to advance free trade globally, regionally, and bilaterally . . . At its most basic level, the competitive liberalization strategy simply means that America expands and strengthens its options. If free trade progress becomes stalled globally – where any one of 148 economies in the World Trade Organization has veto power – then we can move ahead regionally and bilaterally. If our hemispheric talks are progressing stage-by-stage, we can point to more ambitious possibilities through FTAs with individual countries and sub-regions. Having a strong bilateral or sub-regional option helps spur progress in the larger negotiations.

Behind all of these strategies are two kinds of rhetoric. The first is relatively benign, and tends to be targeted at the developed countries and their citizens for the sake of domestic policymaking. It relates national prosperity to innovation and intellectual property. The second is extreme, aggressive and inflammatory, and tends to be directed to developed countries' foreign and trade policy concerning the developing and formerly communist countries. I refer to it as 'the new intellectual property fundamentalism'.

The first kind of rhetoric is based on the current conventional wisdom that the world's most successful nations are those best at producing, acquiring, deploying and controlling valuable knowledge. Knowledge, especially new knowledge unavailable to one's rivals, is key to international competitiveness and therefore to national prosperity. However clichéd such a view may be, the fact is that many policymakers believe it to be true and are acting accordingly. As the United Kingdom government typically expresses it, 'intellectual property is a critical component of our present and future success in the global economy'. Moreover, it asserts, the economic competitiveness of the UK, as of its competitors, 'is increasingly driven by knowledge-based industries, especially in manufacturing, science-based sectors and the creative industries' (Gowers 2006). This view is generally accepted among today's developed countries including those which tend to be net importers of high technology IP protected goods, such as Canada and Australia.

As for the new IP fundamentalism, let us consider a few examples. According to the Office of the United States Trade Representative in 2004:

> Our goal is to control piracy through strong laws and effective enforcement worldwide, and to ensure that protection remains effective as technology develops in the future . . . effective protection of intellectual property rights involves customs, courts, prosecutors and police, commitment by senior political officials; and a general recognition that to copy is to steal and to deprive finance ministries of revenue . . . Our major tools are both bilateral and multilateral.[9]

The whole idea that copying is synonymous with stealing is both dangerous and dishonest. It is dangerous because copying is an essential part of the learning process. If we stop countries copying we may stop them from developing. It is dishonest because the United States itself was a notorious copier nation when it was a developing country, as were several if not all of today's rich nations (see below).

In 2003, Kamil Idris, Director-General of WIPO, pronounced that 'piracy is like terrorism today and it exists everywhere and it is a very dangerous phenomenon'.[10] At a time when public fear of terrorism and loathing of terrorists around the world has never been greater this is not only ludicrous but unnecessarily inflammatory.

Also inflammatory is the dubbing by Washington lobbyists of China, India and Brazil as 'the Axis of IP Evil'. James Glassman of the American Enterprise Institute, in endorsing the phrase, had this to say about these three countries:

> Brazil's own government . . . is in the process of confiscating drug patents. India seems to be getting better. China is another matter. China is making mischief. It is supporting, incredibly, a Brazilian as the next head of the World Trade Organization – Brazil, which was the prime culprit in the collapse of the WTO post-Doha conference in Cancun in 2003.[11]

4. THE STAKES

It is not self-evident that harmonising the international IP rules and making them as responsive as possible to technological evolution is bad for developing countries just because they further the interests of transnational corporations. But making the rules identical and legally binding whether you are a very rich country with enormous balance of payments surpluses in IP-protected goods, services and technologies, or a poor country with highly burdensome trade deficits seems to be tremendously expensive and risky for the latter type of country.

If we consider the expense of it all, while it is impossible to reliably calculate the long-term economic impacts of TRIPS on developing countries and their populations, we can be certain that they will incur short-term costs in such forms as rent transfers and administration and enforcement outlays, and that these will outweigh the initial benefits (Dutfield 2003, p. 49). The cost-benefit balance will vary widely from one country to another, but in many cases the costs will be extremely burdensome (World Bank 2001).

Turning to risk, agreeing to restrict one's freedom to tailor national or regional IP regulations to specific needs and conditions in exchange for market access commitments from the developed countries could turn out to be extremely damaging. At worst, it could place a serious block, perhaps insurmountable, on development.

As for patent harmonisation, if taken to its logical conclusion of a world patent system, Genetic Resources Action International has warned that it could conceivably 'mean the end of patent policy as a tool for national development strategies'.[12] Not only this, but it would represent a radical departure from most of the nineteenth and twentieth centuries, when many countries took advantage of their freedom (pre-TRIPS) to provide statutory subject matter bars on such grounds as infant industry protectionism and the prevention of corporate monopolies on important products like foods and drugs. For example, France only allowed pharmaceuticals to be patented in 1960, Ireland in 1964, Germany in 1968, Japan in 1976, Switzerland in 1977, Italy and Sweden both in 1978, and Spain in 1992. At around the same time, Brazil and India passed laws to exclude pharmaceuticals as such from patentability (as well as processes to manufacture them in Brazil's case).

5. THE NEW IP FUNDAMENTALISM AND THE LESSONS OF HISTORY

Although the rhetoric of IP fundamentalism is most usefully deployed and readily accepted in places like Washington, much of it seems to be inspired by the supposed recalcitrance of developing countries. So let us see what would, or rather what would *not*, have happened if the law in the past had treated all copying as stealing or terrorism by considering a few examples.

Royal Philips Electronics was set up in 1891 to commercially exploit somebody else's invention, Thomas Edison's and Joseph Swan's carbon filament lamp. Commercial success generated considerable revenues that enabled the firm to produce its own inventions and eventually become one of the world's most innovative corporations. How was Philips able to get such a good head start? From 1869 until 1912, Holland had no patent law.

The well-known Swedish mobile phone company, Ericsson, was formed in 1876, the same year as Alexander Graham Bell made his first phone call. Sent some of these new devices to repair, the company worked out how to make them, and by 1878 was selling its own phones to the Swedish public. Bell had neglected to file patents on his invention in Sweden.

In 1960, Texas Instruments filed a patent in Japan on the integrated circuit, arguably one of the most important inventions of the second half of the twentieth century. The Japan Patent Office allowed itself 29 years to grant the patent. By that time Japanese companies, free to read the patent specification 18 months after filing, acquired the technology, improved upon it, and controlled markets worldwide for computer semiconductors. This control includes 80 per cent of the United States market, though this admittedly required Japanese firms to pay royalties to Texas Instruments in that country because of the latter company's many patents held there (Johnson 1995, pp. 74–75).

The point to be made here is that such behaviour broke no international rules of the day. Furthermore, freedom to use such technologies was often beneficial not only to the imitator companies but also to the national economies in which they were based. Indeed, none of the recipient countries remained copiers for long. Eventually they became among the world's most technologically advanced.

Indeed, historical evidence strongly suggests that by depriving developing countries of the freedom to design IP systems as they see fit, the rich countries are, to use the title of a recent book by Ha-Joon Chang, 'kicking away the ladder' (Chang 2002) after they have scaled it themselves. Let us consider a few examples of how differentiation worked well in the past to enable some of today's developed countries to catch up with the technology leaders in the past.

5.1 Japan and the Asian Tigers

It is somewhat ironic that Japan is probably the most ambitious proponent of substantive patent harmonisation given that, only a few decades ago, the government's technology licensing policy was quite aggressive and foreign companies often felt discriminated against by the country's nationalistic trade and industry policy, of which the patent law was an essential component. For example, post-war Japan adopted a policy of aggressively pressuring foreign high technology firms to make their technologies available to domestic industries. In the late 1950s, a Vice-Minister at the Ministry of International Trade and Industry allegedly warned IBM that: '[w]e will take every measure possible to obstruct the success of your business unless you license IBM patents to Japanese firms and charge them no more than a 5 percent royalty' (quoted in Johnson 1982, p. 247). IBM had little choice but to comply.

In a comprehensive study of the evolution of the Japanese patent system, which shows that for almost all of its existence it was very much 'TRIPS minus', Fisher is drawn to conclude that: '[t]he meteoric rise from feudal serf to technological whiz-kid that the country has undergone in less than 150 years is little short of astounding, and poses the question of whether it could be repeated today. The homogenisation of patent law, the claim implicit in TRIPS that one size can, and indeed should, fit all, does not adequately correspond with the picture of Japan's evolution' (Fisher 2004, p. 113).

Research by Kim on the experience of South Korea led him to find that 'strong IPR protection will hinder rather than facilitate technology transfer to and indigenous learning activities in the early stage of industrialisation when learning takes place through reverse engineering and duplicative imitation of mature foreign products'. He also concluded that 'only after countries have accumulated sufficient indigenous capabilities with extensive science and technology infrastructure to undertake creative imitation in the later stage that IPR protection becomes an important element in technology transfer and industrial activities' (Kim 2003, p 5). Similarly, Kumar found that in the East Asian countries he studied (such as Japan, South Korea and Taiwan), a combination of relatively weak patent protection and the availability of other IP rights such as industrial designs and utility models encouraged technological learning. The weak patent regimes helped by allowing for local absorption of foreign innovations. Industrial designs and utility models encouraged minor adaptations and inventions by local firms. Later on, the patent systems became stronger partly because local technological capacity was sufficiently advanced to generate a significant amount of domestic innovation, and also as a result of international pressure.

5.2 The United States

Despite the national treatment rules under the 1886 Berne Convention, nineteenth-century national copyright laws tended to be less friendly towards the interests of foreigners than patent laws. Several reasons can be offered, but one important explanation is that while granting patent-type rights to foreigners was sometimes considered to benefit the country by encouraging the introduction of protected technologies, allowing foreigners to protect their literary and artistic works did not provide such obvious economic advantages to net importers of creative works (Cornish 1993, pp. 48 and 50). For example, for most of the nineteenth century, the United States refused to extend copyright protection to the works of foreigners at all, and was notorious as a pirate nation. Nonetheless, despite the highly TRIPS-incompatible United States copyright regime of the day, a detailed economic study of the nineteenth century book trade by Khan showed that publishers, printers and the reading public all benefited. This led her to conclude that 'the United States experience during the nineteenth century suggests that appropriate intellectual property institutions are not independent of the level of economic and social development' (Khan 2004).

By the late nineteenth century, voices could be heard in literary circles supporting reform. The editors of the *Atlantic Monthly*, for example, noting that 'the rapid increase in the value and importance of American books brings prudence to the aid of morality', advocated that 'on every ground it is important that the barbarous system of pillage should cease', and supported an international copyright convention giving equal rights to domestic and foreign authors (Atlantic Monthly 1872). History, however, shows that the United States wisely held off granting copyright to foreigners as long as the country showed, in terms of balance of trade, a net loss on the import/export ratio of cultural products. It was not yet in the interest of the United States to embrace reciprocal arrangements with foreign publishers. United States copyright law discriminated against foreign works from 1891 until 1986 with the 'manufacturing clause', a protectionist measure intended to benefit American printers. Originally, this required all copyrighted literary works to be printed in the country. Although the clause was weakened over the years, when President Reagan vetoed a four-year extension in 1982 in the face of an unfavourable GATT panel ruling and complaints from Europe, Congress disregarded the ruling and overruled Reagan. The fact that the United States had by that time become by far the world's biggest exporter of copyrighted works suggests that its creative industries were not exactly held back by a copyright system that appears initially to have been inspired by infant-industry protectionism. Significantly, the world's leading producer of entertainment products did not sign the Berne Convention until 1989.

6. THE FUTURE: BACK TO IP AGNOSTICISM?

There is ample historical evidence to indicate that freedom to imitate was an essential step towards learning how to innovate. In addition, numerous examples show that relatively unfettered access to goods, technologies and information from more advanced countries stimulated development in the less advanced ones. Support for both findings comes, as we saw, from the cases of Holland, Sweden, Japan, the United States and the Asian Tigers. It is difficult to see why they would not also be true for today's developing countries.

In reflecting on the implications for policymaking and diplomacy, history would appear to indicate two things that are worthwhile considering. First, it is totally unreasonable for the developed countries to restrict the freedom of developing countries to take full advantage of the vagueness of many of the TRIPS provisions by holding them to rigidly defined TRIPS plus standards. Secondly, the developed countries can justifiably be accused of hypocrisy[13] when they demand that the rest of the world adopt their own patent and other IP standards – or even stronger ones – before the developing countries feel, for very good reason, they are ready for them. Thirdly, and this is much more important, in doing so they are preventing the developing countries from adopting appropriate patent and copyright standards for their levels of development, a freedom today's rich countries made sure not to deny themselves when they were developing countries and may well adopt again if they find themselves being overtaken in certain strategic business sectors.

Indeed, it is perfectly conceivable that if the United States experiences marked increases in the proportion of domestic patents being granted to inventors from advanced developing countries like China and India, something which currently seems inevitable, the tide may well turn back to the patent scepticism of yesteryear, especially if in consequence the reliably massive annual trade surplus in royalties and licence fees is converted into a regular deficit. It also seems highly possible that the United States' and European economies will soon start to haemorrhage not just blue collar jobs but scientific and technical research positions as industry finds it can get cheaper scientists and technicians elsewhere to do the same work for a fraction of the cost. Indeed, this may be starting to happen irrespective of whether the IP systems of the countries concerned meet United States or European standards of enforcement, and of all places, in at least two of the members of the axis of IP evil.[14] And it is conceivable that the very limited limitations to patentability currently permitted under United States law will contribute to this.[15] Furthermore, though this does seem less likely, if the United States finds itself becoming a net importer of entertainment products, educational materials and software from other areas of the world, it may reconsider its stance on copyright as well. The present bout of IP fundamentalism may turn out to be skin deep and fleeting, and something that the United States will in time regret.

ACKNOWLEDGEMENTS

An earlier draft of this chapter was presented at the TRIPS Forum, Griffith University, Brisbane, December 2004. The author is grateful to Justin Malbon, Charles Lawson and to the other participants.

NOTES

1. Commentators often use the term 'strong' or 'weak' with respect to IP protection, but without clarification. For the purposes of this chapter the strength of IP protection varies according to: (i) the extent of the explicit or implicit subject matter exclusions; (ii) the extent to which defences from infringement are available; (iii) the extent to which public interest and other provisions such as compulsory licensing are available and are actually used; and (iv) the extent to which rights can be enforced. So protection is 'strongest' where exclusions are minimal, defences are confined to very limited acts and circumstances, compulsory licensing is either unavailable or never resorted to, and public enforcement measures are carried out efficiently, and private enforcement of rights is inexpensive and uncomplicated.
2. And, one might add, as it is already becoming in respect of one intellectual property right, that of geographical indications.
3. This is not to say that the intellectual property regimes of the developed countries are necessarily TRIPS compatible in their entireties.
4. These include authors, publishers, performers, film production companies, phonogram producers, internet service providers and broadcasters.
5. In the United States, much of the technical assistance is targeted at the enforcement of rights, which in many developing countries are mostly owned by foreigners (often Americans). Some of it is provided through the United States Agency for International Development and is classed as overseas aid: see Sagar 2006.
6. When Brazil or Thailand does this it is accused of 'breaking' a patent. This is despite the fact that the patent-holding firm must be compensated. On the other hand, under the country's antitrust regime, the United States has over the years issued a large number of compulsory licences and continues to do so. Morally, it is difficult to accept that doing so to save lives should be beyond the pale while antitrust-related motivations make compulsory licensing perfectly legitimate.
7. Such as when efforts were made to drive a wedge between India and Brazil on the one side, and the African Group on the other during the negotiations relating to the 2001 Declaration on the TRIPS Agreement and Public Health.
8. Letter from Robert Zoellick to David Walker, Comptroller of the United States, December 2003: http://www.ustr.gov/releases/2003/12/2003-12-03-letter-gao.pdf, visited April 2004.
9. www.ustr.gov, visited January 2005.
10. http://uk.news.yahoo.com/031203/323/efqp 1.html, visited June 2004.
11. Glassman, J.K., 'An Upbeat View'. Speech to Ex-Im Bank's Annual Conference, Omni Shoreham. http://www.exim.gov/news/annualconf/glassman_speech.html, 2005, visited November 2006.

12. GRAIN (2002), 'WIPO Moves Toward "World" Patent System', http://www.grain.org/publications/wipo-patent-2002-en.cfm, visited November 2002.
13. One may of course reasonably counter that the current behaviour of the Americans and Europeans is not hypocrisy but reflects a genuine change of mind. But let us for a moment consider the response of the United States government to the anthrax biological warfare scare in October 2001. The government decided to stockpile vast quantities of Bayer's ciprofloxacin (Cipro) to ensure that up to 10 million people could receive immediate treatment should the need arise. The government was concerned not only about whether it was possible to acquire so much Cipro at short notice but about the cost of doing so. Tommy Thompson, the Secretary of Health and Human Services, threatened Bayer that if they did not halve the price he would simply acquire the drug from other sources. At one stage he even raised the possibility of asking Congress to pass legislation exempting the government from compensating Bayer for ignoring its patent. This tough approach worked. Thompson successfully negotiated a large discount. But, by threatening to override the patent, the United States government, which was at the same time pressuring developing country governments not to issue compulsory licences to generic drug producers, looked hypocritical.
14. For some evidence of this phenomenon, see Santini 2004.
15. In the United States, the scope of the judicially created research exemption attracted critical attention as a result of the judgement in *Madey v Duke University*. The judgement gave rise to concerns that United States courts may have gone too far in interpreting the research exemption into a state of virtual non-existence, and that in doing so it may well hinder universities from conducting the basic research upon which future commercially-oriented research ultimately depends and which the private sector cannot be relied upon to carry out all by itself. A recent *Science* article on the case notes the prediction expressed by some that Congress may respond by imposing its wish 'to have the final word on the right balance between patent holders and the needs of academic researchers', concluding with a warning: '. . . that is, if all the scientists haven't moved to China'. The latter is certainly an exaggeration, but it does suggest, based as it was on the views of scientists interviewed by the article's author, that not only may an excessively narrow research exemption hinder follow on innovation, but may also stop basic research in its tracks, and even drive away scientists to other countries. See Malakoff 2003.

REFERENCES

Atlantic Monthly (1872), 'Politics', *Atlantic Monthly*, 29(173), 387–388.

Chang, H. (2002), *Kicking Away the Ladder: Development Strategy in Historical Perspective*, London: Anthem Press.

Cornish, W. (1993), 'The International Relations of Intellectual Property', *Cambridge Law Journal*, 52(1), 46–63.

Dutfield, G. (2003), *Intellectual Property Rights and the Life Science Industries: A Twentieth Century History*, Aldershot: Ashgate.

Fisher, M. (2004), 'Growth of the Japanese Patent System: A Lesson For Us All?', *Intellectual Property Quarterly*, 22(1), 85–113.

Gowers, A. (2006), *Review of Intellectual Property: A Call for Evidence*, London: HM Treasury.

Johnson, C. (1982), *MITI and the Japanese Miracle: The Growth of Industrial Policy, 1925–1975*, Stanford: Stanford University Press.

Johnson, C. (1995), *Japan: Who Governs? The Rise of the Developmental State*, New York and London: W.W. Norton & Co.

Khan, B. (2004), *Does Copyright Piracy Pay? The Effects of US International Copyright Laws on the Market for Books, 1790–1920*, National Bureau of Economic Research Working Paper W10271, Cambridge, MA: National Bureau of Economic Research Inc.

Kim, L. (2003), *Technology Transfer and Intellectual Property Rights: The Experience of Korea*, Issues Paper No. 2, UNCTAD-ICTSD Project on Intellectual Property Rights and Sustainable Development, Geneva: UNCTAD-ICTSD.

Madey v Duke University, 307 F.3d 1351 (Fed. Cir. 2002).

Malakoff, D. (2003), 'Universities Ask Supreme Court to Reverse Patent Ruling', *Science*, 299(5603), 26.

Musungu, F. and G. Dutfield (2003), *Multilateral Agreement and a TRIPS Plus World: The World Intellectual Property Organization*, TRIPS Issues Paper No. 3, Geneva: Quaker United Nations Office.

Sagar, R. (2006), *Identifying Models of Best Practices in the Provision of Technical Assistance to Facilitate the Implementation of the TRIPS Agreement*, Queen Mary University of London, London.

Santini, L. (2004), 'Drug companies look to China for cheap R&D', *Wall Street Journal*, 22 November 2004.

World Bank (2001), *Global Economic Prospects & the Developing Countries 2002*, Washington DC: World Bank.

4. Last chance? Multilateralism, TRIPS and developing countries

Xu Yi-chong

1. INTRODUCTION

Making rules for the protection of intellectual property rights (IPRs) involves finding a balance between the interests of right-holders and right-users. The first international trade agreement on IPRs protection, the Agreement on Trade-Related Intellectual Property Rights (TRIPS Agreement) is skewed in favour of the interests of intellectual property right-holders and the countries where they reside at the expense of right-users and developing countries.[1] It is, however, not in the interest of developing countries to abandon or to reopen the TRIPS Agreement. This chapter argues that there are three instruments available in the WTO system that may allow developing countries to pursue their interests and address some of the imbalances inherent in the TRIPS Agreement: the TRIPS Council, which is empowered to oversee and monitor the implementation of the Agreement; the dispute settlement mechanism embedded in the WTO Dispute Settlement Understanding (DSU); and the continuing negotiations in adjusting the multilateral trading regime. Two important features of the TRIPS Agreement make the use of these instruments feasible. One is the flexibility of the TRIPS Agreement: like all international agreements, the provisions of the Agreement are broadly, and sometimes even vaguely, defined and their implications therefore depend heavily on the interpretation of these provisions. The other is the 'positive' nature of the required enforcement process: the TRIPS Agreement requires the adoption and adaptation of domestic legislation. The combination of international and domestic politics embedded in the TRIPS Agreement means that its enforcement will inevitably involve a political and diplomatic process within which both active and passive instruments can be utilised to address the imbalanced interests of the right-holders and right-users.

This chapter accepts three established arguments. First, the issue of IPRs protection was brought into the Uruguay Round negotiations under the threat, and reality, of trade sanctions against some developing countries and the withdrawal of their aid particularly by the United States; and the terms of the TRIPS Agreement reflected this unequal bargaining position (Sell 2003). Secondly, implementation of the TRIPS Agreement incurs substantial economic and social costs for developing countries because it involves a significant transfer of resources from consumers and firms in developing countries to those in industrialised countries (United Nations Conference on Trade and Development 1996). Thirdly, the difficulty of effecting technology transfers to developing countries is more acute than ever as developing countries are facing health crises on a massive scale and as the disparity between the rich and the poor is enlarging at an alarming rate. Improving access to effective and affordable medicine and technology is necessary to reverse the rising trend of high mortality and morbidity from infectious and non-communicable diseases. It is also an effective way to alleviate poverty in developing countries.

Despite (and because of) these developments, it is argued in this chapter that undoing or reopening the TRIPS Agreement is not a course of action that would benefit developing nations for several reasons: (a) the Agreement is part of the package of international trade agreements from which developing countries can benefit; (b) without such a multilateral agreement developing countries would be more vulnerable to the tactics of divide and conquer through lopsided bilateral or pluralateral negotiations, as they experienced during the financial crises in the 1980s and 1990s; and (c) long-term, multi-level and multi-channelled coordinated actions can help developing countries enhance their ability to redefine and reshape the understanding and priorities concerning the interests of right-users and to ensure the implementation of intellectual property regimes in a manner appropriate to their needs. Redefining and reshaping the priorities of TRIPS is possible because, as many experts admit, the TRIPS Agreement 'retains flexibility for choosing standards that pay attention to the development needs of particular economies while meeting TRIPS obligations' (Maskus 2000, p. 148). This flexibility is the product of hard bargaining during the Uruguay Round. Broadly and vaguely defined provisions of the Agreement are exhibited by the cross-referencing of existing multilateral conventions and by the standards established specifically in the TRIPS Agreement. Comprehensive coverage and broad governing provisions mean that the implementation of the TRIPS Agreement depends heavily on how the rules and standards are interpreted and 'what these norms and standards actually entail as well as regarding whether a provision of national law correctly reflects such a norm or standard' (Geuze and Hannu 1999, p. 348). This will result in a greater reliance on the DSU, which serves 'to clarify the existing provisions of those agreements in accordance with customary rules of interpretation of public international law' (DSU

Art 3.2). Legalised dispute settlement bodies, however, 'are "passive" organs . . . unable to initiate action by unilaterally seizing a dispute' (Keohane, Moravcsik and Slaughter 2000, p. 462). While the initiatives to engage in debate and reshape the direction of the TRIPS development lie in the hands of states through the DSU, states can also take initiatives through another two active mechanisms – the TRIPS Council and continuing multilateral trade negotiations (MTN) in general.

This being said, it is acknowledged that there is no easy way to address the asymmetric power relationship between the battalions of pharmaceutical and entertainment industries based in developed countries and poor developing countries. Neither is there an easy way to balance the power of a few rich countries with the interests of many small and poor developing countries. The reality of world politics remains power-based: 'the structure of power and interests, the extent of inequality, the divergences of cultures and value systems, and the rigidities of political language make the resolution of many conflicts difficult, if not impossible' (Hurrell 2003, p. 26). Nonetheless, institutionalised negotiations and judicialised trade rules can play a positive role in assisting the weak and the poor. The developing countries can defend their interests and address the existing problems in the TRIPS Agreement by participating in the TRIPS Council and using their collective bargaining power to advance their interests. They can actively bring cases to the DSB process, the outcomes of which bind both weak and strong states. It is under this process that their legal, political and diplomatic interests are often taken into account. Thirdly, they can seek help from the combination of the TRIPS Council, DSB, and other international organisations, especially UNCTAD which has spoken up about the high costs developing countries must incur in implementing the TRIPS Agreement. In addition, assistance can be gained from the WHO and the UN High Commission on Human Rights, both of which are deeply concerned about the impact of the TRIPS Agreement on the public health in poor countries.

The first section of this chapter will briefly discuss the TRIPS Agreement, pointing out the flexibility and options that are available for interpretation and the responsibilities delegated to the TRIPS Council. The second section will discuss the DSU and especially the lesson we can draw from the first TRIPS case, *India – Patents (US)* (the mailbox case; WT/DS50/AB/R). Particular attention will be given to the role and responsibilities of panelists and the members of the Appellate Body. The last section will focus on the issue of implementation and continuing negotiations. The argument presented in this chapter is that these established and institutionalised multilateral channels (the TRIPS Council and the DSB), like all international organisations, and despite their restraints, allow 'for the centralisation of collective activities through a concrete and stable organisational structure and a supportive administrative apparatus [which] increase the efficiency of collective activities and enhance the organisation's ability to affect the understanding, environment, and interests of states' (Abbott and Snidal 1998, pp. 4–5). They therefore provide ample opportunities for affected parties to participate in the deliberation and bargaining over competing goals. The availability of the institutionalised setting through which collective actions can be taken does not by itself guarantee the rebalance of the interests of right-holders and right-users. Developing countries must actively participate in the process by bringing their concerns to the multilateral arena. Multilateral cooperation through formal organisations is the best way to restrain the strong and protect the weak.

2. TRIPS AND THE TRIPS COUNCIL

Intellectual property, by definition, infers monopolies and restriction of competition. Ever since the concept of intellectual property became known in the early 17th century, it has been linked with government-granted monopoly rights and trade restrictions. The fundamental assumption behind the concept of IPRs is that the state has the power to grant the temporary monopoly, leaving society with the obligation to abide by the temporary monopoly rights given to the individual, and to protect these rights from infringement by others. Protection of intellectual rights therefore involves several parties – the state, IPR holders, users and the society as a whole. Two important implications of the nature of IP are: its protection used to be limited within a territory-bound state; and the interests of users are often paid insufficient regard when protection is granted. First, the territorial nature of IPR protection means that how the IPR protection is provided depends heavily on the political and economic system, level of technical and economic development, and the prevailing interpretation of what intellectual property rights are in a given society. Not all states have the same political and economic systems and certainly are not at the same development stage; and neither do they have the same view about what to protect and how to have it protected. There can be disagreement between states as to who are the actors – are they individuals or collectivities who have rights, privileges, duties, power, or liabilities? In what way are these rights protected? All societies have measures to protect public goods, among which intellectual property is one. Yet, what is considered to be protected and how they are to be protected vary greatly. Because of these reasons, it is difficult to internationalise or globalise IP protection. This is one of the main reasons for the difficulties in internationalising or globalising IPRs protection.

Secondly, protection of IPRs involves balancing the interests of right-holders and right-users. In the last quarter of the 20th century there was a steady, yet significant, increase in the protection of the interests of right-holders. For example, patent protection of 14 years was increased to 20 years in 1977 and patent-holders of medicinal products were granted an additional five years. The term of copyright protection was increased in many countries from the life of the author plus 50 years to life plus 70 years. Intellectual property rights relate to public goods. This concept has been used by right-holders who argue that since IPRs are public goods, their access by one person does not exclude the access by others and there is therefore no incentive for people to engage in research and development unless some protection is granted to the right-holders. Furthermore, the value of IPRs will not decline or diminish as they are consumed and therefore an extension of the protection of right-holders after life in the case of copyright at least is necessary. These increases were clear indications that the concept has been exploited by 'the big battalions' – big and powerful copyright or patent holders – often at the expense of the inventor. The UK Law Lord Sydney Templeman of the House of Lords explains: '[a]ll the increases of patent and copyright protection were obtained by powerful lobbies persuading individual governments to take action and then persuading all others to "harmonize" their legislation, thus obtaining world wide monopolies' (Templeman 1998, p. 604). One explanation of the overwhelming influence of the right-holders is that within a state user interests can be protected by deference to local laws when local lawmakers are resolved to promote user values. That resolve 'can easily dissipate in the welter of international lobbying [where] public choice problems are exacerbated because right holders have so far proven better able than user groups to put their demands before multiple legislatures and international lawmakers' (Dreyfuss 2004, p. 26).

Since the mid-19th century, IPR protection has also been subject to the international commitment a country made, such as the Paris Convention (which deals with the protection of industrial property) and the Berne Convention (which deals with copyright). Different countries have different commitment on IPR protection. From the late 1970s the pressure to politicise the issue and link the traditional 'arcane, technical issue' with international trade heated up, primarily because of 'the expressed wishes of the twelve chief executive officers of US-based multinational corporations' (Sell 2003, p. 13). While it had begun incorporating IP protection into its domestic trade legislation, the US 'employed a coercive trade-based strategy, threatening trade sanctions and the denial of trade benefits for countries whose IP regimes were deemed as unacceptably weak' (Sell 2003, p. 13). The ultimate acceptance of the TRIPS Agreement at the end of the

Uruguay Round was therefore a clear indication that governments had been captured by the right-holders, including the pharmaceutical, entertainment and information industries, which 'mobilized their private sector counterparts both at home and abroad to press their governments and the GATT to support and produce an IP code' (Sell 2003, p. 13). Indeed, they 'were largely responsible for getting TRIPS on the agenda, obtained much of what they sought when the negotiations were launched' (Sell 2003, p. 120; Hoekman and Kostecki 2001, p. 297).

3. SUBSTANCE

The original objective of developed countries to pursue the negotiation over trade-related intellectual property rights at the Uruguay Round was 'to limit the capacity of firms in developing countries to make export free-riding copies of high-tech goods produced at great cost in the developed countries' (Reichman 1998, p. 585). By the time the Uruguay Round was concluded, countries had accepted the TRIPS Agreement (if not all the detailed substance, at least the principle), which extended not only the coverage of IPRs but also the coverage period of protection for right-holders. The TRIPS Agreement covers almost all aspects of IP – copyrights and related rights, trademarks, geographical indications, industrial designs, patents, layout designs of integrated circuits and trade secrets. It adopted a patent law minimum well above the previous standards of the 1883 Paris Convention; extended copyrights norms under the Berne Convention to covering new copyrights, such as computer software, databases and sound recording; expanded patent rights to virtually all subject matter, including pharmaceutical products, chemicals, pesticides and plant varieties; and required all signatory countries to observe the Treaty on Intellectual Property in Respect of Integrated Circuits. It also imposed the non-discriminatory 'Most Favoured Nation' principles and national treatment to the IPRs protection on member nations. TRIPS represents the effort of harmonising a wide range of intellectual property protection standards across a wide range of countries at different development stages and provides a multilateral justification for the unilateral pressure on IPR protection.

4. ENFORCEMENT

Like its counterpart, GATS (General Agreement on Trade in Services), the TRIPS Agreement is an agreement that introduces positive obligations to adopt new domestic policy measures. Unlike the GATS, which established the opt-in principle, the TRIPS Agreement established the obligations for all members to adopt a wide range of IPR protection by changing or adopting new domestic legislations. It has moved far beyond the traditional realm of negative integration, which consists of prohibitions of certain trade restricting measures. Instead, it requires members to introduce regulations in areas of public policy traditionally restricted to the sovereign state, and it requires the reform of domestic institutional arrangements. While negative integration under the GATT/WTO regime proceeds via the removal of trade barriers in bilateral deals and reciprocal concessions that are then applicable to all member states, the positive integration in IPR protection requires significant improvement, adaptation and enlargement of legal, administrative and particularly enforcement frameworks in complying with the Agreement.

Furthermore, since the TRIPS Agreement provides a comprehensive code of substantive obligations regarding all major aspects of IPRs protection, it imposes 'detailed obligations regarding private and public enforcement and procedural fairness mechanisms' (Smith 1999, p. 436). Broad enforcement standards are required to be set up by members, as stated in TRIPS Art 41:

> . . . enforcement procedures as specified in this Part are available under their law so as to permit effective action against any act of infringement of intellectual property rights covered by this Agreement, including expeditious remedies to prevent infringements and remedies which constitute a deterrent to further infringements. These procedures shall be applied in such a manner as to avoid the creation of barriers to legitimate trade and to provide for safeguards against their abuse.

Since the role and operation of private and public enforcement of IPRs protection vary greatly across states, harmonisation of enforcement is a major challenge as national laws, institutions and procedures must be brought in line with the provision of the TRIPS Agreement, which could become a demanding endeavour for many developing countries and involve substantial costs (United Nations Conference on Trade and Development 1996). For this reason, TRIPS set different dates for implementation for different countries – 1996 for developed countries, 2000 for developing and transition economies and 2006 (eventually extended to 2016) for least-developed countries (Arts 65 and 66).

5. INSTITUTIONS

The TRIPS Council is charged with monitoring the operation of the Agreement, especially each member's compliance with its obligations

(Art 68). It is empowered to oversee a notification programme of all members' laws and regulations in the fields of intellectual property, which is particularly onerous to members (Art 63), and has the power to grant a waiver of certain obligations (Art 63.2). The Council operates as a forum for consultations on any problems relating to TRIPS which arise between countries, and it has the capacity to clarify and interpret provisions of the Agreement. The aim is, whenever possible, 'to resolve differences between countries without the need for formal recourse to dispute settlement' (Geuze and Hannu 1999, p. 382). The Agreement also requires the TRIPS Council to study the scope and modalities of complaints regarding indirect violation of IPRs under the dispute settlement mechanism (Art 64.3). Art 71.1 of the Agreement calls for a review of its implementation after the expiration of the transitional period (1 January 2000) and at two-yearly intervals thereafter. It is the responsibility of the TRIPS Council to undertake such reviews and suggest changes when new developments warrant the modifications of the Agreement. In addition to these powers, the TRIPS Council has two specific powers: the non-application of the so-called non-violation and situation complaints under the dispute settlement provisions of the DSU; and the special power as related to the special ten-year transition period for the implementation of the TRIPS Agreement granted to the least-developed countries in Art 66.1.

There are several major issues concerning the institutional arrangement of the TRIPS Council. The first is that the TRIPS Agreement contains few examples of functions specifically assigned to the TRIPS Council: it is not clear from the text whether the oversight function grants the TRIPS Council any decision-making power at all; on the other hand, the text on the oversight function 'is so broad that it could encompass almost any kind of decision' (Kuijper 2002, p. 84). The second one is that as the Council is granted the power to extend the waiver to developing countries, it is up to the member states to make a decision which is often subject to negotiations and bargains rather than following strictly the principles set up in the Agreement. Such a process undoubtedly operates in the shadow of the exercise of power. Yet within a multilateral institutional context, power is not as easily abused as in a bilateral environment. The third issue is that as members are afforded the opportunity to consult with the TRIPS Council 'on matters relating to the trade-related aspects of intellectual property rights' (Art 68), it is the Council's responsibility to decide whether a member has or has not complied with the Agreement. Though its decision is not binding, as are decisions made by the DS panelists and the Appellant Body, it does carry political and diplomatic weight. Finally, the TRIPS Council is open to all WTO members to participate who are willing to engage in the administration of the TRIPS Agreement. This means when the issue of reviews, modifications or approvals of the establishment of panels or the adoption of the panel reports arises, the Council members will inevitably engage in the normal process of negotiations and bargaining.

6. DISPUTE SETTLEMENT MECHANISM

While the TRIPS Council offers the opportunity for WTO members to engage in institutionalised bargaining, the dispute settlement mechanism allows them to 'delegate the task to third-party tribunals charged with applying general legal principles' (Keohane, Moravcsik and Slaughter 2000, p. 457). This institutionalised legalislation may assist developing countries rebalance the interests in the TRIPS Agreement because 'institutions for selecting judges, controlling access to dispute resolution, and legally enforcing the judgments of international courts and tribunals have a major impact on state behaviour' (Keohane, Moravcsik and Slaughter 2000, p. 458). The effective resolution of trade disputes is vital for the smooth operation of the world trade system and the dispute settlement mechanism, no matter how primitive it might be, was developed as soon as the GATT became operational (see Xu and Weller 2004). Under the GATT, dispute settlement was based on voluntary and consensus principles – that is, the GATT as an institution could not handle a dispute unless the disputing parties agreed to allow it to do so. Even after the dispute was assessed and a decision was made, the resolution could not be automatically adopted. To improve the dispute settlement mechanism, countries adopted the Understanding on Rules and Procedures Governing the Settlement of Disputes at the Uruguay Round. Under the new procedure, disputing countries can no longer block the establishment of a panel or the adoption of panel reports. Consequently, not only did the decisions of panels and Appellate Body become binding, but also their adoption is automatic unless the decisions are rejected by consensus of the members of the DSB (which is highly unlikely to ever occur).

Part of the reason for the US and some developed countries insisting on placing IP protection under the umbrella of the GATT was that, under the WIPO Paris-Berne regime, dispute resolution procedures can only be adopted on a voluntary and consensual basis by any parties (individuals or firms) that wish to avail themselves of WIPO's dispute-resolution services: mediation, arbitration and expedited arbitration. By contrast, an important component of TRIPS 'is that it folds disputes over IPRs into the integrated dispute settlement mechanism that lies at the heart of the WTO' (Maskus 2000, p. 26). That is, in contrast to the multilateral agreements on trade in goods and the GATS, the TRIPS Agreement does not include additional dispute settlement provisions on, for example, the composition of the panels and on the relationship between the WTO dispute settlement system and dispute settlement provisions in conventions on IPR outside the WTO, such as WIPO. The TRIPS Agreement (Art 64.1) provides that the rules of Arts XXII and XIII of GATT 1994, as elaborated by the Dispute Settlement Understanding (DSU), will apply to consultations and dispute settlement under the TRIPS Agreement. Disputes under TRIPS are settled through the same process as under the general DSU.

If the TRIPS Agreement is seen as a type of soft international law because it is drafted in vague and broad terminology, its incorporation of the broad WTO DSU processes can be seen as an attempt to move in the direction of hard international law as it would enable disputes to be resolved by legally binding rulings. 'By using hard law to order their relations, international actors reduce transaction costs, strengthen the credibility of their commitments, expand their available political strategies, and resolve problems of incomplete contracting' (Abbott and Snidal 2000, p. 422). Even though all international laws operate in the shadow of power, it is much harder to capture a passive body of a governing system, say the judicial system, than the active one, such as the general decision-making body. Indeed, the process of legalising the selection of judges, the control of access to dispute resolution procedure, interpreting the contracts or covenants and their enforcement has an effect on the behaviour of states, large and small, rich and poor, and developed and developing ones (Goldstein, Kahler, Keohane and Slaughter 2000).

7. CASES

Between 1995 and 2003, there were 304 cases under DSU and 25 of these concerned provisions of TRIPS (merely 8 per cent).

Six of these 25 cases involved the US and the EC and 17 of the 25 cases were between developed countries. The eight cases (less than one-third) that involved a developed and a developing country covered five developing countries – Argentina, Brazil, India, Indonesia and Pakistan – and in only one of them was the developing country the complainant (IP/D/24). One explanation of this small number of developing countries involved in the disputes over TRIPS is that the Agreement allows for a five-year transition period for developing countries, and a ten-year period for less developed countries. Another reason is that despite the creation of the Advisory Centre on WTO Law which offers *pro bono* services, developing countries do not have the human and economic resources to engage in such legal cases. In the seven cases where developing countries were the respondents,

Table 4.1 Between 1995 and 2003, there were 304 cases under DSU and 25 of these concerned provisions of TRIPS (merely 8 per cent)

Dispute	Complaint	Defendant	IP area	Date
IP/D/1	US	Japan	Copyright	1996
IP/D/2	US	Pakistan	Patents	1996
IP/D/3	US	Portugal	Patents	1996
IP/D/4	EC+MS	Japan	Copyright	1996
IP/D/5	US	India	Patents	1996
IP/D/6	US	Indonesia	Trademarks	1996
IP/D/7	EC+MS	India	Patents	1997
IP/D/8	US	Ireland	Copyrights/enforcement	1997
IP/D/9	US	Denmark	Enforcement	1997
IP/D/10	US	Sweden	Enforcement	1997
IP/D/11	EC+MS	Canada	Patents	1998
IP/D/12	US	EC	Copyrights/enforcement	1998
IP/D/13	US	EC	Enforcement	1998
IP/D/14	US	EC	Enforcement	1998
IP/D/15	Canada	EC+MS	Patents	1998
IP/D/16	EC+MS	US	Copyrights	1999
IP/D/17	US	Canada	Patents	1999
IP/D/18	US	Argentina	Patents	1999
IP/D/19	US	EC	Trademarks	1999
IP/D/20	EC	US	US domestic law	1999
IP/D/21	EC	US	US domestic law	2000
IP/D/22	US	Argentina	Patents	2000
IP/D/23	US	Brazil	Patents	2000
IP/D/24	Argentina	US	Patents	2001
IP/D/25	Australia	EC	Trademarks	2003

the US was the complainant for six of them. Since only the government can bring the cases to the DSB, it is evidence that the American government was fighting on behalf its pharmaceutical and entertainment industries against 'loopholes, alternative interpretations of vague language, and perhaps, most importantly, effective resistance to further expansion of global IP rights' (Sell 2003, p. 122).

Large developing countries were particularly targeted by the EC and US to ensure their compliance with the TRIPS Agreement on the provisions over the patents of pharmaceutical industries. IP/D/2, 5 and 7 concerned the same provisions of the TRIPS Agreement, namely Arts 70.8 and 70.9. The three cases the US brought against Argentina and Brazil 'go to the heart of the "access to essential medicines" campaign' (Sell 2003, p. 136). Two arguments can be made: (a) some large developing countries, such as

Brazil and India, are sufficiently competitive in the field that their counterparts in the developed countries are concerned; and (b) the active participation of large developing countries in the dispute settlement procedure can have substantial impact on the evolution of the interpretation and implementation of TRIPS. That is, if a system can be used to defend a particular regime, it can also be used to redirect the underlying principles of the regime. It is therefore the obligation of large developing countries to make the effort, at least, to raise the world's attention and concern through various channels, including the DSU, over the implications of the TRIPS Agreement on the developing countries.

8. PROCEDURES

The dispute settlement procedure under the TRIPS Agreement is the same as in other areas of dispute settlement in the WTO. It follows an established format: initiation of consultations, consultations, request for the establishment of a panel, third party participation, establishment of terms of reference, submission of pleadings and evidence, proceedings before the panels, possibilities for expert consultation, and final decision making. The DSU sets out a four-stage process for WTO members to resolve their differences over the implementation of the various WTO agreements. First, members must make efforts to resolve their differences through bilateral consultation, and if that fails, through the conciliation and mediation facilities offered by the Director-General. The objective is 'to enable the dispute parties to understand the factual situation and the legal claims and hopefully to settle the matter bilaterally' (Hoekman and Kostecki 2001, p. 76).

The second stage, if resolution is not reached, is to request a panel. The complaining party may request the establishment of a panel, which cannot be blocked by the complained party. According to Art 8 of the DSU, the Secretariat (specifically the legal affairs division, with consultation on the relevant division – the TRIPS division in this case) proposes a slate of panelists to the disputing parties. If the parties concerned do not accept the panelists within 20 days after the establishment of the panel, it is the responsibility of the WTO Director-General to appoint a panel of three from the list of candidates prepared by the Legal Affairs division. These candidates can be lawyers, former and current state delegates, diplomats, or other government officials or non-government (academic in particular) individuals who have the knowledge and experience which allow them to work as panelists.

The third stage involves the panel at work. Panelists are required to make an objective assessment of the matter before them, including the facts of the case and the applicability of the covered agreements. Another two important aspects of the panel procedure are: panelists can seek information and technical advice from any individual or body and consult experts to obtain their opinion; and panel deliberations are confidential. The panel is required to draft a report that includes conclusions and recommendations. The final report will be issued to the disputing parties and the Dispute Settlement Body (DSB), which consists of all WTO members.

The fourth stage involves the adoption of the report or an appeal. The panel report must be adopted within 60 days or rejected by consensus by the DSB. A party concerned can appeal the report to the Appellate Body (AB) but only over legal issues, not on facts. The AB is a permanent body, consisting of seven members who serve a four-year term, renewable for another term. Three of the seven will serve on a specific case. The AB report becomes the Dispute Settlement Body's ruling or recommendation within 60 days unless a consensus rejects it. Despite the effectively automatic nature of DSB rulings and recommendations, this does not remove the DSB from politics. The bargaining over the establishment of a panel or the selection of panelists allows individual governments to exercise a certain degree of underlying control over the legal promulgation and implementation of judgments.

9. ESTABLISHING A PANEL

As 'an extraordinary achievement that comes close to a miracle' (Ehlermann 2003b, p. 639), the DSU reversed the voluntary dispute settlement mechanism under the GATT regime to a more automatic system. Under the new WTO dispute settlement procedure, panels will be established if a potential plaintiff so wishes. The provision of the TRIPS Agreement as such, however, cannot be the direct and sole basis of a claim by a private party. Unlike disciplines formed under GATT 1947 that were primarily directed at the treatment of the goods of other countries, rules under the TRIPS mainly deal with the treatment of nationals of other WTO members. In addition, any action that charges non-compliance with the rules of TRIPS Agreement can only be taken by other WTO members, not by individuals or firms (Reiterer 1994; Hoekman and Kostecki 2001). Consequently, when a conflict over IPR protection arises, right-holders can only 'lobby' their governments to bring the disputing country to the DSU process. Governments, especially under the democratic system, may or may not always subject themselves to extremely narrow or secondary interest groups, as Keohane and his colleagues have argued:

> In state-controlled systems, the individual or group must typically lobby a specialized government bureaucracy, secure a majority in some relevant domestic

> decision-making body, or catch the attention of the head of the government. State officials are often cautious about instigating such proceedings against another state, since they must weigh a wide range of cross-cutting concerns, including the diplomatic costs of negotiating an arrangement with the foreign government in question (Keohane, Moravcsik and Slaughter 2000, p. 463).

There is, therefore, no guarantee that individuals or firms will be able to convince their government to 'espouse' their claims as a state claim against another government.

Secondly, over the procedural issue, countries cannot impose trade sanctions against another country without going through the proper dispute settlement process and gaining the authorisation of the DSU. That is, WTO members can only seek remedies with respect to other WTO members when authorisation is obtained from the DSB; and authorisation can only be obtained after a complaint has been filed under the DSU and a panel or AB report has been adopted by the DSB that recommends that the complained country comply with the panel or AB decision.

Thirdly, over each complaint, the panel makes its independent decision and the finding of the previous panels or AB cannot automatically extend to the cases on the same matter. In other words, panelists are not strictly bound by precedent, although obviously prior WTO decisions on similar matters are persuasive. The WTO has not adopted *stare decisis*, which is very much part of the judicial system in the common law system. In the matter of *India – Patents* (WT/DS79/R), 'on the same matter the Panel did not consider itself bound by the Panel and Appellate Body Reports in the dispute between the US and India, although it took them into account' (Geuze and Hannu 1999, p. 463). This principle undoubtedly creates another set of opportunities for developing countries to bring cases to the DSU to redress some original imbalances in the Agreement.

All in all, the DSU may be a powerful instrument for governments to protect their interests or even to 'coerce' others to subject to their policy pursuits. It is, however, important to note that the WTO dispute settlement body, like all judicial institutions, is no more than a 'passive' body of the whole governing structure, waiting for disputes to be brought in for resolution. Given this, if countries want to use the DSU to protect themselves, they will have to make the effort to go through the process. There are, of course, costs involved.

10. SELECTING PANELISTS

With an institutionalised adjudication system, a third party is required to make a decision over a particular dispute if the parties cannot reach agreement between themselves. The third party under the WTO are panelists and the AB. Panels are required to be 'composed of well-qualified government and/or non-governmental individuals, including persons who have served on or presented a case to a panel, served as a representative of a Member or of a contracting party to GATT 1947 or as a representative to the Council or Committee of any covered agreement or its predecessor agreement, or in the Secretariat, taught or published on international trade law or policy, or served as a senior trade policy official of a Member' (DSU Art 8.1). To assist the selection process, the Secretariat keeps a roster of candidates, based on their specialty, publication and work experience.

Given the process of selecting panelists often runs into a political stalemate, the disputing countries prefer to ask the Secretariat for help. It is not uncommon that when one party selects the panelists, the other opposes automatically because of the perceived and real differences in views over the issue concerned. Neither is it uncommon for one country to demand lawyers as panelists while the opponent wants economists; or for a country to want economists or lawyers while its opponent tries hard to make sure that the panelists are non-lawyers and non-economists, but practitioners who are more politically and diplomatically sensitive. Helping the disputing countries select panelists requires delicate diplomacy for the WTO Secretariat: its Legal Affairs division often discusses the selection of panelists not only with disputing countries but other operating divisions of WTO, which know specialists in the fields.

Countries concerned have 20 days to agree on a list of panelists. If there is no agreement (which occurs in about one-third of the cases), the Director-General will appoint the panelists. Once the disputing countries accept the panelists, the Secretariat contacts the individuals and checks whether there are any conflicts of interest. It is always useful to have at least one panelist from Geneva, whether it is a delegate to the WTO or someone from outside, to help with the administrative details. The panelist selection process is one indication of the effect of 'political filter' in the dispute settlement process. Some have argued that to avoid delays or potential biases, it is better to create permanent panelists. For now, however, 'the flexibility of the current ad hoc selection system serves to address one of the key objectives of a party to a WTO panel proceeding – to compose a panel that appears likely to rule in its favour – better than would a permanent panel body' (Shoyer 2003, p. 203). This flexible selection process allows disputing parties to settle for neutrality whilst creating a perception that the selection is 'more than neutral'. Perception is crucial in international diplomacy.

A similar spirit exists in relation to the Appellate Body whose first team 'was a cocktail with ingredients from all branches of government (the legislative, the executive and the judiciary branches) international organisations (regional and world-wide), academia, private law practice, and private arbitration' (Ehlermann 2003b, p. 608). Two of the first seven members of the AB elected in 1995 were not lawyers. Julio Lacarte (Uruguay) had been at the original Havana conference 1946/47 and incarnates the history of GATT and the WTO, and is a long-time believer that 'diplomacy and international negotiations have traditionally thrived on discretion and secrecy; indeed, they could not exist if they were deprived of them' (Lacarte 2004, p. 683; see also Oxley 1990, p. 136). Four of the members of the AB had previous careers as senior bureaucrats or diplomats. The current members of the AB are not all trade specialists. The chairman, George Abi-Saab from Egypt, has had a wide experience in working on international bodies including the IMF Administrative Tribunal, and the Appeals Chamber of the International Criminal Tribunal for the former Yugoslavia. Mr A.V. Ganasan is a life-time domestic civil servant from India.

Art 8 of the DSU allows the selection of panelists from other international Organisations, including WIPO and the European Patent Office (Petersmann 1997). The concern is whether panelists from WIPO and the European Patent Office institutions which specialise in intellectual property law should have the authority to interpret the TRIPS Agreement. In principle, the WIPO secretariat is not authorised to interpret any multilateral conventions it administers, at least not officially. The second concern is whether panelists from these institutions can interpret the Agreement fairly because normally those who work for specific international Organisations often share the principal philosophy of the Organisation. Those who work for WIPO tend to be believers in the protection of intellectual property rights and the interests of right-holders. Consequently, it should be taken for granted that the WIPO staff will not be able to balance the interests of right-holders and right-users and the concern of selecting panelists from WIPO or other Organisations in charge of IP issues is real.

11. INDEPENDENCE

Panelists and members of the AB are independent of their home countries. Members of the AB in particular are 'appointed by all the Members of the WTO to speak for all the Members of the WTO by speaking solely for the WTO trading system as a whole' (Bacchus 2002, p. 1024). They work in a quasi-judicial system. It is judicial because panelists and members of the AB do make judicial decisions over the disputes. In that sense it is quasi-judicial because the rulings of the panel and AB must be adopted by the members of the WTO through the DSB. The rulings of the AB will not be adopted only if all the members of the WTO decide by 'consensus' that they should not be – including the member or members in whose favour AB may have ruled. Thus far, this has unsurprisingly never happened.

According to those who have served at panels or AB, their utmost objective is to 'gain credibility, acceptability, and legitimacy, combined with the paramount concern for independence' (Ehlermann 2003b, p. 696). To uphold the credibility of panels and AB as an institution, Arts 14 and 17.11 DSU require the deliberations of panels and the AB to be confidential. Individual opinions are allowed, provided they are expressed anonymously. Consensus decision-making is considered necessary to maintain the independence of the institution. As described by the AB member Fiorentino Feliciano (the Philippines):

> [Independence] has at least two aspects: firstly, independence and impartiality need to be constantly felt and lived, and manifested in every adjudication rendered. A second aspect relates to the independence and impartiality of the institutions of dispute settlement themselves, the Appellate Body and panels. Institutional independence implies acceptance of some costs and some restraints on the part of all involved but it is entirely indispensable for the maintenance and development of the kind of dispute resolution institutions and processes you have put in motion (Bacchus 2002, p. 696).

Building such independent quasi-judicial institutions does not mean that panelists and members of the AB have any intentions or illusions about contributing to the 'World Trade Constitution'. Indeed, closed-door deliberations and consensus decision-making processes allow them to make decisions based on a combination of political, legal, diplomatic and economic considerations. As another member of the AB (James Bacchus) once commented in relation to 'GATT old hands': 'GATT hands tend to the real world. GATT hands are practical. GATT hands are as mundane as the mundane pose of the GATT itself. We are realists' (Bacchus 2003). To them the aim is 'to gain credibility, acceptability, and legitimacy, combined with the paramount concern for independence'. This is more important than pursuing 'any constitutional aspirations (Ehlermann 2003a, pp. 696 and 698).[2] The 'quasi-judicial' nature of the WTO dispute settlement mechanism sets the parameters within which they make their decisions. That is, the key in the decision-making process is the interpretation of the WTO agreements as well as the dispute settlement procedures. Although the DSU has some explicit provisions relating to some of the issues raised, 'on other procedural issues, the DSU says very little or nothing at all' (Steger 2002, p. 487).

12. INTERPRETATIONS

12.1 The Secretariat

Once a panel is formed and the work starts, a key issue is how the panelists 'adjudicate' the dispute. Panels are not standing bodies, but ad hoc tribunals created pursuant to predetermined procedures under the DSU. To ensure consistency in making judgments on cases, the Secretariat is always present, providing panelists with summaries and analyses of the cases and lists of questions. When experts are needed, the Secretariat will provide the list of names for panelists to choose from. After the last round of meetings (often two to three rounds depending on the nature of the disputes), the panelists will tell the Secretariat what they want and what they do not want in the final reports. The Secretariat will then draft the outlines of the final report. The scope for initiative to be taken by the Secretariat will depend on how detailed panelists' instructions are. The Secretariat then will go through the outline with the panelists and make the necessary changes. If panelists are less experienced in adjudicating such cases, the Secretariat can have significant influence in the process as well as the final reports. When panelists are state delegates, according to some staff at the Legal Affairs division, the panelists might handle the politics while the Secretariat might research and write up the law. If the panelists are academics, the reverse might be the case. When panelists are the current state delegates or trade officials, their time constraints may require that the Secretariat play a major role in the process.

12.2 Difficulties

In trade disputes, parties frequently disagree on the rules, particularly the interpretation of rules and their application to their particular circumstances. They need a neutral third party to intervene and interpret the rules so that one party has the necessary justification for changing its behaviour.[3] In making judgment, the understanding and the interpretation of the disputes and the law are essential. The TRIPS Agreement covers two main sets of legal provisions – those of the existing multilateral covenants relating to IPRs protection which it incorporates by reference into the Agreement, such as specified provisions in the Berne Convention and the Paris Convention, and those that are specific to the TRIPS Agreement. This means that the panels not only need to understand the two sets of provisions but, more importantly, must be able to interpret them in a coherent way, as required by Art 3.2 DSU. It states that the dispute settlement procedure serves to clarify the existing provisions of the covered agreements 'in accordance with customary rules of interpretation of public international law' and Art 31.1 of the Vienna Convention on the Law of Treaties. The Law on Treaties became effective on 27 January 1980, stating: '[a] treaty shall be interpreted in good faith in accordance with the ordinary meaning to be given to the terms of the treaty in their context and in the light of its objective and purpose'. The three criteria set up in the Convention are ordinary meaning, objective and purpose. Panels and the AB have 'certainly attached the greatest weight to the first, such as "the ordinary meaning of the terms of the treaty" ' (Ehlermann 2003b, p. 651).

Secondly, disagreements over whether intellectual property should be brought under the umbrella of the GATT rules can, at least partially, explain some of the ambiguous provisions of the Agreement and the continuing debate over its implementation. In other words, as the first international agreement trying to harmonise IPR protection, flexibility is not only necessary but also inevitable. Art 30 of the TRIPS Agreement declares:

> Members may provide exceptions to the exclusive rights conferred by a patent, provided that such exceptions do not unreasonably conflict with a normal exploitation of the patent and do not unreasonably prejudice the legitimate interests of the patent owner, taking account of the legitimate interests of third parties.

Vested with the power to interpret the rules, and TRIPS in particular, the panels and the Appellate Body can shape the direction of the development of TRIPS. As in the matter of *India – Patents (US)* over patent protection for pharmaceutical and agricultural chemical products, the panel decided, 'when interpreting the text of the TRIPS Agreement, the legitimate expectation of WTO Members concerning the TRIPS Agreement must be taken into account, as well as standards of interpretation developed in past panel reports in the GATT framework, in particular those laying down the principle of the protection of conditions of competition flowing from multilateral trade agreement' (WT/DS50/R 1997).

The terms 'flexibility' and 'without prejudice' were formally integrated into the Doha Declaration and even WTO directors-general encourage countries to use this flexibility to ensure that medicines reach the world's poorest and most vulnerable people. Finally, the TRIPS Agreement provides a framework for legislation, but does not set out operative provisions that are directly imported into national law. In some cases, there is considerable room for interpretation as to the meaning of TRIPS provisions. For example, the concept of 'exclusive marketing rights' contained in Art 70.9 is undefined. Art 27.3(b) allows members to develop an 'effective *sui generic* regime' for plant varieties that may be designed without following any specific model. Even in those cases where the standard of protection is clearly stated, members must decide how to implement it according to their own legal systems (Art 1). Flexible implementation of the Agreement will inevitably lead to disputes among states. Room for differences of opinion about the meaning and import of TRIPS provisions is not necessarily negated by the broad requirement under the Vienna Convention on the Law of Treaties, 'WTO panels are to interpret and apply the provisions of WTO agreements in light of their object and purpose' (Shaffer 2004, p. 467). The TRIPS objects are very broad and to an extent contradictory.

The WTO dispute settlement system is not rigidly legal even with dispute outcomes leading to the binding Dispute Settlement Body recommendations and rulings. The efficacy of the WTO DSB system still depends ultimately on the will of governments to make it work. This 'quasi-judicial' nature of the dispute settlement process requires panels and members of the Appellate Body to take into consideration political, diplomatic, economic and legal aspects of the disputes with which they are required to deal. This is particularly the case if we accept the argument that the WTO dispute settlement process is not designed to facilitate punishment, but rather to constrain it (if it is believed we should). The DSU can be used as a vehicle for developing countries to engage in renegotiation of provisions of the Agreement. It may well give at least some developing countries 'meaningful hostages in their relations with developed countries' in the continuing negotiations over the exchange of market access in goods and services and concessions regarding the protection of IPRs (Ethier 2004, p. 456).

12.3 'Soft' Law

The standards of interpretation vary according to matters being dealt with as well as who serves in the panels. A panel 'could stringently apply the specific provisions of the TRIPS Agreement . . . as setting a "floor" for international intellectual property protection that all members must meet'. It could also 'take a more active role in flexibly applying open-ended provisions of the TRIPS Agreement to assess the costs and benefits of competing public goods concerns in a specific factual context (Shaffer 2004, p. 468).

'The language of the relevant WTO agreement has been strictly interpreted where a strict interpretation has served a panel's or the Appellate Body's trade policy preference', commented a WTO observer. 'But where the agreement contains language that, fairly read, allows a WTO Member discretion to interpret the relevant agreement in a way that offends a panel's or the Appellate Body's policy sensibilities, both have been happy to read the offending language out of the agreement' (Greenwald 2003, p. 113). Neither member states nor panelists and AB have any hesitation in using their 'interpretation' power to promote their favoured policies. They may do so to exercise their policy-making power on a global level and/or to maintain institutional credibility. The practice, however, makes some happy when they win a dispute while others grumble when their cases are ruled out. This is not unique to the WTO dispute settlement mechanisms. All international dispute resolution procedures leave plenty of room for interpretation so that the 'legal system' created by states will not collapse with states' occasional violation of the rules. An international system built on a combination of strict rules and regulations and flexible interpretation, implementation and adjudication of the rules, provides states with the opportunities to pursue their national interests while respecting the rules and regulations. The combination of legal and diplomatic mechanisms allows multilateral cooperation, as in the case of the WTO, to survive.

13. MULTILATERAL ARENA

The GATT/WTO system is not intended to be a rigid system. It has evolved through continuing negotiations that are highlighted with the major rounds. The TRIPS Agreement not only represented a revolution in international intellectual property law but also 'carried the developed countries well beyond their initial goal, which was to limit the capacity of firms in developing countries to make and export free-riding copies of high-tech goods produced at great cost in the developed countries' (Reichman 1998). But the law of unintended consequences has been at work and has both heightened and expanded the conflictual aspects of the Agreement. What was not really evident in 1994 at the conclusion of the Uruguay Round was the acceleration of the biotechnology revolution that has brought to the forefront environmental and food safety issues (genetically modified organisms and so on). With the spread of the HIV/AIDS pandemic, the implementation of the TRIPS Agreement has become a human rights issue that needs to be addressed not only by the WTO but also with the participation of other Organisations.

Indeed, during the Uruguay Round, when intellectual property rights were brought to the negotiation tables, few developed and developing countries were aware of the full implications of the potential rules. With the exception of UNCTAD and WIPO, other international Organisations, such as the WHO, whose interest in public health overrides its concern for the interests of pharmaceutical industries, and the UN High Commission on Human Rights, which treats the deprivation of medicine for HIV/AIDS as a human rights violation, were excluded from the negotiations.[4] Finally, some serious issues, particularly HIV-AIDS, at the time were exclusively the concerns of the developed countries and therefore little attention was paid to the potential impact of the Agreement on such problems. For these reasons, continuing negotiations over the specific provisions and the implementation of the Agreement are inevitable and have been and will be conducted under quite different circumstances.

Furthermore, TRIPS is a component of an elaborate system of international institutions and rules concerning protection of intellectual property rights. In addition to WIPO, which is the primary Organisation providing a range of services aimed at facilitating or strengthening the protection of intellectual property at the international level, the World Bank, the Food and Agriculture Organization (FAO), the International Telecommunications Union (ITU), the United Nations Conference on Trade and Development (UNCTAD), the United Nations Development Program (UNDP), and the World Health Organization (WHO) are deeply involved in IPRs-related work. Some other Organisations, such as OECD, African Regional Industrial Property Organization, the European Patent Office and the North American Free Trade Agreement (NAFTA) also 'play prominent roles in developing and implementing IPRs standards, as well as in the formation of research and development programs' (Abbott 1998, p. 500). The involvement of all these institutions in protecting IPRs means that there are various avenues for developing countries to coordinate strategies to offset the relentless bilateral pressure from the developed countries, especially the US, to ratchet up global patent rights over the longer term through constant forum-shifting.

With the participation of a variety of international institutions, developing countries would also be able to 'enlarge the policy space in which they may implement domestic regulatory regimes to suit their interests, and gain confidence in their ability to ward off US and EC legal threats to these choices' (Shaffer 2004).

14. CONCLUSION

The TRIPS Agreement has become synonymous with the debate on the rich versus the poor, developed versus developing, greedy pharmaceutical industries versus dying AIDS patients in many developing countries. Some see the TRIPS Agreement as the necessary condition for continuing research and development in technology while others see it as the product of patent and copyright holders trying to obtain worldwide monopolies. The concept and practice of protecting intellectual property are at least as controversial as the TRIPS Agreement itself. From the point of view of the consumer and the general public, a patent right is a grant of a monopoly and copyright is a grant of restriction on trade.

With the adoption of the Declaration on the TRIPS Agreement and Public Health in Doha in 2001, ministers from WTO member states acknowledged the link between TRIPS and public health and agreed that TRIPS must be interpreted and implemented in a way to support public health by 'promoting both access to existing medicines and the creation of new medicines'. The real challenge, however, is to ensure the Declaration is implemented in good faith. Negotiations on related issues, such as geographical indications and transfer of technology to least-developed countries, have been ongoing. Meanwhile, dispute settlement processes will play a more important role in ensuring what is called health apartheid will not take place in the coming years and that developing countries will be able to address their concerns through the process. This chapter discusses the flexibility and options available in TRIPS and their interaction with the WTO dispute settlement system.

Up to now, 'most disputes about matters of compliance with the requirements of the TRIPS Agreement are resolved in bilateral consultations between the members concerned, either in Geneva or in capital, without invoking the dispute settlement procedures in the DSB' (Geuze and Wager 1999, p. 375). Countries sometimes have no choice but to be 'dragged' into a bilateral agreement. This is especially so when the country being complained about is a relatively small and weak country that does not have much leverage against the country pursuing the bilateral agreement or is not in a position to force the case to the DSB either because of their economic dependence or the political ties. To avoid being 'coerced' to accept specific conditions, the weak or small developing countries can actively participate in the multilateral negotiation process in pursuing their interests. Large developing countries which have the human and economic resources should participate actively in the WTO dispute settlement system in order to be better 'positioned to effectively shape the law's interpretation and application over time' (Shaffer 2004, p. 470).

NOTES

1. A large body of literature on the TRIPS Agreement focuses on its negative impacts on developing countries. See, for example, United Nations Conference on Trade and Development 1996; Maskus 2000; Sell 2003; Shaffer 2004; Templeman 1998.
2. For the debate on the merits of a permanent body of dispute settlement or the current ad hoc system, see Davey 2003, pp. 177–186; Shoyer 2003, pp. 203–209.
3. This is essential for any controversial policies to be adopted when there is strong domestic opposition. Governments often need 'external' pressure to justify their policies and/or

domestic pressures to justify their bargaining positions at the international arena. See Putman 1998; Moravcsik 1991.

4. See a resolution on 'Intellectual Property and Human Rights' adopted by the Sub-Commission on Human Rights, UN Office of the High Commissioner for Human Rights (16 August 2001) at http://www.unhchr.ch/Huridocda/Huridoca.nsf/0/c462b62cf8a07b13c12569700046704e?Opendocument, visited 17 May 2007.

REFERENCES

Abbott, F. (1998), 'The Enduring Enigma of TRIPS: A Challenge for the World Economic System', *Journal of International Economic Law*, 1(4), 497–521.

Abbott, F. (2003), 'Trade Diplomacy, the Rule of Law and the Problem of Asymmetric Risks in TRIPS', Occasional Paper No. 13, Geneva: Quaker United Nations Office.

Abbott, K. and D. Snidal (1998), 'Why States Act through Formal International Organisations', *Journal of Conflict Resolution*, 42(1), 3–32.

Abbott, K. and D. Snidal (2000), 'Hard and Soft Law in International Governance', *International Organization*, 54(3), 421–456.

Bacchus, J. (2002), 'Table Talk: Around the Table of the Appellate Body of the World Trade Organization', *Vanderbilt Journal of Transnational Law*, 35(4), 1021–1039.

Bacchus, J. (2003), 'The Appeals of Trade: The Making of an Old GATT Hand', address to International Trade Law Congress of the American Bar Association, Georgetown University Law School, 31 January 2003, at www.worldtradelaw.net/articles/bacchusgatthand.pdf, visited 17 May 2007.

Bacchus, J. (2004), 'Open Doors for Open Trade: Shining Light on WTO Dispute Settlement', Mayflower Hotel, Washington DC: National Foreign Trade Council.

Davey, W. (2003), 'The Case for a WTO Permanent Panel Body', *Journal of International Economic Law*, 6(1), 177–186.

Dreyfuss, R. (2004), 'TRIPS-Round II: Should Users Strike Back', *University of Chicago Law Review*, 71(1), 21–35.

Ehlermann, C-D. (2003a), 'Reflections on the Appellate Body of the WTO', *Journal of International Economic Law*, 6(3), 695–708.

Ehlermann, C-D. (2003b), 'Six Years on the Bench of The "World Trade Court" – Some Personal Experiences as Member of the Appellate Body of the World Trade Organization', *Journal of World Trade*, 36(4), 605–639.

Ethier, W. (2004), 'Intellectual Property Rights and Dispute Settlement in the World Trade Organization', *Journal of International Economic Law*, 7(2), 449–458.

Foot, R., J. Gaddis and A. Hurrell (2003), *Order and Justice in International Relations*, Oxford: Oxford University Press.

Geuze, M. and W. Hannu (1999), 'WTO Dispute Settlement Practice Relating to the TRIPS Agreement', *Journal of International Economic Law*, 2(2), 347–384.

Goldstein, J., M. Kahler, R. Keohane and A-M. Slaughter (2000), 'Legalization and World Politics', *International Organization*, 54(3), 385–399.

Greenwald, J. (2003), 'WTO Dispute Settlement: An Exercise in Trade Law Legislation?', *Journal of International Economic Law*, 6(1), 113–124.

Hoekman, B. and M. Kostecki (2001), *The Political Economy of the World Trading System: The WTO and Beyond*, 2nd edn, Oxford: Oxford University Press.

Hurrell, A. (2003), 'Order and Justice in International Relations: What is at Stake?' in R. Foot, J. Gaddis and A. Hurrell (eds), *Order and Justice in International Relations*, Oxford: Oxford University Press.

Keohane, R., A. Moravcsik and A-M. Slaughter (2000), 'Legalized Dispute Resolution: Interstate and Transnational', *International Organization*, 54(3), 457–488.
Kuijper, P. (2002), 'Some Institutional Issues Presently Before the WTO', in Kennedy and Southwick 2002.
Lacarte, J. (2004), 'Transparency, Public Debate and Participation by NGOs in the WTO: A WTO Perspective', *Journal of International Economic Law*, 7(3), 683–686.
Maskus, K. (2000), *Intellectual Property Rights in the Global Economy*, Washington DC: Institute for International Economics.
Moravcsik, A. (1991), 'Negotiating the Single European Act: National Interests and Conventional Statecraft in the European Community', *International Organization*, 45(1), 19–56.
Oxley, A. (1990), *The Challenge of Free Trade*, London, UK: Harvester Wheatsheaf.
Petersmann, E-U. (1997), *International Trade Law and the Gatt/WTO Dispute Settlement System*, Studies in Transnational Economic Law, London: Kluwer Law International.
Putnam, R. (1988), 'Diplomacy and Domestic Politics: The Logic of Two-Level Games', *International Organization*, 42(3), 427–460.
Reichman, J. (1998), 'Securing Compliance with the TRIPS Agreement after US v India', *Journal of International Economic Law*, 1(4), 585–601.
Reiterer, M. (1994), 'Trade-Related Intellectual Property Rights', in Organisation for Economic Co-operation and Development, *The New World Trading System*, Paris: OECD Publishing.
Sell, S. (2003), *Private Power, Public Law: The Globalization of Intellectual Property Rights*, Cambridge: Cambridge University Press.
Shaffer, G. (2004), 'Recognizing Public Goods in WTO Dispute Settlement: Who Participates? Who Decides? The Case of TRIPS and Pharmaceutical Patent Protection', *Journal of International Economic Law*, 7(2), 459–482.
Shoyer, A. (2003), 'Panel Selection in WTO Dispute Settlement Proceedings', *Journal of International Economic Law*, 6(1), 203–209.
Smith, P. (1999), 'A Long and Winding Road: Trips and the Evolution of an International Competition Framework', *Journal of International Economic Law*, 2(3), 435–440.
Steger, D. (2002), 'The Appellate Body and its Contribution to WTO Dispute Settlement', in D. Kennedy and J. Southwick (eds), *The Political Economy of International Trade Law: Essays in Honour of Robert E. Hudec*, Cambridge: Cambridge University Press.
Templeman, S. (1998), 'Intellectual Property', *Journal of International Economic Law*, 1(4), 603–606.
United Nations Conference on Trade and Development (1996), *The TRIPS Agreement and Developing Countries*, New York: United Nations Conference on Trade and Development.
WT/DS2/AB/R (1997), *India – Patent Protection for Pharmaceutical and Agricultural Chemical Products*, Geneva: World Trade Organization.
WT/DS79/R (1998), *India – Patent Protection for Pharmaceutical and Agricultural Chemical Products*, Geneva: World Trade Organization.
Xu, Y-C. and P. Weller (2004), *The Governance of World Trade: International Civil Servants and the Gatt/WTO*, Cheltenham, UK, Northampton, MA, USA: Edward Elgar Publishing.

5. Intellectual property protection after TRIPS: An Asian experience

Jakrit Kuanpoth

1. INTRODUCTION

Intellectual property (IP) was until recently the domain of specialists and producers of IP rights. The Agreement on Trade-Related Aspects of Intellectual Property Rights (TRIPS) concluded during the Uruguay Round negotiations in 1994, signalled a major shift in this regard. The incorporation of IP rights into the multilateral trading system has elicited great concern over its pervasive role in people's lives and in society in general. TRIPS is a comprehensive agreement containing new multilateral rules and disciplines with relatively high standards of IP protection. Developing countries that are members of the World Trade Organization (WTO) have fewer policy options for protecting IP rights, and are enjoying less flexibility than that enjoyed by developed countries in using IP rights to support their national development. However, TRIPS is not the end of the story. Significant new developments are currently taking place at the regional and bilateral level that build on and strengthen the IP standards through the progressive harmonisation of technologically advanced countries.

Developing countries face the challenge of constraint optimisation on ways of implementing the TRIPS Agreement that minimise socio-economic costs and maximise national benefits. The developing states are now facing increased pressure towards higher standards of IP protection (such as the so-called TRIPS-plus). The attempts of the developed countries to evolve the TRIPS-plus regime, which appears in the form of free trade agreement (FTA), provide opportunities for those countries to negotiate rules and commitments that go beyond what was not possible on the multilateral level.

By entering into an FTA with developed countries, developing countries see some advantages in tariff reductions of agricultural, clothing and other products. Doing so closes down the opportunity to put forward the issues of concern through the WTO forums. These issues include the harmonisation of TRIPS and the United Nations Convention on Biological Diversity

(CBD), access to medicines, the protection of genetic resources, Farmers' Rights and the recognition and protection of traditional knowledge (TK). This chapter explores the development of IP protection in the post-TRIPS era, particularly the controversial TRIPS-plus issues under various FTAs that pose many challenges to the developing countries. It analyses the TRIPS-plus standard imposed on Asian countries, particularly the rules under an FTA between Singapore and the United States (SUSFTA), a bilateral trade agreement between Vietnam and the United States (VUSBTA) and the proposed FTA between Thailand and the United States (TUSFTA). This chapter also explores major TRIPS-plus issues and considers the broad implications of such rules under various headings, including the patenting of living organisms, the effects on access to medicines, and the protection of test data, trade marks and digital technologies.

2. INTELLECTUAL PROPERTY DEVELOPMENT IN THE POST-TRIPS ERA

Most developing countries in Asia are signatories to the WTO agreements. In order to comply with the WTO commitments, those countries must reform their laws and regulations in several areas. They have to reduce the tariff rates on certain industrial and agricultural products, and convert non-tariff measures (for example, quotas and other quantitative restrictions) to tariffs on certain agricultural products such as rice, corn, soybean, sugar and garlic. In the area of foreign investment, the WTO Agreement on Trade-Related Investment Measures (TRIMS) provides that Members may apply certain investment measures such as performance and local content requirements, but such measures must not amount to barriers to trade or distort trade. The WTO Agreement on Trade in Services (GATS) does not oblige Members to liberalise their market for services, but requires them to enter into negotiations with a view to gradually liberalising service trade under the principle of progressive liberalisation. Whether or not a country has an obligation to amend any existing laws in the service sectors depends on its commitments with the WTO.

The WTO obligations that require significant reform of the law are those found in TRIPS. Member countries are obliged to substantially eliminate IP infringements and to bring IP laws up to the TRIPS standards. This requires implementing measures that include amending patent, trademark and copyright laws and adopting new laws to protect geographical indications, trade secrets and layout-designs of integrated circuits.

Although the rapid development of IP law in Asia may partly be due to TRIPS' multilateral obligations, the developments were primarily due to external pressures exerted by developed countries. In the late 1980s, the United States exerted bilateral pressure, by withdrawing the Generalised System of Preferences (GSP) and threatening trade sanctions to increase IP standards outside the General Agreement on Tariffs and Trade (GATT) processes. A number of countries in Asia, including Taiwan, Korea, India, Thailand and Indonesia, were placed under tremendous pressure by the world's largest trading bloc whom they were unable to withstand. Several Asian countries decided to revise their IP laws even before the Uruguay Round of multilateral trade negotiations was concluded.

The United States has recently launched negotiations for an FTA with a large number of countries, including Chile, Jordan, Morocco, Singapore, the Central American countries, the Andean countries, Thailand, Panama, Bahrain and Southern African countries. Up until now, the United States has signed bilateral trade treaties with two South East Asian countries, namely Singapore and Vietnam, and is engaged in negotiations with Thailand. The United States is also looking at three other ASEAN countries, namely Indonesia, the Philippines, and Malaysia, as its next targets for bilateral FTAs.

The agreements the United States has signed with Singapore and Vietnam contain several IP provisions that far exceed obligations under the TRIPS Agreement. The countries concluding a bilateral or regional treaty with the United States are required to provide for more stringent IP regimes than those existing in any other country, in exchange for greater access for their exports to the United States market (Roffe 2004; Vivas-Eugui 2003).

During the deadlock of WTO multilateral talks, the developed nations have demanded further IP commitments from the developing countries under bilateral and regional trade deals. The inclusion by the United States of an IP chapter in the FTAs it has entered into or is negotiating is due to lobbying by industry groups. The groups include the International Intellectual Property Alliance, the Biotechnology Industry Organization and the Business Software Alliance. The Advisory Committee on Intellectual Property Rights for Trade Policy Matters (IFAC-3), which plays the most important role in advising and influencing US trade policy, comprises large multinational companies such as Eli Lilly, Merck, Pfizer, Anheuser-Busch and Procter & Gamble.

The United States, in particular, evidently perceives bilateral and regional trade talks as offering a very important strategic opportunity to demand greater trade commitments from its trade partners (Drahos 2002, p. 765). The tightening of IP laws in foreign countries as a result of bilateral trade negotiations, together with the use of trade leverage under US trade laws, will likely assist the United States in establishing a framework for negotiating the terms of the Doha Round agreements. The United

States successfully employed this strategy during the Uruguay Round of trade negotiations, which led to the adoption of TRIPS.

The United States' objectives in FTA negotiations are reflected in the United States Trade Representative (USTR)'s Letter of Notification for FTA negotiations with Thailand:

> The United States is concerned about intellectual property protection in Thailand. The United States has worked with Thailand on intellectual property rights issues under the Trade and Investment Framework Agreement (TIFA). While some progress has been made, bringing Thailand's intellectual property regime up to the standards set in other recent FTAs that the United States has negotiated will be a high priority of these negotiations (United States Trade Representative 2004).

Similarly, the USTR formal notification letters to Congress state that the aim of the negotiations is to:

- Seek to establish standards to be applied in Thailand that build on the foundations established in the WTO Agreement on Trade-Related Aspects of Intellectual Property Rights and other international intellectual property agreements, such as the World Intellectual Property Organization (WIPO) Copyright Treaty, the WIPO Performances and Phonograms Treaty, and the Patent Cooperation Treaty.
- In areas such as patent protection and protection of undisclosed information, seek to have Thailand apply levels of protection and practices more in line with U.S. law and practices, including appropriate flexibility.
- Seek to strengthen Thailand's laws and procedures to enforce intellectual property rights, such as by ensuring that Thai authorities seize suspected pirated and counterfeit goods, equipment used to make such goods or to transmit pirated goods, and documentary evidence (United States Trade Representative 2004).

The bilateral treaties concluded between the United States and its trade partners are built largely upon the provisions of the North American Free Trade Agreement (NAFTA), the World Intellectual Property Organization (WIPO) treaties and the basic rules embodied in United States legislation. United States FTAs generally focus on the following issues: (i) providing for greater patent protection for new subject matter, (ii) restricting the grounds for compulsory licensing, (iii) prohibiting the revocation of patents, (iv) restraining parallel importation, (v) extending the patent term, (vi) creating a global patent system, (vii) providing for exclusivity for test data and relevant undisclosed information, (viii) providing higher level of protection for trade marks, and (ix) providing high levels of protection for digital technologies. Some of these issues will now be discussed in further detail.

3. PATENTING OF BIOTECHNOLOGICAL INVENTIONS AND PLANT VARIETIES

Patent law was initially introduced to protect inventions in the fields of inanimate matters, such as chemistry, physics and engineering. Although biological processes and products have been used in industries for a long time, biotechnological inventions were normally excluded from patentability (Beier 1985, p. 25). In 1969, the German Supreme Court accepted in the *Red Dove* case that an animal-breeding technique was patentable. It held, apparently for the first time in a European court, that a biotechnological method was capable of patent protection. However, the Court ultimately denied the grant of patent because the claimed invention did not fulfil the particular condition of a written description by lack of a repeatable feature.

In 1980, the United States Supreme Court in a landmark case, *Diamond v Chakrabarty*, ruled that a bacteria, in which a plasmid from another strain had been inserted, was patentable subject matter. The Court went further by holding that the statute did not distinguish living matters from inanimate things, but only between the products of nature and man-made inventions. In other words, an alleged subject matter must not be denied patentability merely because it was alive. It was held also that the patentable subject matter included 'anything under the sun made by man', which means that the problem of patentable subject matter under United States patent law did not depend on whether or not the claimed invention was living matter, but on whether it was a result of nature or made by a human.

In Europe, the patenting of particular types of biotechnology is prohibited by the European Patent Convention (EPC). Art 53(b) of the EPC states, inter alia, that:

> European patents shall not be granted in respect of: . . .
> (b) plant or animal varieties or essentially biological processes for the production of plants or animals; this provision does not apply to microbiological processes or the products thereof.

The excluded subject matters include plant varieties, animal varieties and essentially biological processes. But microbiological processes and the products thereof are patentable. The only exclusion regarding the protection of micro-organisms is when the claim is merely a discovery rather than an invention.

Art 27.1 TRIPS states that 'patents shall be available for any inventions, whether products or processes, in all fields of technology'. However, Art 27.3(b) allows Members to exclude plants and animals, but not micro-organisms, from patent protection. Further, essentially biological processes for the production of plants or animals other than non-biological and microbiological processes are also denied protection. But countries must provide protection for plant varieties. Since 1999 this specific provision has been up for renegotiations by WTO Members. It could be reworded, deleted or modified in any way.

Like other developing countries, most Asian developing countries exclude plant varieties, animal varieties and essentially biological processes from patentability. Extracts from living organisms such as genes and gene sequences are also excluded. However, the rule that bans life patenting could be substantially altered if the bilateral TRIPS-plus agreements are introduced.

United States FTAs oblige contracting parties to change their national laws to allow for patents over life forms. SUSFTA, for example, provides that 'each party may exclude inventions from patentability only as defined in Arts 27.2 and 27.3(a) of the TRIPS Agreement' (SUSFTA, Art 16.7(1)). The draft IP text which the USTR submitted to Thailand in the sixth round of FTA negotiations in January 2006 also requires Thailand to provide protection for plants, animals, biological processes and products, genes and gene sequences.[1] This TRIPS-plus provision is designed to allow for the patentability of the by-products of genetic engineering and other biotechnological methods without linking the patentability issues to ethical, social, economic and environmental considerations. The patenting of life could have a considerable socio-economic impact on the developing countries. The granting of patents on biological materials such as genes will confer monopolistic power on large biotechnology companies and will disrupt the access to essential products. Stricter protection for IP rights would increase monopoly powers of the right-holders, generally multinational firms, allowing them to gain far greater control over the production chain of crops and food.

Moreover, gene patenting will have detrimental effects on the research environment and generate negative effects on downstream innovation and could impede discovery and innovation in the fastest-growing field of technology (Heller and Eisenberg 1998). The patents on biotechnological technology would act as a barrier to the transfer of technology. Developing nations view scientific and technological advancement as the vehicle for industrialisation and economic development. Patenting such products would override the technological and economic requirements of a developing country as it will increase the cost of modern technologies and provide innovative disincentives for local research agencies.

With regard to plant variety protection, Art 27.3(b) of TRIPS gives Member countries the option to protect plant varieties by patents, an effective *sui generis* system, or both. The International Union for the Protection of New Varieties of Plants (UPOV) system is recognised to be one, but not the definitive means, for establishing a *sui generis* system. The ambiguity of the term 'effective *sui generis* system' under TRIPS allows developing countries to avoid having to develop full IP laws covering plant varieties. Each Member is free to adopt the term of protection as it sees fit. For example, the *sui generis* system provided for in Art 27.3(b) may be implemented by including Farmers' Rights into the system. The concept of Farmers' Rights adopted by the Food and Agriculture Organization (FAO)[2] has an aim of compensating farmers who have been conserving plant genetic resources for the past centuries, and have thereby contributed to the development of plant varieties. In other words, the *sui generis* system may be aimed at promoting not only the creation of new varieties of plant but also the conservation and encouragement of the agricultural practices in countries that have adopted it (Correa 1999). Some developing countries in Asia, such as Thailand and India, have flexibly implemented the TRIPS provision by incorporating the Farmers' Rights and the access and benefit sharing system under the CBD into their national legislation.

Thailand has so far resisted ratifying the UPOV system or adopting it as the standard for its plant variety protection law. This is because plants are vitally important for agriculture, which is still regarded as the backbone of the Thai economy. Its current law, the Plant Variety Protection Act BE 2542, is notable for not following the UPOV system. Unlike the UPOV system, the Thai law aims at promoting not only the creation of new varieties of plant but also the conservation and encouragement of agricultural practices in the country. The law protects breeders' rights and recognises the rights of farmers and local communities over the grant of IP rights over plant genetic resources. It also adopts legal requirements such as prior informed consent and access and benefit sharing, which allows individuals and communities to claim compensation for their contribution to the resources.

It seems that in the current legal framework countries can adapt and change the plant variety protection system to suit the local conditions in their agriculture and farming sectors. United States FTAs no doubt attempt to limit this flexibility by requiring the trade partners to implement the UPOV 1991 Act (for example SUSFTA, Art 16.1.2(a)(ii)). The UPOV system will leave Thailand and other FTA partners with few options regarding the scope of protection, as the 1991 Act provides the least discretion to the signatory states in choosing how to protect plant varieties.

According to Art 14 of the UPOV 1991 Act, the protection must be extended to all plant varieties. The exclusive rights must cover vegetative or reproductive propagating material, and extend to essentially derived varieties and harvested material. The rights of farmers to save, use, exchange or sell farm-saved seeds are constrained. The full-scale monopoly rights will adversely affect the food and agricultural sectors, and adversely affect the interests of poor farmers, in particular when their right to save seeds is removed. Moreover, the accession to the UPOV 1991 Act will prohibit the inclusion of provisions, which are currently enshrined under the plant variety protection law of Thailand, requiring applicants to prove that a plant variety is safe and does not cause any harmful effects to the environment (Thailand's Plant Variety Protection Act BE 2542, s. 13).

4. PROTECTION OF TRADITIONAL KNOWLEDGE AND GENETIC RESOURCES

Governments around the world currently place a high priority on traditional knowledge, as well as biological resources. Often, customary and informal knowledge has been made publicly available and exploited without adequate compensation, and occasionally researchers or companies have claimed the IP rights to the knowledge (United Nations Development Program 1999; Crucible Group 1994). By claiming ownership, these companies can charge anyone who uses their patented items, including those in the country where the plants originate and the people who, in the belief knowledge is to be shared, taught them the plants' healing or other useful properties. Such illicit and uncompensated appropriation of traditional knowledge is exploitative and is cause for concern among developing country governments as well as among indigenous and local communities (Roht-Arriaza 1996, pp. 930–931).

International attempts to strengthen the control of developing countries over biological resources and associated knowledge date back to 1992 with the signing of the Convention on Biological Diversity (CBD). It is increasingly apparent that self-determination as a necessary corollary to the attainment of people's human rights must broadly include the ability to determine their political, economic and social progress, independent of any external manipulation (UNEP/CBD/COP/6/20). Protection of traditional knowledge has also become an integral part of the work of other intergovernmental organisations, including the WTO, the World Intellectual Property Organization (WIPO), the United Nations Conference on Trade and Development (UNCTAD) and the World Health Organization (WHO).

TRIPS does not require the protection of informal knowledge systems like traditional knowledge. No direct tools to establish a link between IP protection and the principles of the CBD can be found under the Agreement. However, nothing in the Agreement would appear to either prevent or promote the development of additional measures that provide for the sharing of benefits with countries and communities providing resources or traditional knowledge, as long as those measures do not contravene TRIPS provisions. TRIPS also leaves plenty of room for nations to move with regard to the recognition and adoption of *sui generis* rights (Watal 1998).

For developing countries in Asia contemplating traditional knowledge protection, the first issue to consider was which legal system should be applied to protect the informal knowledge system (Blakeney 1999). The IP system is not designed to protect traditional knowledge and may not suit the needs of indigenous and local communities in protecting their traditional knowledge. The current IP systems adopt standards of protection that are too high and the criteria for protection are difficult to satisfy by innovations generated at the community level. For example, a traditional knowledge-based product, which generally comprises active substances found in nature rather than a pure form of substance, would not be considered new and inventive and would hence be denied patent protection. On the contrary, when researchers and companies take the next step by using the same knowledge in laboratories, such as by isolating, altering or purifying an active chemical of the herbal plants, the substance would become a novel and inventive piece of knowledge and thus patentable.

In addition, the objective of IP protection which aims to protect individual and corporate interests is different from the objective for traditional knowledge protection (Reid et al. 1995). The protection of traditional knowledge can be viewed as part of the effort for environmental conservation. Informal knowledge and biological materials are deemed as valuable resources for the international community and held in trust by local communities (Urbanski 1995, p. 179). The use of market-based IP rights may lead to heavy commercialisation of knowledge and resources, thus eroding the pool of valuable herbs and wild species. Stevenson argues that 'the individuality upon which patents are based could seriously disrupt that indigenous community or neighbouring indigenous communities' (Stevenson 2000, p. 1140).

Under patent law, local communities, farmers and traditional practitioners who are the rightful owners of traditional knowledge are usually not considered joint inventors under the concept of joint inventorship. According to patent law, in order to claim joint inventorship, each joint inventor must have contributed to the inventive thought and to the final result (Stevenson 2000, p. 1145). This condition creates difficulties for the traditional knowledge holders, who may not have a demonstrable role in the final conception of the traditional knowledge-based innovation.

Some developing countries in Asia adopted a law to protect traditional knowledge, notably the *sui generis* law of Thailand that was adopted to protect informal knowledge systems in the field of medicines. The Traditional Thai Medicinal Intelligence Act BE 2542 (1999) lays down conditions on access to medicinal genetic resources and Thai traditional knowledge. The law establishes the rights of traditional healers to retain control over traditional medicinal knowledge through public registration.

There are three categories of traditional medicinal knowledge protected under the law: (i) general formula, (ii) national formula, and (iii) personal formula. The general formula of traditional Thai medicine is knowledge that is already in the public domain and is free for everyone to use. It includes traditional medicinal knowledge that has been widely used and is widely available. It also includes the medicinal formula of which patent protection has expired. The Act stipulates that the Ministry of Public Health has authority to announce that a specified formula of traditional Thai medicine is a national formula. The traditional formula announced must offer significant benefit or have special medical value. After the announcement, the rights over such a formula belong to the State. Anyone who wants to use the national formula for the commercial production of drugs or for research and development must receive permission from a relevant government official. A person who uses the national formula for commercial purposes without authorisation is subject to criminal sanctions under the Act. Private formulation of traditional Thai medicine can be registered under the Act. People who may apply for registration of a personal formula include: (i) an inventor or developer of the formula; or (ii) an inheritor of the inventor or developer of such a formula.

The Traditional Thai Medicinal Intelligence Act provides for the examination of the application as to its substance. If it appears that the application for registration does not comply with the rules and procedures or that the claimed formula is not registrable (for example, the formula is a national formula or has been registered as a personal formula by another person), the registrar may reject the application. The Act affords exclusive rights by allowing the owner of the registered personal formula to use the formula for research and to sell and distribute any product developed or manufactured by using the formula. However, there are certain limitations and exceptions to the exclusive rights. The rights over a registered personal formula subsist throughout the life of the applicant and continue to subsist for a further period of 50 years from the date the applicant dies.

The Traditional Thai Medicinal Intelligence Act also provides for the protection of a particular type of biological resources, namely herbs and medicinal plants. Thailand's Ministry of Public Health has authority to put a plant or herb it considers at high risk of extinction on the Extinction List. No one is entitled to use the listed plant or herb without proper authorisation from the authority concerned.

Although attempts have been made to protect traditional knowledge at the national level, there has been no unified international legal protection of traditional knowledge, genetic resources and biodiversity under TRIPS. The TRIPS-plus terms adopted under various FTAs, including the proposed TUSFTA, provides no protection for the informal innovations of traditional knowledge. By contrast United States FTAs call for a high level of protection for biotechnology and new plant varieties. By ratifying a TRIPS-plus bilateral treaty, Thailand might open the door for the United States biotechnology industry, the largest biotechnology industry in the world, not only to dominate its farming sector but also to exploit its abundant biological resources. Although it is endowed with plentiful amounts of biological resources, Thailand will not be able to take advantage of the resources as a source of economic growth and poverty alleviation. The UPOV system would impose the mandatory components of plant variety protection and restrain the country's sovereign rights over its biological resources and its ability to regulate access to the biodiversity. Under the TRIPS-plus and UPOV regimes, Thailand's attempts to balance the IP protection and to maintain the alternative rights system would be reduced.

5. PATENT PROTECTION FOR PHARMACEUTICALS

Patent protection for pharmaceuticals is of particular concern to many developing countries. Pharmaceuticals are a basic requirement for their deprived populations. Stricter protection would allow firms to increase market share and will lead to overpricing and the restricted supply of an essential product (Correa 2000). This was the reason why pharmaceutical products were excluded from patenting under the law of many countries before 1994, when TRIPS was introduced. The question of constraints, as regard to pharmaceutical patenting, has been a subject of serious concern and has been intensely debated in the WTO meetings. The request from a group of African countries for a special session on access to medicines led to the adoption in November 2001 of the Doha Declaration on the TRIPS Agreement and Public Health (WT/MIN(01)/Dec/2; Abbott 2005). The Declaration expresses the concern of WTO members over 'the gravity of the public health problems afflicting many developing and least-developed countries, especially those resulting from HIV/AIDS, tuberculosis, malaria and other epidemics'. It clarifies some of the ambiguities with respect to the relationship between the TRIPS Agreement and Members' rights to protect public health. For example, Art 6 of TRIPS has been clarified to acknowledge that each Member is free to establish its own regime for the use of exhaustion of rights to encourage parallel import of pharmaceuticals with the lowest price.

The Declaration reaffirms the 'right of WTO members to use, to the full, the provisions in the TRIPS Agreement', including taking advantage of the compulsory licensing provision. The Declaration also makes it very clear that a problem relating to public health can represent 'a national emergency or other circumstances of extreme urgency'. Members may interpret the 'emergency situation' as either a short-term problem, or a long-lasting situation. This is a significant step forward in view of public health, because it clarifies the ambiguous terms of Art 31(b) of TRIPS.

The Declaration has extended the provisional period for the least-developed countries (LDCs) to comply with TRIPS obligations until 2016. But the countries that did not provide patents for pharmaceutical products before TRIPS entered into force were granted a grace-period until 2005. This means that after 2005 major exporters of generic products such as India may no longer be allowed to produce cheap versions of medicines, especially newly developed medicines for the treatment of the mutated HIV virus or other diseases. Because of this problem, the Doha Declaration instructed the TRIPS Council to find an expeditious solution to the problem of the difficulties that WTO Members with insufficient or no manufacturing capacities in the pharmaceutical sector could face in making effective use of compulsory licensing.

After several rounds of negotiations, the Council on TRIPS reached an agreement on 30 August 2003. The Decision, which is the solution to the problem addressed under paragraph 6 of the Declaration, permits a country that has issued a compulsory licence to export the drugs produced under licence to eligible importing countries, provided that a number of conditions are fulfilled (Vandoren and Eeckhaute 2003). Despite the Declaration, problems remain as a result of Art 31(f) and (h) which permit Members to grant compulsory licences to supply foreign markets but limit exports to less than half of the production and require payment of adequate remuneration to the patent-holder when such licences are issued. This led to the decision by the WTO General Council in December 2005 (followed by approval of the Ministerial Council) to amend the TRIPS Agreement permitting production for export under a compulsory licence and waiving the payment requirement in the eligible importing Member. This amendment effectively and permanently implements the waiver of TRIPS Art 31(f) and (h) created by the WTO General Council Decision of 30 August 2003.

A number of developing countries in Asia adopt available measures in their national laws to deal with abuses of IP rights. These measures include compulsory licensing, revocation of patents and parallel import to deal with situations such as a patent-holder not exploiting the patent or maintaining artificially high prices for patented articles. However, the FTAs introduced by the United States aim to limit the options the countries have under the current legal framework and to allow the patent-holders to secure monopolisation and avoid competition. On patents and pharmaceuticals, United States FTAs focus mainly on three major aspects: (i) limiting the use of compulsory licensing, (ii) prohibiting the revocation of patents, and (iii) restraining parallel importation.

5.1 Compulsory Licensing

Compulsory licensing refers to a non-voluntary licence issued by the State to a third party to perform acts that are covered by the patent's exclusive rights (for example, rights to license manufacturing, selling or importing of the patented product), on the condition that the licensee pays reasonable remuneration to the patent-holder in return. Multinational companies always oppose compulsory licensing. They argue that the use of patents against the will of the right-holder is tantamount to free-riding by other companies, which they claim will result in trade distortions (Singham 2000, p. 406). Nonetheless, the compulsory licensing which the multinationals regard as trade distorting is the very cornerstone of the patent system. The experience of many countries including the United States, Canada and Brazil has shown that compulsory licensing is an effective mechanism to limit abusive practices by the patent-holder and helps to force prices down.

Countries, according to TRIPS, are free to use the compulsory licensing of patents, provided that certain conditions are fulfilled (Art 31). In practice, the countries that intend using compulsory licensing have always been under considerable economic pressure. With the adoption of the Doha Declaration on TRIPS and Public Health, it now seems obvious that WTO Members can legitimately employ this legal mechanism to improve access to medicines.

Limiting the right of a country to use the compulsory licensing is probably the most significant of the constraints under United States FTAs. The TRIPS-plus rules attempt to make the compulsory licensing provisions difficult to apply, as they set more stringent conditions than the TRIPS standards. SUSFTA, for example, confines the permissible use of compulsory licences to three circumstances only, namely (i) to remedy anti-competitive practices, (ii) in the case of public non-commercial use, and (iii) in the case of national emergency or other circumstances of extreme urgency (SUSFTA, Art 16.7(6)).[3] The FTAs prevent parties from issuing compulsory licences in circumstances other than those mentioned above. Issuing a compulsory licence on the ground of non-working or insufficient working of patents is also prohibited, despite the fact that the use of compulsory licences for the local operation of patents is the cornerstone of most countries' patent laws and is a use explicitly enshrined in the Paris Convention (see Art 5(A); see also Penrose 1951; Vaitsos 1972).

According to SUSFTA and the proposed TUSFTA, a compulsory licence may be issued to remedy an anti-competitive practice only after the patent-holder has been adjudged by judicial or administrative process, under the competition laws, as carrying out an anti-competitive practice (SUSFTA, Art 16.7(6)(a)). This requirement would render the compulsory licensing practically unworkable against anti-competitive behaviour, as the patent-holders can challenge directly sovereign conduct that injures them, through a judicial or administrative channel. The compulsory licence system will not do much to provide a means to safeguard consumer interests if the patentee's alleged abuse of patent rights can be bitterly contested by the proceedings and grants of the licence in court or before the antitrust authority

In the case of public non-commercial use or national emergency or other circumstances of extreme urgency, a compulsory licence can be granted only in accordance with these conditions under a typical TRIPS-plus FTA:

- A compulsory licence can be issued only to the public sector or third parties authorised by the government.
- The patent-holder shall receive full compensation with reference to the TRIPS provision for the compulsory licence.
- There must be no requirement for the transfer of undisclosed information or for the disclosure of know-how without the consent of the right-holder (SUSFTA, Art 16.7(6)(b)).

No doubt, the TRIPS-plus provisions attempt to introduce language that would limit an essential measure such as compulsory licensing to certain situations and make the procedure for issuing a compulsory licence intricate and prolonged. The constraints imposed on the developing countries will threaten to restrict the measure those countries can take to pursue affordable drugs, and will affect ability of many countries to promote access to medicines. Thailand's signing an FTA with the United States will result in limited access to medicines not only in Thailand itself but also in its neighbouring countries, including Vietnam, Myanmar, Cambodia and Laos, which have been relying on Thailand as an important source of drug supply. With its obligations to the United States under the FTA, Thailand will not be able to issue a compulsory licence and export the compulsorily licensed drugs to those countries that have no or insufficient capacity in drug production, denying their rights as reaffirmed by the Doha Declaration on TRIPS and Public Health.

5.2 Prohibiting Revocation of Patents

While revocation of patents is compatible with TRIPS, the TRIPS-plus requirements introduced by the United States prohibit the trade partner from revoking patents on grounds other than those that would have justified a refusal to grant the patent. Typically this is restricted to lack of patentability, insufficiency of or unauthorised amendments to the patent specification, non-disclosure or misrepresentation of prescribed, material particulars, fraud, or misrepresentation (SUSFTA, Art 16.7(4)). Revocation of patents is not possible in cases where compulsory licences were not sufficient to curb abuses of patent rights or non-working as provided by the Paris Convention (Art 5(A)(3)). Limited compulsory licensing therefore becomes only one mechanism that the trade partner can use to curtail the abusive practices of the patent-owners.

5.3 Restraining Parallel Import

FTAs proposed by the US allow the patent-holders to prevent the products they have marketed in one country from being exported to another. US FTAs demand the trade partners to provide a right to the patent-holders to restrict parallel importing in either of the following ways:

- it must adopt a system of national exhaustion only, thus prohibiting international exhaustion in which the first sale of an object embodying IP rights in a foreign country exhausts the right-holder's exclusive rights; or
- it must permit the right-holders to take legal action against the import or export of the patented product by a party who knows or has reason to know that such product is or has been distributed in breach of a contract between the right-holder and a licensee, regardless of whether such breach occurs in or outside its territory.[4]

According to Art 6 of TRIPS, countries may implement the exhaustion principle differently. Some may apply the national exhaustion principle, but other countries (notably within the European Union) place no restrictions on the import of a product if it is put on sale within the community. This is known as regional exhaustion. Under the international exhaustion doctrine, the right-owner cannot use his IP rights to prevent further distribution of goods that have been placed into commerce anywhere by himself or herself, or with his or her consent. Since the TRIPS-plus arrangements prohibit international exhaustion, parallel importing is regarded as an IP infringement and cannot be carried out without the authorisation of the right-holders.

The FTA between the United States and Singapore does not explicitly prohibit the international exhaustion rule, but does provide an opportunity for patent-holders to restrain parallel importation through contractual arrangements. The FTA partners are barred from invalidating product distribution agreements that limit distributors' freedom to resell the supplied products (SUSFTA, Art 16.7(2)). Thus, the patent-owners can impose restrictions on the resale of patented goods and thus limit the possibility of exporting the product from Singapore, or importing the product to Singapore when it is sold in a foreign market. Although such restrictions have an anti-competitive character, Singapore is prohibited from voiding the restrictions on parallel importing.

Prohibiting parallel importation is no doubt being introduced in an attempt to block the trade partners from importing cheap medicines and other goods, in disregard of the humanitarian and economic needs of a partner country. For a number of years, developing countries like Thailand have been progressively promoting parallel importation through court cases and national legislation.[5] These developments will be of no avail after it signs the TRIPS-plus trade treaty with the United States. Recent experiences of the country regarding pharmaceutical patents and access to HIV/AIDS medicines should prompt Thailand and other developing countries to exercise considerable caution before entering into any new commitments.[6]

6. REVISING THE PATENT SYSTEM

6.1 Extension of Patent Term

The 20-year patent term under TRIPS is supposed to reward the inventor for his or her innovative efforts. Some products, such as pharmaceuticals and agrochemicals, require official authorisation before they can enter a market, and the approval process normally takes several years. The law of the United States and some other developed countries now provides for the so-called patent term restoration, in order to provide compensation for the loss of patent term due to the approval process.[7] The rationale behind the patent term extension is to allow the patent-holders to capture economic benefits that could not be obtained during the period a government agency (for example, the FDA) reviews the safety and efficacy of the patented product.

Based on its laws, the United States demands that its FTA partners restore a portion of the patent term. Under the VUSBTA, the patent term extension is not mandatory but may be provided at the discretion of the trade partners

(VUSBTA, Art 7.10). By contrast, the SUSFTA requires patent term extension not only in cases of a delay caused by a regulatory approval process but also when there are unreasonable delays in the grant of patent (SUSFTA, Art 16.7 (7), (8) and 16.8(4)).

The extension of the patent term will allow multinationals to monopolise the market longer than the conventional patent rule, despite the fact that those companies can utilise various marketing techniques, such as brand name advertisement and trade mark protection, to secure their monopoly position even after the expiration of the patent term. Extending patent term will delay the potential introduction of affordable generic medicines and defer the day when consumers can reap the benefit of generic competition. Developing countries, which have already experienced hardship from patents on pharmaceuticals, will find the extension of a period of protection in these essential products risky to the well-being of their people.

6.2 Creating a World Patent System

Patent-granting procedures in most countries are based on the 'examination system' which requires prior search and examination as to the validity of the claimed invention before a patent is granted. However, due to the growing sophistication of applicable inventions, full search and examination of applications has become more and more difficult and it has led to an overloading of many patent offices.

The Patent Co-operation Treaty (PCT) was signed in June 1970 in Washington and came into effect in June 1978. It was modified twice, in 1984 and 2001. The Treaty provides for a system of international filing of patent applications in different countries. It allows inventors to secure protection in several countries through a single examination procedure which significantly reduces the costs of patent applications.

A functioning system of patent protection in developing countries is still far short of the level in the developed countries. The PCT, it is claimed, can assist developing countries by increasing efficiency and reducing the costs of patent examinations. However, the system provides a lot more benefit to multinational companies as they can seek patent protection for an invention simultaneously in a large number of countries by filing a single application. The United States intends to use the negotiation opportunities to demand that all its trade partners participate in the single patent filing system of the PCT 1984 (see, for example, SUSFTA, Art 16.1(2)(a)(v)).

Joining the PCT means that developing nations must surrender their right to conduct and implement their own patent laws, and this will make them dependent on the patent offices of the developed countries. In fact, accession to the PCT is part of the developed countries' patent agenda, in which they seek to further harmonise patent law and to create a global patent system with the aim of transforming the trilateral patent offices (such as USPTO, EPO and JPTO) into the world patent office (GRAIN 2002). The patent examination carried out by those offices will most likely serve the interests of the developed countries and their nationals. Nothing can guarantee that the foreign offices will carry out prior search and examination of patent applications to the developing countries' benefit.

The international preliminary examination system under the PCT may serve requirements of the rich countries and their multinationals to achieve worldwide protection, but will not fully operate to accommodate and protect the interests of the developing countries.

7. PROTECTION OF MEDICINAL AND AGRICULTURAL DATA

Law of most nations requires pharmaceutical and agrochemical products to be registered before they can be put on the market. The company that seeks registration must submit data relating to the products' quality, safety and efficacy, the so-called test data, with the relevant regulatory authority. Since the origination of the data involves considerable effort, international agreements demand protection for the data.

Art 39.3 of TRIPS stipulates that Members must protect the undisclosed data submitted for marketing approval. Legal protection must be available to protect new chemical entities against 'unfair commercial use' and 'disclosure' of the data. TRIPS does not require Member parties to provide exclusivity protection to the first person who submits the marketing approval data with a drug regulatory authority (Correa 2002). This has left WTO Members with considerable room to determine rules for the protection of undisclosed test data. For example, a WTO Member's legislation may not prevent third parties from using the test data, if that use does not constitute 'unfair commercial use' or does not breach the 'non-disclosure' obligation in the framework of unfair competition law. In addition, the regulatory authorities may rely on the data submitted by the originator company or on the evidence of a registration made in a foreign country to grant marketing approval for subsequent applications on a similar product.

Some developed countries, including the United States, grant TRIPS-plus protection on the basis of data exclusivity in order to maintain the technological and economic superiority of their multinationals.[8] Multinational drug companies have long been pushing hard for Art 39.3 of TRIPS to be interpreted as requiring data exclusivity. The United States is responding to the demand by requiring all its FTA partners to enforce the data exclusivity for at least five years. The bilateral agreements that the US has signed with Singapore and Vietnam contain provisions relating to data exclusivity.

Under SUSFTA, the parties are required to provide exclusivity for test data submitted to a government for the purpose of product approval for a period of five years for pharmaceuticals and ten years in case of agricultural chemicals (Art 16.8). VUSBTA also obliges Vietnam to prohibit third parties (such as generic companies seeking to introduce generic versions) from relying on the test data previously submitted by the first company (such as an originator company) in support of an application for product approval for at least five years (Art 9.6). The requirement is tantamount to granting exclusivity protection to the originator company.

Furthermore, while TRIPS requires protection only for new chemical entities, the bilateral agreements do not contain such a limitation. Exclusivity protection must be provided for all kinds of data submitted for marketing approval, including data with respect to compositions, dosage forms and new uses of a known drug. This TRIPS-plus commitment will limit the country's ability in flexibly implementing Art 39.3 of TRIPS.

Granting data exclusivity will allow the multinationals to dominate all markets, whilst at the same time creating a barrier to the entry of generic products. Manufacturers of generic products, most of which are small companies in developing countries, will have to enter a long and costly testing process and complete the registration trials before the marketing approval of a generic drug can be obtained. Moreover, since the relevant and essential data are not available due to the exclusivity protection, the possibility for the country to issue compulsory licences will be diminished. Finally, the obligation to provide data exclusivity will prohibit the regulatory authorities from relying on marketing approvals in other countries, despite the fact that most developing countries lack capacity to review data for the purposes of granting marketing approval.

The TRIPS-plus data exclusivity is a means of delaying generic competition and constitutes a barrier to compulsory licensing. For countries considering entering into the TRIPS-plus world, the socio-economic implications for introducing data exclusivity will need careful consideration.

8. GLOBAL PROTECTION FOR TRADEMARKS

According to Art 15 of TRIPS, a trademark is a sign used by any person in the course of business or trade to distinguish his goods or services from those of others. A trademark can be personal names, letters, numerals, figurative elements, colours and any combination of these. A registrable trademark must be distinctive (such as it is capable of distinguishing the goods or services of the owner from other goods or services).

Most US FTAs define trademarks in the broadest manner. According to SUSFTA, for example, the parties have to protect non-visually perceptible trademarks, including scent marks (Art 16.2(1); see Chaudri 2003). This obligates Singapore to change its existing law, which requires that a trademark must be a visually perceptible sign. The new trademark regime will allow anyone to register signs identifiable by their sound, texture and smell as trademarks. No doubt, this requirement is an attempt to bring other countries' trademark law to the level of US legislation.

United States FTAs also requires the trade partners to give effect to Arts 1 to 6 of the Joint Recommendation Concerning Provisions on the Protection of Well-Known Marks (1999), which is an international standard adopted by the Assembly of the Paris Union for the Protection of Industrial Property and the General Assembly of the WIPO, and the WIPO Trademark Law Treaty (Art 16.1(b)). This requirement offers unregistered well-known marks wider protection, as a framework for determination of well-known marks under the Joint Recommendation apparently discriminates against local trademarks in favour of foreign well-known marks.

Strong trademark protection will benefit trademark owners, particularly those producing textile, perfumery and cosmetic products. Pharmaceutical companies will also benefit from the greater protection of trademarks because in this area there are many potentially conflicting trademarks. In addition, trademarks are employed heavily by the pharmaceutical industries. Pharmaceutical companies generally employ brand intensive advertising by using sophisticated techniques to build up a brand loyalty for their trademarks and brand names (Brannon 1999).

A common marketing technique widely used in the pharmaceutical industry involves the launch of a product in different packaged forms and the use of more than one brand name for a single therapeutic drug (British Medical Association 1988; Brown 1999). Each drug has a single generic name, which is a generally accepted name for a drug and reflects the therapeutic class to which the drug belongs. No one can have a monopoly over the generic name. Unlike the generic name, the brand name is a proprietary name which belongs to one owner only. To the extent that a brand name is used to proclaim ownership, a drug company is able to have its brand name displace the generic name, and the drug will be known by the name that is the property of the firm (Lang 1974, p. 31). The brand name is then advertised to consumers, or in the case of prescription drugs, to doctors, in order to build up brand loyalty. The multiplicity of brands causes confusion in consumers' minds. Consumers and doctors tend to believe that the branded drug is different from, and cannot be substituted by, another lower-priced generic drug. The proliferation of branded products, together with intense advertising, enables large companies to create and sustain goodwill as well as maintain leading market positions to protect them against small generic firms.

Unlike the time-limited patent rights, the trademark rights will create indefinite commercial and marketing power for a company through its brand promotion activities. This is because the legal status of trademarks is different from other IP rights, as it can exist forever. As there is no term of protection for trademarks, the company will continue to monopolise the market, even though its products no longer enjoy patent or other IP protection. A comprehensive study of drug prices carried out by Statman reveals that the prices of most patent drugs do not decline after patent expiry due to the brand loyalty built upon their trademarks (Statman 1981, pp. 140–150).

9. PROTECTION OF DIGITAL TECHNOLOGIES

TRIPS does not incorporate minimum standards on specific IP issues in cyberspace. In 1996 the WIPO adopted two 'internet treaties': the WIPO Copyright Treaty and the WIPO Performances and Phonograms Treaty. These two treaties create an entirely new body of IP law relating to the internet. They establish important international norms relating to rights to make a work available to the public through interactive media. They also provide for the protection of rights management information and technological measures used to guard copyrighted and non-copyrighted works. Pressuring all trade partners to adopt the very dynamic digital agenda of WIPO is one of the main objectives in current US trade policy.

The US digital agenda has focused on, inter alia, the following issues:

- The country entering into an FTA with the US must comply with the essential provisions of the Convention Relating to the Distribution of Program-Carrying Signals Transmitted by Satellite (1974), the WIPO Copyright Treaty (1996) and the WIPO Performances and Phonograms Treaty (1996) (see, for example, SUSFTA, Art 16.1).
- The trade partner must provide a longer term of protection than the TRIPS standard (such as the term of protection shall not be less than the life of the author and 70 years after the author's death) (see, for example, SUSFTA, Art 16.4(4)(a)).
- The trade partner must provide adequate protection against the decoding of encrypted program-carrying satellite signals, as well as

any reception or further distribution of decoded signals, without the owner's authorisation. Again, this protection is not covered by TRIPS (see, for example, SUSFTA, Art 16.6; VUSBTA, Art 5).

- While TRIPS does not impose obligations concerning technological protection measures (TPMs), all FTAs proposed by the United States stipulate that parties must provide adequate legal protection and effective legal remedies against acts of circumventing TPMs and against devices which could be used for circumvention, regardless of the intended use of the device (see, for example, SUSFTA, Art 16.4(7)). This means in effect that the United States is now creating a new concept of copyright protection by extending the conventional economic rights of the author to the right to use and distribute circumventing devices.
- The TRIPS-plus commitment of 'rights management information' is also imposed on the contracting parties. All US FTAs demand that the trade partner impose criminal and civil liability on anyone who provides false information, or removes or alters copyright management information (see, for example, SUSFTA, Art 16.4(8)).
- United States FTAs provide greater protection than TRIPS for works in digital form. For example, temporary reproduction such as temporary storage in electronic form is deemed a copyright infringement under the bilateral trade deal between the United States and Singapore (SUSFTA, Art 16.4(1)) and the proposed TUSFTA (but not under VUSBTA). This provision clearly extends the author's right over their works on the internet.
- United States FTAs have gone further than TRIPS by permitting the right-holders to take a legal action against the internet service provider (ISP) for the copying of works by subscribers (see, for example, SUSFTA, Art 16.9(22)).[9] Further, the trade partner must ensure that the owner of copyright can track every use made of digital copies and trace where each copy resides on the network and what is being done with it at any time. These two requirements will greatly affect the public right of fair use with respect to the digital works.

This new area of IP protection will no doubt allow content owners to enjoy greater protection than conventional copyright rules would afford. The provisions on prohibition of circumventing TPMs and devices, for example, will enable the owners to extend greater control over access to and distribution of works that copyright law expressly leaves unprotected in order to stimulate further creativity, including works that have fallen into the public domain. The scope of fair use online will be narrowed down, as the owners can require payment for any use or excerpting of a digital work, regardless of the user's purpose. The use of the internet and digital works for educational or private non-commercial purposes, or the use by educational and library organisations, will be increasingly hindered because of this prohibition (Cohen 1998).

The worst situation arises when a temporary reproduction clause is incorporated into national law. Compared with the conventional copyright rules that no control of reading is given to the right owner, the prohibition of temporary reproduction will allow the copyright owner to control the use of the internet. This is because every use of an internet browser, which requires a few seconds storage in the random access memory (RAM) of a user's computer, will constitute copying. While the use of conventional copyright works, such as reading a book, is not considered infringement, the browsing or using of the internet will be barred on the ground of violation of copyright.

10. CONCLUSION

In light of the considerable and long-term efforts by developing countries to minimise the impact of TRIPS, one might conclude that most developing countries oppose the high degree of IP protection. That conclusion, however, is contradicted by widespread and enthusiastic support of many developing countries for entering into FTAs that demand higher commitments on IP protection.

Given the fact that developing countries have often suffered from the weakening prices of raw materials, foods and semi-manufactured products, which are their main foreign exchange earners, any single developing country would have a strong incentive to sign an FTA with the United States, as it no doubt believes that such a treaty will help it to secure access to the world's most lucrative market. However, by signing an FTA, the developing country agrees, in a binding treaty under international law, to respect any obligations contained in the agreement it has entered into. The treaty can be harmful to the country because it leads to a world in which TRIPS-plus obligations are imposed. In making decisions with respect to bilateral or regional deals, policy-makers will have to weigh the economic benefits of FTAs against the importance of protecting the health and social interests of their populations.

In conclusion, increased national protection of IP rights should be made on the ground of its assistance for the promotion of national technological and economic development, rather than in exchange for the uncertain benefits under the FTA. Any bilateral trade negotiations should be viewed as an opportunity to address a much broader range of concerns of the developing countries, including abuse of IP rights, technology transfer and capacity building, protection of traditional knowledge, and the control and regulation of access to and use of genetic and biological resources.

NOTES

1. The United States draft proposal submitted to Thai negotiators is available on: http://www.bilaterals.org/article.php 3?id_article=3677, visited 17 May 2007.
2. The concept of Farmers' Rights has an aim of compensating farmers who have been conserving plant genetic resources for the past centuries and thereby have contributed to the development of plant varieties. Farmers' Rights are officially adopted by the International Treaty on Plant Genetic Resources for Food and Agriculture (2001), 9.
3. Likewise, the proposed TUSFTA also limits the circumstances in which a compulsory licence can be issued to three circumstances.
4. The former is found in the FTA that the US signed with Australia, as well as the proposed draft FTAA, while the latter is constituted under the SUSFTA. No such provisions are constituted under the proposed TUSFTA.
5. See Supreme Court decision, Case No 2817/2543. See also Patent Act BE 2522, section 36(7).
6. Thailand has had problems of accessibility to essential medicines, especially regarding antiretroviral drugs. It jointly proposed a draft text for a ministerial declaration on the TRIPS Agreement and Public Health in 2001. See the Submission by the African Group, Barbados, Bolivia, Brazil, Cuba, Dominican Republic, Ecuador, Honduras, India, Indonesia, Jamaica, Pakistan, Paraguay, Philippines, Peru, Sri Lanka, Thailand and Venezuela: IP/C/W/296. See Kuanpoth 2006.
7. See United States Drug Price Competition and Patent Term Restoration Act of 1984, generally known as the Hatch-Waxman Act.
8. US laws adopt an absolute exclusivity regime for pharmaceuticals and a limited-exclusivity regime for pesticides. See Correa 2002, p. 8.
9. This provision is basically taken from United States Digital Millennium Copyright Act of 1998. There are three newly introduced copyright rules under the Act: the liability of the ISP, protection against anti-circumvention devices and protection against satellite signal theft.

REFERENCES

Abbott, F. (2005), 'The WTO Medicines Decision: World Pharmaceutical Trade and the Protection of Public Health', *American Journal of International Law*, 99(2), 317–358.

Beier, F.-K. (1985), *Bio Technology and Patent Protection: An International Review*, Paris: Organisation for Economic Co-operation and Development.

Blakeney, M. (1999), 'Intellectual Property in the Dreamtime – Protecting the Cultural Creativity of Indigenous Peoples', Oxford Intellectual Property Research Centre, Research Seminar, 9 November 1999, www.oiprc.ox.ac.uk/EJWP1199.pdf, visited 17 May 2007.

Brannon, L. (1999), 'Regulating Drug Promotion on the Internet', *Food and Drug Law Journal*, 54(4), 599–615.

British Medical Association (1988), *The British National Formulary*, London: British Medical Association.

Brown, R. (1999), 'Advertising and the Public Interest: Legal Protection of Trade Symbols', *Yale Law Journal*, 108(7), 1619–1659.

Chaudri, A. (2003), 'Graphically Speaking: Registering Smell, Colour and Sound Marks in the UK and Europe', *Trademark World*, 157, 26–29.

Cohen, J. (1998), 'Lochner in Cyberspace: The New Economic Orthodoxy of "Right Management"', *Michigan Law Review*, 97(2), 462–563.

Correa, C. (1999), *Access to Plant Genetic Resources and Intellectual Property Rights*, Background Study Paper No. 8, Rome: Commission on Genetic Resources for Food and Agriculture.

Correa, C. (2000), *Integrating Public Health Concerns into Patent Legislation in Developing Countries*, Geneva: South Centre.

Correa, C. (2002), *Protection of Data Submitted for the Registration of Pharmaceuticals: Implementing the Standards of the TRIPS Agreement*, Geneva: South Centre.

Crucible Group (1994), *People, Plants and Patents: The Impact of Intellectual Property on Biodiversity, Conservation, Trade and Rural Society*, Ottawa: International Development Research Centre.

Diamond v Chakrabarty, 447 US 303 (1980).

Drahos, P. (2002), 'Developing Countries and International Intellectual Property Standard-Setting', *Journal of World Intellectual Property*, 5(5), 765–789.

GRAIN (2002), 'WIPO Moves Toward "World" Patent System', http://www.grain.org/publications/wipo-patent-2002-en.cfm, visited 17 May 2007.

Heller, M. and R. Eisenberg (1998), 'Can Patents Deter Innovation?: The Anticommons in Biomedical Research', *Science*, 280(5364), 698–701.

Helms, R. (ed.) (1981), *Drugs and Health*, Washington DC: American Enterprise Institute for Public Policy Research.

IP/C/W/296 (2001), *Submission by the African Group, Barbados, Bolivia, Brazil, Cuba, Dominican Republic, Ecuador, Honduras, India, Indonesia, Jamaica, Pakistan, Paraguay, Philippines, Peru, Sri Lanka, Thailand and Venezuela*, Geneva: World Trade Organization.

Kuanpoth, J. (2006), 'Patents and Access to Medicines in Thailand: The ddI Case and Beyond', *Intellectual Property Quarterly*, 2, 149–159.

Lang, R. (1974), *The Politics of Drugs*, Hants: Saxon House.

Penrose, E. (1951), *The Economics of the International Patent System*, Baltimore: Johns Hopkins Press.

Red Dove case (1970), *International Review of Industrial Property and Copyright Law*, 1, 136.

Reid, W., C. Barber and A. La Vina (1995), 'Translating Genetic Resource Rights Into Sustainable Development: Gene Cooperatives, the Biotrade and Lessons From the Philippines', *Plant Genetic Resource Newsletter*, 102, 1–2.

Roffe, P. (2004), *Bilateral Agreements and a TRIPS-plus World: The Chile-USA Free Trade Agreement*, Ottawa: Quaker International.

Roht-Arriaza, N. (1996), 'Of Seeds and Shamans: The Appropriation of the Scientific and Technical Knowledge of Indigenous and Local Communities', *Michigan Journal of International Law*, 17(4), 919–965.

Singham, S. (2000), 'Competition Policy and the Stimulation of Innovation: TRIPS and the Interface between Competition and Patent Protection in the Pharmaceutical Industry', *Brooklyn Journal of International Law*, 26(2), 363–415.

Statman, M. (1981), 'The Effect of Patent Expiration on the Market Position of Drugs', in Helms 1981.

Stevenson, G. (2000), 'Trade Secrets: The Secret to Protecting Indigenous Ethnobiological (Medicinal) Knowledge', *New York University International Journal of Law & Policy*, 32(4), 1119–1174.

UNEP/CBD/COP/6/20 (2000), *Report of the Sixth Meeting of the Conference of the Parties to the Convention on Biological Diversity*, Montreal: Conference of the Parties to the Convention on Biological Diversity.

United Nations Development Program (1999), *Human Development Report*, New York: United Nations.

United States Trade Representative (2004), *Letter of Notification of USTR to US Congress of Intent to Initiate Free Trade Agreement Negotiations with Thailand*, 12 February 2004, http://www.ustr.gov/Document_Library/Press_Releases/2004/February/USTR_Notifies_Congress_of_Intent_to_Initiate_FTA_Negotiations_with_Thail.html, visited 18 July 2007.

Urbanski, A. (1995), 'Chemical Prospecting, Biodiversity Conservation, and the Importance of International Protection of Intellectual Property Rights in Biological Materials', *Buffalo Journal of International Law*, 2(1), 131–182.

Vaitsos, C. (1972), 'Patents Revisited: Their Function in Developing Countries', *Journal of Development Studies*, 9(1), 71–97.

Vandoren, P. and J. Eeckhaute (2003), 'The WTO Decision on Paragraph 6 of the Doha Declaration on the TRIPS Agreement and Public Health: Making it Work', *Journal of World Intellectual Property*, 6(6), 779–793.

Vivas-Eugui, D. (2003), *Regional and Bilateral Agreements and a TRIPS-plus World: The Free Trade Area of the Americas (FTAA)*, TRIPS Issues Papers 1, Geneva: Quaker United Nations Office.

Watal, J. (1998), 'The TRIPS Agreement and Developing Countries – Strong, Weak or Balanced Protection', *Journal of World Intellectual Property*, 1(2), 281–307.

WT/MIN(01)/DEC/2 (2001), *Declaration on the TRIPS Agreement and Public Health*, Geneva: Ministerial Conference of the World Trade Organization.

6. The development-balance of the TRIPS agreement and enforcement of intellectual property rights

Ermias Tekeste Biadgleng

1. INTRODUCTION

The intellectual property (IP) and development discourse invokes an intriguing debate that intersects the assumed objectives of promoting innovation with concerns about the actual cost for industrialisation and public welfare in developing countries. The developed countries as major inventors continue to maintain an advantageous position regarding the utilisation of the Agreement on Trade-Related Aspects of Intellectual Property Rights (TRIPS). Developing countries, with limited exceptions, have yet to see the promised better days under TRIPS. They are primarily concerned about gaining IP benefits from learning, reverse engineering and the acquisition of existing technologies. Despite the development concerns arising from TRIPS, the G-8 leaders and the United States (US)–European Union (EU) summit adopted a trans-Atlantic agenda on worldwide enforcement of IP rights. The agenda underlines the shift in the position of the advanced countries from setting the standards towards monitoring the enforcement of IP rights in developing countries (European Union 2006). The enforcement of TRIPS requires an assessment of the level of adjustment expected of developing countries, the degree that TRIPS facilitates technology transfers and the extent of the reward for the contribution of developing countries in terms of biological resources, traditional knowledge and cultural expression.

There is a link between TRIPS and IP rights in general with normative justifications for the promotion of innovation through reward systems, including through the institution of legal rights to reward the fruits of labour (Menell 2000). The normative justifications continue to be weighted against the cost of the IP system and questions arise as to whether the system can deliver on its promises of promoting innovation. In the context of TRIPS, the result of analysis justifying or rejecting the assumptions of

TRIPS would be important to all participating countries. If TRIPS is justified for the objectives it assumes, it has to be implemented by all irrespective of the fact that countries differ in their capacity to benefit from its implementation. The rejection of the assumptions of TRIPS provides the participants only with the option to denounce it.

Apart from the normative justifications, TRIPS from its inception has faced fundamental questions of balance. Okediji describes the competing interests and the required balance in the IP system in terms of the 'domestic-international balance' and a 'balance between authors and users' (in case of copyright, which was the subject of her writing) (Okediji 2006, pp. 5–6). The question of balance of interests among users and right-holders encompasses the users in the developed countries, including generic pharmaceutical manufacturers. The 'international-domestic balance' could cover the process of national policymaking that responds to domestic competing interests and the role of the level of economic development of each country in determining the extent to which a one-size-fits-all set of international standards could be sustainable. Right-holders and users in the developed world, in the process of defining their respective interests, could achieve an equilibrium reflecting the cost of knowledge production, purchasing power and the accessibility of technological products. Where the standards that achieved the equilibrium in advanced countries are adopted as the multilateral norm, disequilibrium will occur, unduly burdening developing countries. International obligations and flexibility in domestic policymaking requires a different approach to assessment of the balance of interest based on levels of development, which is described here as 'the development balance'. The Millennium Project Task Force on Science, Technology and Innovation of the United Nations recommended differentiation of countries based on level of development for protection of IP rights (Juma and Yee-Cheong, 2005, p. 112). The importance of the level of development in defining the balance of interest lies in the fact that some of the developed countries, such as the US, require the implementation of IP rights protection in developing countries to the same level available in their country (United States Bipartisan Trade Promotion Authority Act of 2002, § 3802).

The analysis of the 'development balance' of TRIPS in this chapter contributes to the debate about the basic governance structure of TRIPS in the context of enforcing IP rights. This chapter focuses on the question of balance of interests arising from the implementation of TRIPS, as opposed to evaluating the assumed objective of TRIPS. However, since TRIPS lacks any formalised process for evaluating any of its assumed benefits, the relative relevance of its basic assumptions could be useful in examining the allocation of costs and benefits by its implementation. The next section discusses the basic premises of TRIPS and its relation with balance of interest and levels of development, with a reflection on recent developments on the practices of developed countries. The third section reviews the panels and Appellate Body approaches to interpretation of TRIPS provisions in light of development balance. The fourth section discusses enforcement of IP rights and questions of development. The study concludes after synthesis of the various issues and outline of major recommendations.

2. THE BASIC PREMISES OF TRIPS AND THE DEVELOPMENT BALANCE

During the negotiation of the draft Havana Charter in the late 1940s, countries were much more concerned about the unfair and trade restrictive use of IP rights by multinational corporations and the need to regulate such practices than they were when negotiating TRIPS (see, for example, United Nations 1948, Arts 46(3) and 49(1)). Conversely, the General Agreement on Tariffs and Trade (GATT) largely provided exceptions to trade rules to enable parties to ensure compliance with their IP laws (GATT 1994, Arts XII(3), XVIII(10), XX(d)). GATT also provided for the examination of the restrictive business practices of multinational corporations through a panel of experts (GATT Council 1960). However, considering the lack of progress in the international regulation of the anti-competitive practices of multinationals affecting the transfer of technology, many developing countries adopted mechanisms that enable greater access to technologies by limiting the scope of protection of IP rights and closely regulating the exercise of such rights (UNCTAD-ICTSD 2005, p. 3). The developed countries, especially the US, on the other hand, pursued policies to secure the protection of their industries' IP rights. This led to tensions between developed and developing countries. Reflecting these tensions, TRIPS recognises balancing the competing interests as a guiding principle, among others, in setting the multilateral framework. It does this by defining the scope of obligations, flexibilities for implementation, and recognising the relationship between IP rights and trade barriers (TRIPS, Preamble and Arts 7 and 8).

2.1 Balancing Interests as a Basic Principle for Implementing TRIPS

The WTO recognises various objectives for multilateral trade relations. It recognises the objectives of raising standards of living, and the expansion of production and trade in goods and services in accordance with the objective of sustainable development in a manner consistent with the respective needs and concerns of countries at different levels of economic development (Marrakesh Agreement Establishing the World Trade Organization, Preamble and paras 1 and 2). The WTO trading system contributes to the achievement of these objectives by requiring members to enter into reciprocal and mutually advantageous arrangements directed at the substantial reduction of tariffs and other barriers to trade, and to the elimination of discriminatory treatment in international trade relations (Marrakesh Agreement Establishing the World Trade Organization, para 3). This calling for mutually advantageous arrangements fails the realist premise of fairness as leading to 'mutual advantage' (Albin 2001, p. 6). Hence, the WTO as a rule-based trading system can have an automatic claim to its rules as a mutually advantageous arrangement. The permissible debate in a rule-based regime such as the WTO is limited to the strict observation of the rules.

The mutual advantageousness of the WTO rules leading to arrangements for negotiated outcomes extends to its various agreements. The Agreement on Agriculture underlines the objective of establishing a fair and market-oriented agricultural trading system. The preamble and Art 20 of this agreement dealing with the continuation of the reform of agricultural trade reflects this objective as a guiding principle for the negotiations in agricultural trade. As an outcome of negotiation with established objectives – the Agreement on Agriculture – can have an outright claim for being fair and market-oriented, despite the major controversies on existing subsidies and tariffs. Whatever the outcome of the implementation, it can be validly assumed that the members agreed on the text upon satisfying the objective to establish a fair and market-oriented trading system. A mutually advantageous or fair outcome of negotiations imposes an obligation to honour and comply with freely negotiated agreements.

The WTO Agreements also refer to 'fair and equitable' requirements as standard of trade practice or conduct among the member states. GATT, for example, refers to the object of attaining equitable shares of world export trade in primary products and equitable shares from the international supply of products for all member states. Accordingly, it seeks to prevent members from providing export subsidies for primary products that result in them gaining a more than equitable share of the export trade (GATT, 1994, Art XVI(3)). When countries apply measures for the acquisition or distribution of products from the global market, they are required to abide by the principle that all countries are entitled to an equitable share of the international supply of the products (GATT 1994, Art XX(j)). GATT also requires fair and equitable treatment to the trade of other members with respect to the importation by state trading enterprises of products for consumption in government use (GATT 1994, Art XVII(2)). In contrast, the

Agreement on Textiles and Clothing requires fair and equitable trading conditions by countries implementing dumping and anti-dumping rules and procedures, subsidies and countervailing measures, and protection of IP rights (Agreement on Textiles and Clothing, Art 7(1)(b)). Unlike the Agreement on Agriculture, these standards require continuous evaluation of the fairness and equitability of trading practices.

When it comes to TRIPS, Art 7 defines the objective of the agreement as balancing competing interests and envisaging mutual advantage of the producers and users of technologies. It reads:

> The protection and enforcement of intellectual property rights should contribute to the promotion of technological innovation and to the transfer and dissemination of technology, to the mutual advantage of producers and users of technological knowledge and in a manner conducive to social and economic welfare, and to a balance of rights and obligations.

Whether this provision is limited to the negotiating process or to continuously evaluating the balance in the IP system was the subject of the debate in *Canada – Patent Protection of Pharmaceutical Products*. Canada relied on Art 7 to justify its patent law that provided exceptions to rights conferred by patents for regulatory approval and stockpiling before the expiry of the patent. Canada submitted that Art 7 declares that one of the key goals of TRIPS was a balance between IP rights created by the agreement and other important socio-economic policies of WTO member governments. Art 8 elaborates upon the socio-economic policies with particular attention to health and nutritional policies. With respect to patent rights, Canada argued, these purposes call for a liberal interpretation of the conditions stated in Art 30 of TRIPS, so that governments would have the necessary flexibility to adjust patent rights to maintain the desired balance with other important national policies (WT/DS114/R, para. 7.24). The EU countered this argument and submitted that Art 7 is a statement that describes the balancing of goals that had already taken place in negotiating the final texts of TRIPS (WT/DS114/R, paras 7.24 and 7.25).

The submissions of the two parties with respect to the stated objectives of IP rights protection in a manner conducive to social and economic welfare, and to balancing the rights and obligations of members was crucial for the determination of the extent of balance under TRIPS. The submissions could be paraphrased as saying that the objectives of TRIPS as stated under Art 7 are achieved in negotiating the final texts (the EU) or that the objectives continue to influence and guide the implementation of TRIPS (Canada). In the first instance, the balancing of goals was limited to the process of negotiation, in which case the goals are already balanced in the final text, and what is left is the strict implementation of the agreement. In the second case, as argued by Canada, the balancing of goals remains a task to be achieved during implementation.

The Panel observed that the prohibition of discrimination against technologies under Art 27.1 of TRIPS limits the ability to target certain products in dealing with important national policies referred to in Arts 7 and 8. The Panel read this as a deliberate limitation rather than a frustration of purpose. It concurred with the EU argument that 'the TRIPS Agreement would want to require governments to apply exceptions in a non-discriminatory manner, in order to ensure that governments do not succumb to domestic pressures to limit exceptions to areas where right holders tend to be foreign producers' (WT/DS114/R, para. 7.92). This observation of the Panel does not provide the full picture of what its analysis would be if Canada had limited its argument to Art 7 without referring to Art 8. In this regard, UNCTAD-ICTSD has observed that:

> The Panel suggests that Arts 7 and 8.1, and the policies reflected in those articles, are bounded by the principle of non-discrimination in Art 27.1 with respect to patents. Presumably the Panel is invoking the specific non-discrimination requirement of Art 27.1 as a control on the more general policies stated in Arts 7 and 8.1, and also invoking the consistency requirement of Art 8.1. It is not clear how far this idea of giving precedence to specific obligations over more general policies should be extended (UNCTAD-ICTSD 2005, p. 129).

The Panel also accorded more weight to the balance created by Arts 28 and 30 of TRIPS. Art 28 determines the scope of rights conferred by a patent. Art 30 authorises limited exceptions to rights conferred by a patent. It saw that Arts 7 and 8 play a limited role. As a result, the problem is more than whether Arts 7 and 8 are subject to the principle of non-discrimination. Instead it may involve the assumption that Arts 7 and 8 proclaim that TRIPS itself balances member states' interests but does not allow members themselves to re-evaluate the balance of interests under their domestic norm-setting. The Panel seems to support the EU's argument when it states that:

> In the Panel's view, Art 30's very existence amounts to a recognition that the definition of patent rights contained in Art 28 would need certain adjustments. On the other hand, the three limiting conditions attached to Art 30 testify strongly that the negotiators of the Agreement did not intend Art 30 to bring about what would be equivalent to a renegotiation of the basic balance of the Agreement. Obviously, the exact scope of Art 30's authority will depend on the specific meaning given to its limiting conditions. The words of those conditions must be examined with particular care on this point. Both the goals and the limitations stated in Arts 7 and 8.1 must obviously be borne in mind when doing so as well as those of other provisions of the TRIPS Agreement which indicate its object and purposes (WT/DS114/R, para. 7.26).

Here the Panel supports the claim about the achievement of the balance of interests through Art 30, which provides exceptions, and at the same time considers the conditions attached to the exceptions as confirming the final delineation of the scope of deviation. The Panel indicated that the objectives under Art 7 and the principles under Art 8 should be *borne in mind* in determining the exact scope of Art 30. It is not clear how this kind of interpretation provides any role for Arts 7 and 8 in determining the exact scope of Art 30.

Based on the Panel's interpretation of Arts 7 and 8.1 in *Canada – Patent Protection of Pharmaceutical Products* the balance of competing interests under domestic norm setting should strictly fall under the relevant provisions of TRIPS. The relevance of general policy statements and objectives regarding the balance and promotion of public interest under Arts 7 and 8 is very limited. Canadian patent policy was attempting to enable the entry of generic drugs into the market as early as possible. In this context, the room for promoting robust exceptions to patents, considering the level of development and the public welfare in developing countries, could be relatively narrow. However, the Panel's interpretation could be re-examined where the party to the dispute is a developing country with well-established concerns about the need for an interpretation that takes into account levels of development when balancing the interests of private right-holders and the public welfare. In addition, the Panel's conclusion could be revisited based on the Declaration on the TRIPS Agreement and Public Health (the Declaration; also known as the 'Doha Declaration' – WT/MIN(01)/DEC/2) adopted in 2001.

The fourth ministerial conference of the WTO adopted the Declaration providing interpretive guidelines and affirming the rights of states to use fully the flexibilities under TRIPS. The Declaration adopts the agreement of the member states as to the interpretation of TRIPS in relation to measures to protect public health. The Ministers agreed that TRIPS does not and should not prevent members from taking such measures and reaffirmed that TRIPS can and should be interpreted and implemented in a manner supportive of WTO members' right to protect public health, and, in particular, to promote access to medicines for all. This unanimous Declaration by WTO members contributes to the jurisprudence on TRIPS.

The Declaration requires each TRIPS provision to be interpreted in light of the agreement's objects and purposes. It gave particular attention to Art 7 (objectives) and Art 8 (principles) of TRIPS. Abbott noted that the Declaration effectively restates Art 31(1) of the Vienna Convention on the Law of Treaties, and the interpretive principles discussed by the Panel in *Canada – Patent Protection of Pharmaceutical Products* (Abbott 2004, p. 447). Correa, on the other hand, observed that:

> In fact, the Doha Declaration goes beyond merely confirming the relevance of Arts 7 and 8 for the interpretation of the TRIPS Agreement. It provides an *understanding* about the purpose of the TRIPS Agreement in relation to public health issues, which should guide any future rulings by Panels and the Appellate Body dealing with such issues (Correa 2002, pp. 14–15).

The Declaration helps developing countries in protecting public interests, at the minimum by requiring the interpretation of conditions on adoption of limited exceptions to IP rights in light of the objective of promoting balance. This might require, for example, a panel dealing with the same issues as in *Canada – Patent Protection of Pharmaceutical Products* to examine the scope of deviation under Art 30 in light of Art 7 of TRIPS. In which case, panels might consider the cumulative conditions under the article for adoption of exceptions in light of the desire to promote balance in the IP system in accordance with Art 7 and in a manner supportive of measures taken to protect public health. Ultimately, to factor the level of development of a particular country in the implementation of the TRIPS Agreement, it is necessary that the interpretation of TRIPS moves away from the rather literal and textual approaches. The relevance of Art 7 as a gateway for promotion of balance in the domestic IP law-making largely depends on the scope of obligation and the nature of permitted deviation from the rules. Member nations should ultimately ensure that any deviation from the rules promotes a balance between the interests of uses and right-holders, and not merely frustrates the protection and enforcement of IP rights. The next section discusses the scope of the obligations of member states under TRIPS.

2.2 Scope of Obligation and the Development Balance

Article 1 of TRIPS is the core provision determining the nature of obligation and rights. It provides that members shall 'give effect' to the provisions of the agreement and may, but are not obliged, to implement under their laws more extensive protection than is required by TRIPS. Members are also free to determine the appropriate method of implementing the provisions of TRIPS within their own legal system and practices.

The obligation to 'give effect' to TRIPS provisions is obviously broader than implementing the minimum protection of each category of IP rights. The interpretation of the obligation to give effect to the provisions clearly links with the mandatory obligations on the protection of subject matter, and the entitlement to determine the scope and terms of protection. However, TRIPS also contains mandatory limitation or exclusionary provisions; Art 9(2) excludes providing copyright protection to ideas, procedures and methods of operation or mathematical concepts as such.

Countries can give effect to Art 9(2) by excluding the same subject matters from copyright protection. Giving effect to provisions providing optional methods of compliance can also involve implementing one of the alternatives provided. For example, Art 27 of TRIPS provides options to protect plant varieties by patents or an effective *sui generis* system or by both. To give effect to Art 27, countries should make the decision to adopt one (or both) of the options provided for the protection of plant varieties. Furthermore, giving effect to the provisions of TRIPS on the enforcement, availability and maintenance of IP rights also includes the enforcement of the obligations of right-holders. These include the requirements to comply with reasonable procedures, preventing the abuse of enforcement procedures and furnishing necessary evidence as a basis for administrative and judicial reviews.

TRIPS limits the obligations of countries to protect IP rights to those specifically provided for under its provisions. In *Indonesia – Certain Measures Affecting the Automobile Industry*, the Panel's reading of Indonesia's national treatment obligations under Art 3.1 and its footnote with respect to the use of trademarks was restricted to the use specifically addressed in TRIPS in accordance with Art 20 (WT/DS54/R, para. 14.273). The AB in *India – Patent Protection for Pharmaceutical and Agricultural Chemical Products* also confirmed that the reading of the national treatment provision does not extend to legitimate expectations of other members as it does under GATT (WT/DS50/AB/R, para 57).

The national treatment (Art 3) and most-favoured nation (MFN) treatment (Art 4) obligations also restrict the obligations in respect of the rights of performers, producers of phonograms and broadcasting organisations to the rights provided under TRIPS. The incorporation of the Berne Convention and the Paris Convention by reference under TRIPS preserves important aspects of material reciprocity in a manner that limits the obligations of states to the existing system in their country. Where the Berne Convention (1971) or the Rome Convention allow material reciprocity, a consequential exception to MFN treatment is also permitted under Art 4 of TRIPS. Furthermore, Art 5 of TRIPS also provides that the national treatment and MFN obligations do not apply to procedures provided in multilateral agreements concluded under the auspices of the World Intellectual Property Organization (WIPO) relating to the acquisition or maintenance of IP rights. This includes the Madrid Agreement and Protocol concerning the International Registration of Marks, the Hague Agreement concerning the International Deposit of Industrial Designs, the Patent Cooperation Treaty, the Patent Law Treaty, the Trademark Law Treaty and the Budapest Treaty on the International Recognition of the Deposit of Microorganisms for the purposes of Patent Procedure. The utility of provisions restricting or limiting the obligation of countries to those specifically provided for under TRIPS is significant for developing countries, especially for determining their rights and obligations with a reasonable degree of certainty.

The second sentence of Art 1.1 of TRIPS, in the words of a Panel, confirms that TRIPS is a minimum standards agreement in respect of IP rights (WT/DS170/R, para. 6.87). The article authorises countries, but does not oblige them, to extend protection more extensively than provided under TRIPS. With the emergence of free trade agreements (FTAs) promoting the extension of IP rights, loose applications of criteria for granting IP rights, and the erosion of flexibilities, the limitations to the level of protection more extensively than provided under TRIPS have particular relevance for the developing world. The only limitation available under Art 1.1 to the upward movement of IP rights protection is that such protection should not contravene any provision of TRIPS. 'More extensive protection' in the context of Art 1.1 that does not contravene TRIPS within the definition of 'protection' under footnote 3 would mean expanding the availability and scope of IP rights, facilitating the procedural requirements for the acquisition and maintenance of IP rights, strengthening the enforcement of IP rights and reducing matters affecting the *use* of IP rights specifically addressed under TRIPS.

There is no direct link between the provision of more extensive protection and the objective of promoting balance as provided under Art 7. In as much as Art 30 provides for exceptions and limitations to patent rights under Arts 28 and 33, one would expect the proportional expansion of limitations and exceptions to the extent of the more extensive protection of patents. However, TRIPS authorises only the expansion of the protection of IP rights as recognised under TRIPS. It does not allow members to expand (under a FTA or their domestic legislation) the limitations and exceptions of those rights beyond the limitations and exceptions provided for in TRIPS.

The Panel in *US – Section 110(5) Copyright Act* considered exemptions provided for in section 110(5) of the US Copyright Act under Art 13 of TRIPS. The 'business' exemption provided for in the Act allowed the amplification of music broadcasts, without an authorisation and a payment of a fee, by food service and drinking establishments and by retail establishments, if their size did not exceed a certain square footage limit or use of certain equipment. In addition, the 'home-style' exemption allows small restaurants and retail outlets to amplify music broadcasts without an authorisation of the rights-holders and without the payment of a fee, if they use equipment of a kind commonly used in private homes. The EU contended that the Act was inconsistent with the US obligations under Arts 1–21 of the Berne Convention and Art 13 of TRIPS (WT/DS160/R, para.

6.17). The latter allows certain limitations or exceptions to exclusive rights of copyright holders, subject to the condition that such limitations are limited to certain special cases, do not conflict with a normal exploitation of the work in question and do not unreasonably prejudice the legitimate interests of the right-holder.

The Panel confirmed the consistency of the 'home-style' exemption with Art 13 of TRIPS after considering the limits imposed on the beneficiaries of the exemption. However, the 'business' exemption did not meet the requirements of Art 13 of TRIPS and was thus inconsistent with Arts 11*bis*(1)(iii) and 11(1)(ii) of the Berne Convention. This is because a substantial majority of eating and drinking establishments and close to half of retail establishments in the US were covered by the business exemption (WT/DS160/R, paras. 6.252–6.266 and 6.267–6.272). However, section 110(5) of the US Copyright Act was the result of domestic arbitrage involving different interest groups. It extended the copyright term by 20 years accompanied by the business and home-style exemption to balance the various competing interests. Leaving aside whether the net result of the domestic law-making process had fairly balanced competing interests in copyright protection in the US, the Panel's analysis never alluded to the domestic law's history and objectives or to the compromise it attempts to achieve (see further discussion in Dinwoodie and Dreyfuss 2005). As a result, TRIPS provides rights and obligations only to the extent provided under its provisions. However, the balance of the rights and obligations strictly provided under the agreement lacks supportive norms that place a check on the shift of balance that results from providing more extensive protection than required under TRIPS.

2.3 Participatory and Compensatory Regime for Developing Countries under TRIPS

The other way of looking at the issue of balancing interests is to consider whether developing countries can transform their knowledge system and share the gains that TRIPS accords to developed countries. During the finalisation of the Uruguay Round, the developing countries anticipated that they would only have a limited capacity to participate under TRIPS but expected gains from other parts of the package. Strongly put arguments that developing countries would benefit from an IP rights system rested on claims that they would benefit from technology transfers and flows of foreign investment (Organisation for Economic Co-operation and Development 2003).

The ability of the developing countries to reciprocate and share the benefit of the system of IP rights protection under TRIPS is not promising in the short term. The patent filing trends under the Patent Cooperation Treaty (PCT) of WIPO and the Organisation for Economic Co-operation and Development indicator of triadic patent families shows that only a handful of developing countries have engaged in the IP system, and even then only to a limited extent (WIPO/PR/2006/436).

Similar situations arise in relation to all other fields of IP rights. There is, for example, a limited prospect of developing countries benefiting from implementing geographic indications laws. Europe has already more than 700 foods, agricultural and beverage products protected under its laws. It would require quite a long period to establish a similar number of products linked to geographic region in developing countries with the value comparable to the European products. The same is true for building trademarks and brands in developing countries that can capture the global markets for quality products. Valuable trademarks and brands are associated with established businesses with high-tech technologies enabling the supply of quality products and services, in which the developed country enterprises have a clear advantage over developing country enterprises. Copyright dependent enterprises in the developed countries also have capital and developed market advantages that do not exist for developing country enterprises (UNCTAD-ICTSD 2005, p. 136).

There are certain norms that attempt to strike a balance between the implementation of TRIPS and the level of development. The first relates to providing a transition period for the implementation of the agreement and transitional arrangements in relation to product patents in areas of technology not protected by a developing country on the date of application of TRIPS in accordance with Arts 65(2) and (4) and 70(8) and (9). The second targets the need for flexibility to create viable technologies by delaying the implementation of TRIPS and prompting and encouraging technology transfer for least developed countries (LDCs) in accordance with Art 66. The third relates to technical assistance arrangements for the implementation of TRIPS in accordance with Arts 65(2) and 67. While the first flexibility has expired for developing countries, the provisions of technical assistance has a limited role in creating a nexus between the protection of IP rights and development as demonstrated by its implementation. The flexibility allowing the creation of a viable technological base in LDCs by providing for a transition period and the promotion of technology transfers is supplemented by subsequent decisions of the Council for TRIPS. The utility of these flexibilities, however, depends on how much LDCs are able to use them and on the way developed countries implement their obligations on technology transfer.

The flexibilities in terms of substantive rights and obligations that take account of the level of a country's development are uniquely incorporated under Art 9(1) of TRIPS and the Annex to the Berne Convention, which among other provisions authorises the use of compulsory licensing, for the reproduction of copyrighted material and for its translation into a local language.

The remainder of the flexibilities under TRIPS broadly cover all countries and users of technology both in developed and developing countries. The particular advantage of the flexibilities for developing countries lies in the fact that their level of development can benefit from the utilisation of the flexibilities. The flexibilities address some aspects of the controversies about the impact of IP rights on innovation and creativity, abuse of dominant power and restrictive business practices. Some of these TRIPS flexibilities include the flexibility:

(1) to adopt limited exceptions to rights conferred by IP rights under Arts 13, 14(6), 17, 26(2) and 30 of TRIPS and other provisions under the treaties incorporated by reference under TRIPS;
(2) to provide options to exclude certain subject matter from protection based on grounds for the protection of the public interest and the environment under Arts 27(2) and 39(3) and certain inventions related to methods of treatment and plants and animals under Art 27(3), and to choose methods of compliance under a patent system or an effective *sui generis* system for plant varieties;
(3) to adopt conditions for the granting of protection, such as registration and use requirement to confer trademarks, publication or fixation requirement to confer copyrights, and the requirement for the disclosure of the status of foreign application in the case of patents;
(4) for the determination of the specific content of threshold criteria for the grant of IP right protection under Art 27 and other provisions of TRIPS;
(5) for other uses of IP rights without the consent of the rights-holder under Arts 31 (as amended) and 37 of TRIPS and Art 13 of the Berne Convention and its Appendix as applicable to subject matters protected as copyright such as computer programs and compilation of data under Art 10 of TRIPS as well as Art 15 of the Rome Convention;
(6) to determine the regime of exhaustion under Art 6 of TRIPS as clarified by the Declaration.

The narrow scope of some of the obligations and the strict limitations of obligations to the extent provided by TRIPS is also an important flexibility. The protection of pharmaceutical test and other data under Art 39(3) of TRIPS is, for example, limited to data on new chemical entities. The protection from unfair commercial use is another important flexibility. The overall assessment of these flexibilities embodied under TRIPS and its relation with the level of development raises at least two systematic questions, in addition to the question of governance discussed below.

2.3.1 The effectiveness of the flexibilities

The question of effectiveness addresses the viability of some of the flexibilities in the face of their national-level use in the global political economy context. Most of the flexibilities are left for determination at the national level. However, the feasibility of national-level flexibilities could be seriously affected by the nature of IP laws in the most innovative countries. The protection of public morality, the environment and human health by excluding certain inventions from patentability can be frustrated easily if another country decides to protect the offending invention.

Most importantly, although countries strictly adhere to the criteria for granting IP rights to protect the public domain, the loose application of the criteria, the expansion of the subject matter and terms of protection in the advanced countries would seriously affect the supply to the global market of technological goods, and the shrinking of the public domain. The developing countries can prevent the patenting of pharmaceuticals that do not adequately satisfy the novelty, inventive steps and industrial applicability standards. However, the lack of adequate manufacturing capacity can force them to acquire from the international market at higher prices the same pharmaceutical products they have excluded from patentability.

In contrast, the flexibility adopted by the Protocol amending TRIPS in order to enable the exportation of products produced under compulsory licences for the benefit of developing countries with no or limited manufacturing capacity has faced practical problems regarding implementation. The amendment has its own birth problems reducing the incentive for generic manufacturers to engage in production of pharmaceuticals for export to developing countries. In addition, the measures taken by the potential exporting countries for its implementation are criticised for failing to provide sufficient flexibilities and economic incentives for generic producers (Musungu and Oh 2006, p. 70). These show the extent of the dependence of the utilisation of the TRIPS flexibilities on the cooperation of the technologically advanced countries.

Some of the conditions attached to the flexibilities themselves make them difficult to implement domestically. The Appendix to the Berne Convention authorises a special compulsory licence regime for developing countries for the reproduction and translation of copyrighted materials. However, the implementation of the Appendix requires a three to seven-year waiting period and an additional 'grace period' to give the original owner every opportunity to supply that particular local market. In addition, the developing countries have to establish a 'competent authority' to utilise the flexibility under the Appendix. The compulsory licence for translation is allowed only for teaching, scholarship and research purposes. Applicants for licences under the Appendix are required to prove that permission requested from the copyright owner was denied or that the copyright owner could not be located after inquiry. The result of these conditions is that a very limited number of developing countries express interest in using the system (Okediji 2006, p. 15).

2.3.2 Institutional capability and the economic space dilemma

Another strategic question relates to the ability of developing countries to maximise the development advantage arising from the use of flexibilities. Musungu and Oh have identified the increasing use of TRIPS flexibilities by developing countries (Musungu and Oh, 2006, Executive Summary). However, they have also identified:

(1) Lack of simplified legislative and administrative procedures and sometimes inadequate determination of grounds for the use and administration of compulsory licence for the public and non-commercial use of patents (Musungu and Oh, 2006, pp. 32 and 46).
(2) Inadequate use of limited exceptions, including under Art 30 of TRIPS (Musungu and Oh, 2006, pp. 62–63).
(3) Inadequate domestic laws on the scope of the patentability criteria, which lack clarity on whether the protection for process covers 'uses' or 'methods of use', and the institutional shortcomings in carrying out substantive examination of patent claims (Musungu and Oh, 2006, pp. 61–62).
(4) Failure to comply with notification requirements, such as the notice of intention by countries to the WTO and the necessary legal changes in developing countries for the use of the system of exportation of generic pharmaceuticals to countries with no or limited manufacturing capacities (Musungu and Oh, 2006, p. 71).

The critical problems of utilisation of TRIPS flexibilities in developing countries are not solely attributable to institutional weakness. Of course, many of the flexibilities require flexible and dynamic administrative capability, continuous review and the balancing of interests. Since IP rights in developing countries have evolved as institutions without parallel or comparable development of institutions of competition, and a supporting technological base, the developing countries require technical assistance to balance the various goals during the implementation of TRIPS. However, technical assistance in the field of IP rights from rich nations is often confined to IP right maximisation. Even the UN specialised agency WIPO has a very narrow focus on IP rights protection rather than upon assisting with the development of institutions and laws necessary to enrich the IP system and the utilisation of flexibilities.

2.4 IP and Barriers to International Trade

TRIPS promotes the objective of ensuring that measures for the protection and enforcement of IP rights do not themselves become a barrier to international trade. With respect to the granting of IP rights protection, TRIPS does not provide specific guidelines as to what countries should consider for preventing barriers to international trade. Instead, Art 41 requires the application of the IP rights enforcement procedures in a manner to avoid the creation of a barrier to legitimate trade and to provide safeguards against their abuse. This will enable countries to challenge legal measures and practices in the enforcement of IP rights where the applications of the procedures were arbitrary and with a view to preventing or increasing the cost of importation from foreign markets. Art 40 of TRIPS also provides flexibility for the domestic regulation of competition and restrictive practices without any substantive obligation of multilateral collaboration.

There are also concerns related to product standardisation and the incorporation of protected inventions in the standard and their impact on international trade. The EU imposed a standard on cigarette lighters that incorporated patented technology to block the importation of lighters from China, which arguably forms a technical barrier to trade (China Electronic Standards Institute 2003). Similarly, information technology standards set by industrial associations in the developed countries and international organisations, environment standards that require the use of certain technology available only in the domestic market, and labelling and packaging requirements could affect international trade. The requirements for disclosure and licensing of technologies under standards set by organisations are an important means for controlling the possible adverse effects of IP-centric standards (International Telecommunication Union 2005, p. 4).

The WTO Committee on Technical Barriers to Trade (TBT) discussed the relationship of IP rights, standard setting and international trade. China cautiously expressed the view that 'the combination of IP [Rights] with standards could bring about negative impacts on standardization and international trade' (G/TBT/M/38, para. 141). The particular concern involved the insufficiency of disclosure of IP rights and cases where the holder of rights to essential technologies uses unreasonable and arbitrary or discriminatory licensing practices (G/TBT/M/38, para. 145). China appropriately identified that the real problem is lack of adequate rules to respond to IP rights issues in standardisation. This requires the active and effective participation of developing countries and their industries in international, regional and domestic industrial standard setting. Otherwise, the countries with the most advanced technological infrastructure will be in the most advantageous position to influence product standardisation and benefit from the gap in TRIPS to prevent IP rights from functioning as trade barriers. Countries with the most advanced technological infrastructure could use the IP system for trade protectionist purposes without any meaningful safeguards existing for developing countries. This brings the discussion to a more political analysis of the development balance and the impact of TRIPS in international relations.

2.5 The Political Governance of IP and the Development Balance

A reduction of the tension on IP rights protection through a multilateral framework of standard making and dispute settlement was one of the major contributions countries expected from TRIPS (Abbott 1996, p. 472). To what extent TRIPS provides a practical mechanism to address these tensions is an important element for its continued legitimacy. In this regard, the WTO designed the Understanding on Rules and Procedures Governing the Settlement of Disputes (the Understanding) with elements to minimise aggressive resort to seeking redress outside the multilateral system. WTO members are required to abide by the rules and procedures set under the Understanding in seeking redress. Art 23 of the Understanding requires members not to make a determination of violation, impairment or nullification of benefits or impediment of the attainment of any objective of the WTO agreements, except through its rules and procedures. It further prohibits any suspension of concessions or other measures taken seeking to redress a WTO violation prior to the relevant authorisation by the Dispute Settlement Body (DSB). The basic tenet of the multilateral system to ensure governance in international relations concerning trade could be jeopardised where countries maintain unilateral mechanisms in order to address the alleged violations of the WTO agreements, such as TRIPS. Art 23 of the Understanding does not exclude unilateral enforcement mechanisms with respect to TRIPS-plus obligations arising from treaties other than the WTO, including the WIPO treaties not incorporated into the TRIPS Agreement by reference, and bilateral agreements.

The US maintains a unilateral mechanism for ensuring protection of US IP rights under a unilateral trade barriers review mechanism (called Section 301 Trade Act). The mechanism was the subject of dispute under the Understanding. The WTO panels often exercised moderation when it came to claims against the possible use of discretionary laws in violation of the WTO Agreements. The Panel in *US – Section 301 Trade Act* stated that the very discretion to make determinations covered under Art 23(2)(a) of the Understanding on its face precludes the US from abiding by its obligations. However, the Panel relied on the undertakings of the US administration that it would base its determinations on whether there has been a violation or denial of US rights on findings of the Panel or AB. Accordingly, the Panel concluded that the discretionary power for taking action under the trade review mechanism cannot be presumed to be used in violation of the US obligations under the WTO Agreements (WT/DS152/R, para. 7.109).

As a result, more than a decade after the adoption of TRIPS, the tension between the developed and developing countries on the level of IP rights protection remains very high. The 2005 G8 leaders' statement and the US–EU summit of June 2006 reflects the high-level political attention accorded by the developed world to IP rights protection in the developing countries (G8 Gleneagles 2005). In recent years, a wave of FTAs promoted a US standard of protection of IP rights in poor countries. The US has concluded FTAs with Chile, Morocco, Jordan, Central American countries and Dominica, Peru, Colombia and Australia and is negotiating FTAs with Thailand, the remaining Latin American countries, the Middle East countries, Malaysia and Korea. Moreover, the US is not only interested in the enforcement of TRIPS and the utilisation of the dispute settlement mechanisms but also in the enforcement of standards of IP rights higher than TRIPS and the use of unilateral and bilateral mechanisms to secure compliance. Under its FTAs, the US requires the ratification of WIPO treaties, not required by TRIPS (Roffe, 2004, p.13). The EU is following in the footsteps of the US to secure the highest international standards of protection for its right-holders. The EU has concluded an FTA with the South African Customs Union (SACU) and Association Agreements with Mediterranean countries and is negotiating FTAs with the Association of South East Asian Nations (ASEAN) and other countries in Latin America. It has launched an Economic Partnership Agreement with the African, Caribbean and Pacific (ACP) countries with TRIPS-plus standards (South Centre 2007). Japan, Australia and others also have bilateral and unilateral mechanisms to maximise IP rights.

Equally, certain uses of the TRIPS provisions themselves can exert undue pressure on other members, even in the absence of supporting legal provisions. The US, for example, requested consultation with Japan on alleged violations of Art 14.6 of TRIPS and the rules for retroactive protection under Art 18 of the Berne Convention for the Protection of Literary and Artistic Works (1971) (WT/DS28/1). The US alleged that Japan was required to provide retroactive protection to all US sound recordings that met the criteria of Art 18(1) – that is, recordings that had not entered into the public domain in the US through the 'expiry of the term of protection'. However, the US copyright law never protected sound recordings fixed before 1972. The US argued that, as of the entry into force of TRIPS, Japan was in violation of its TRIPS obligations for not retroactively protecting its pre-1972 recordings. Some observers argued that:

> . . . the whole case was but a show with four intended audiences: Americans skeptical about the benefits of WTO membership, a Japanese bureaucracy known for dragging its feet, Japanese consumers who would have to pay higher prices for oldies, and the governments of developing countries, which were understandably nervous about the power of the new TRIPS agreement (Obenski 2002, p. 194).

No panel was established to consider the US claim. Japan bilaterally agreed with the US to protect such rights, though the same content is not protected in the US. Similar and assertive invocations of TRIPS were utilised by the developed countries and their pharmaceutical companies against a South African amendment of patent law to import medicines from other countries in case of a national emergency by issuing compulsory licence or to produce the medicine locally and against similar reform in Brazil (Abbott 2004, p. 444). Several instances in which the developed countries and their enterprises had asserted claims of violation of TRIPS against developing countries measures relating to public health prompted the Doha Declaration.

The practice of reading TRIPS in the most favourable way to maximise IP rights and to allow extra-legal mechanisms to invoke the change of laws in the developing world undermined the expectation that TRIPS would reduce tensions in the protection of IP rights and discipline unilateral actions. These expectations are critical for developing countries, which are vulnerable to political and economic pressure as a result of developed countries' use of development aid and preferential trade arrangements. The Doha Declaration is the first attempt after the adoption of the TRIPS Agreement at dealing with tensions over the protection of IP rights. Doha is unique in addressing the freedom of countries to determine the grounds for compulsory licensing, and what constitutes a national emergency or other circumstances of extreme urgency, and establishes a regime for exhaustion of IP rights. The upholding of freedoms in making policy decisions, however, does not answer the question whether a member can legally assert its freedoms so as to inhibit another member from exercising its freedoms.

The Declaration recognised that a public health crisis exists where there are circumstances amounting to a national emergency. It has also clearly shifted the burden of proving otherwise to the WTO member disputing the various determinations made by the other state. This will prevent other members from placing undue influence upon the country exercising the freedom to decide that a national emergency exists or disputing the determination of a public health crisis as a national emergency. However, the Declaration may well end up only making a minimal contribution towards managing the tensions between developed and developing countries with respect to the political economy of IP rights. This is because TRIPS is little more than a reference point to the more pressing issues of development for countries that have signed FTAs with higher standards of protection of IP rights. The IP rights and investment chapters of many of the FTAs, and the post-TRIPS WIPO treaties have implemented higher standards of protection or eroded some of the flexibilities available under TRIPS for developing countries (Levis 2006, p. 58). Moreover, recent studies show that the FTAs and legislation in developed countries derailed the implementation of the Declaration and subsequent decisions by the WTO's General Council regarding the exportation of pharmaceutical products produced under compulsory licence (Musungu and Oh 2006, p. 99).

3. THE PANEL AND AB INTERPRETATION OF TRIPS AND BALANCE OF INTERESTS

The limited number of cases under TRIPS provides important insight as to the approach of the WTO panels and the AB on the treatment of domestic IP policies and the balance of interests. The first case under TRIPS was against India involving claims of violation of transitional arrangements for developing countries that required adequate 'mailbox' arrangement to receive and maintain applications pending the availability of patent protection for pharmaceuticals and agricultural chemical products. The AB agreed with the Panel's conclusion that India failed to implement its obligations under TRIPS Art 70(8) and (9). The AB, however, emphasised the text of TRIPS in interpreting India's obligations under the agreement and rejected the Panel's broad interpretive approach, which was based on 'legitimate expectations' – a concept derived from GATT 1947 jurisprudence on adverse treatment of imported products (WT/DS50/AB/R, para. 57). Similarly, the AB in *Canada – Terms of Patent Protection* confirmed the Panel's approach in relying on the plain language of Art 70(1) and (2) (WT/DS170/AB/R, paras 54–59).

The AB in *India – Patent Protection for Pharmaceutical and Agricultural Chemical Products* and the Panel in *EC – Protection of Trademarks and Geographic Indications for Agricultural Products and Foodstuffs* referred to the Preamble of TRIPS as an interpretive guideline. Their focus was on the need to promote effective and adequate protection of IP rights and the need for new rules and disciplines concerning the applicability of the basic principles of GATT 1994 and relevant IP treaties (WT/DS50/AB/R, 1997 para. 57; WT/DS290/R, para. 7.181; and WT/DS174/R, para. 7.131).

The AB in *India – Patent Protection for Pharmaceutical and Agricultural Chemical Products* and the Panel in *Canada – Terms of Patent Protection* reviewed Art 1.1 of TRIPS and construed the freedom to determine the appropriate method of implementing TRIPS. The AB limited India's obligations to the textual reading of the article as requiring the provision of a 'means' through a sound legal mechanism to implement its mailbox obligations (WT/DS50/AB/R, para. 59). In *Canada – Terms of Patent Protection*, the Panel emphasised that the freedom to determine the appropriate method of implementing specific requirements does not mean freedom to ignore the requirement in order to implement another obligation (WT/DS170/R, para. 6.94).

The Panel in *United States – Section 211 Omnibus Appropriation* examined the legislative history of the Paris Convention on the Protection of Industrial Property, and requested, and received a factual report from the WIPO regarding its negotiating history (WT/DS176/R). The AB concurred with the Panel on the contextual and textual interpretation of Arts 15 and 16 of TRIPS (WT/DS176/AB/R, para. 158). The AB, after agreeing to the arguments that factual circumstances leading to less favourable national treatment under Art 3.1 are remote, concluded that the existence of the possibility of foreign nationals facing double hurdles is inherently less favourable than the fact that US nationals face only one procedure. In doing so, the AB agreed with the Panel in relying on GATT jurisprudence with respect to national treatment and made a similar assertion with respect to most-favoured nation treatment (WT/DS176/AB/R, paras 240 and 265).

The *Indonesia – Certain Measures Affecting the Automobile Industry* case concerned the consistency of Indonesia's National Car Programme with several WTO agreements, including claims that the provisions of the programme discriminated against nationals of other WTO members with respect to trademarks, in violation of Art 3.1. The Panel cautioned against construing the national treatment obligation under Art 3 of TRIPS as being a *de facto* tariff, subsidy or other measure with respect to domestic companies that could have an indirect impact on the maintenance of trademark rights by foreign nationals. The Panel stated that:

> We consider that considerable caution needs to be used in respect of 'de facto' based arguments of this sort, because of the danger of reading into a provision obligations which go far beyond the letter of that provision and the objectives of the Agreement. It would not be reasonable to construe the national treatment

> obligation of the TRIPS Agreement in relation to the maintenance of trademark rights as preventing the grant of tariff, subsidy or other measures of support to national companies on the grounds that this would render the maintenance of trademark rights by foreign companies wishing to export to that market relatively more difficult (WT/DS54/R, para. 14.273).

In *EC – Protection of Trademarks and Geographic Indications for Agricultural Products and Foodstuffs*, the Panel recalled previous panel decisions in determining the appropriate standard of examination under Art 3.1 of TRIPS as that enunciated by the GATT panels (WT/DS174/R, para. 7.299). Accordingly, it placed emphasis on the 'effective equality of opportunities' in respect of the application of laws, regulations and other requirements (WT/DS174/R, para. 7.335). The Panel also considered it appropriate to base its examination under Art 3.1 of TRIPS on the fundamental thrust and effect of the EC Regulation, which was the subject of the dispute, including an analysis of its terms and its practical implications. However, as far as TRIPS is concerned, the Panel indicated that the relevant practical implications are those opportunities with regard to the protection of IP (WT/DS174/R, paras 7.182–7.187).

With respect to Art 27 of TRIPS, the Panel in *Canada – Patent Protection of Pharmaceutical Products*, advised against using the term 'discrimination' whenever 'more precise standards are available':

> The primary TRIPS provisions that deal with discrimination, such as the national treatment and most-favoured-nation provisions of Arts 3 and 4, do not use the term 'discrimination'. They speak in more precise terms. The ordinary meaning of the word 'discriminate' is potentially broader than these more specific definitions. It certainly extends beyond the concept of differential treatment. It is a normative term, pejorative in connotation, referring to results of the unjustified imposition of differentially disadvantageous treatment. Discrimination may arise from explicitly different treatment, sometimes called '*de jure* discrimination', but it may also arise from ostensibly identical treatment which, due to differences in circumstances, produces differentially disadvantageous effects, sometimes called '*de facto* discrimination'. The standards by which the justification for differential treatment is measured are a subject of infinite complexity. 'Discrimination' is a term to be avoided whenever more precise standards are available, and, when employed, it is a term to be interpreted with caution, and with care to add no more precision than the concept contains (WT/DS114/R, para. 7.94).

Given the very broad range of issues that might be involved in defining the word 'discrimination' in Art 27.1 of TRIPS, the Panel decided that it would be better to defer attempting to define that term at the outset, but instead to define the concept of discrimination to 'the extent necessary to resolve those issues' (WT/DS114/R, para. 7.98). However, the Panel went on to analyse the claims of *de facto* discrimination under Art 27.1 of

TRIPS based on standards used in GATT cases, namely, the existence of discriminatory effects and discriminatory objectives or purposes (WT/DS114/R, paras 7.101–7.104). Although the Panel did not find *de facto* discrimination from the evidence furnished to it, it did not employ the cautionary approach taken by the Panel in *Indonesia – Certain Measures Affecting the Automobile Industry* in applying GATT's approach on *de facto* discrimination to IP rights.

The Panel applied a restrictive interpretation of the limitations and exceptions to rights conferred by patent under Art 30, by adopting cumulative applications of conditions and applying textual interpretations of terminologies under the article (WT/DS114/R, paras 7.20–7.21 and 7.31). The Panel referred to the negotiating history of TRIPS and applied equal weight to both empirical and normative justifications when defining the meaning of the term 'normal exploitation' and 'legitimate interests' under Art 30. The Panel distinguished regulatory exceptions limited for the purpose of research and submission for approval purposes and the manufacturing and stockpiling of patented inventions, which was limited to within six months of the expiration of the patent. The Panel concluded that the exception permitting the stockpiling of patented inventions did not qualify as a limited exception since it lacked quantitative restrictions, whereas the regulatory exception was in line with all the elements of Art 30 (WT/DS114/R, paras 7.32–7.33).

There are systemic questions arising from the interpretation of TRIPS by panels and the AB. The WTO panels and the AB have followed largely formalistic approaches, thereby limiting themselves to the plain language of the text. Sometimes they adopt incremental approaches on a decision-by-decision basis, but these incremental steps only take the narrowest possible grounds and only move forward to the shortest extent necessary. The formalistic approach of interpretation may in some respects have a positive effect for developing countries that want to limit their obligations under TRIPS. Their freedom to implement TRIPS is limited by a plain language interpretation of the agreement and not by the expectations of the demanders of IP rights. On the other hand, it narrows down the agreement's scope for promoting legitimate public goals. The frequent choice and preference of formalism by the panels and the AB also reflect:

(1) The overall inclination or preference to protect and enforce IP rights as the single most important objective of TRIPS, rather than the agreement's other stated objectives.
(2) A preference for borrowing interpretive guidelines from GATT jurisprudence, especially in cases of national treatment and MFN treatment.

(3) An inadequate consideration of normative justifications for TRIPS and the dynamism of domestic IP policymaking.

However, the jurisprudence is gradually beginning to weigh up the complex policy and legal issues embedded in TRIPS. This is reflected in *Canada – Patent Protection of Pharmaceutical Products* and the restrictive approach to *de facto* discrimination claims in *Indonesia – Certain Measures Affecting the Automobile Industry*. These systemic questions have relevance in determining to what extent development-related policies influencing IP rights can find supportive interpretation under TRIPS. The most important lesson learned from the cases is that countries have to consider the plain language of the provisions of TRIPS in adopting IP policies with development objectives.

4. ENFORCEMENT OF IP AND DEVELOPMENT

TRIPS lays down minimum standards that must be reflected in the domestic laws of WTO member states for the enforcement of IP rights. The TRIPS standard on enforcement of IP rights does not attempt to harmonise members' laws and practices. The general provisions under Section 1 Part III of TRIPS establish the obligation that members of the WTO shall ensure the availability of enforcement procedures under their laws. The availability of the enforcement procedures under domestic laws must be fair and equitable and must permit effective action against any act of infringement of IP rights covered by TRIPS. However, the application of the enforcement procedures shall be in a manner as to avoid the creation of barriers to legitimate trade and to provide for safeguards against their abuse. Art 41.5 of TRIPS confirm that the obligation for the availability of enforcement procedures does not create any obligation to put in place a judicial system and for allocation of resources for enforcement of IP rights as distinct from enforcement of law in general. TRIPS is specific on obligations of WTO members to make available effective mechanisms for enforcement, without putting standards on measuring the operational and functional aspects of the mechanisms in each country. It requires:

(1) Countries *to make available* to right-holders civil judicial procedures concerning the enforcement of any IP right covered by TRIPS, and criminal procedures and penalties at least in cases of wilful trademark counterfeiting or copyright piracy on a commercial scale.
(2) Countries *to adopt procedures* to enable a right-holder to lodge an application with competent authorities, for the suspension of the

release into free circulation of goods validly suspected to involve trademark counterfeiting or copyright piracy.

(3) The judicial authorities *to have the authority* to order disclosure of evidence, injunctions, damages, prompt and effective provisional measures and disposition of infringing goods and materials and implements the predominant use of which has been in the creation of the infringing goods.

However, the trans-Atlantic agenda of the EU and the US on enforcement of IP rights through cooperation in the Council for TRIPS (the Council) introduces new challenges for developing countries. The enforcement issues advanced by the developed countries in the Council, if accepted, would constitute a critical post-TRIPS development in international norms on IP rights (IP/C/W/468). The agenda aims at dealing with a number of interrelated issues including requiring (1) the Council to monitor the actual operational performance and effectiveness of TRIPS, (2) the exchange of information and other forms of cooperation among customs authorities, and (3) the development of best practices (IP/C/W/468, paras 7 and 9). Bilaterally, the US and EU will coordinate their enforcement of IP rights in China and Russia, as well as other allegedly infringing countries and transshipment areas of key concern in Asia, Latin America and the Middle East (European Union 2005).

The US has recently submitted a request for consultations with China regarding its measures affecting the protection and enforcement of IP rights (WT/DS362/1, IP/D/26 and G/L/819). The request for consultations relates to a wide range of Chinese laws on criminal procedures, disposal of goods and copyright enforcement. The enforcement issues identified by the US in the request for consultation are also the main elements promoted in its FTAs. The US FTAs provide further specificity to standards that were to be determined by each country in accordance with TRIPS (see, for example, United States – Central America Free Trade Agreement, Art 15.11(26).

Balancing the enforcement agenda for IP rights with promoting the advancement of developing countries is complicated for various reasons. First, the agenda tilts the cost burden onto public institutions, whereas IP rights are essentially private rights and the primary responsibility for enforcement should lie with the private right-holders. Secondly, the laws of the developed countries on boarder measure is a factor that could shape IP rights enforcement as a trade barrier for goods originating from the developing countries. As a result, the agenda for enforcement of IP rights under the TRIPS Council for higher standards through bilateral agreements could create more problems than it solves. It targets less developed countries and undermines further the basic premise of TRIPS that avoids the possibility of an enforcement mechanism requiring additional public resources or being used for protectionist purposes.

5. A MATTER OF INTERPRETATION OR A GOVERNANCE ISSUE: SYNTHESIS OF THE CHALLENGES OF DEVELOPMENT BALANCE

TRIPS has failed in its promise to establish a multilateral framework that adequately handles the tension between developed and developing countries on the protection of IP rights. Unilateral and bilateral norm setting mechanisms altered and prevailed over many of its objectives and principles. The failure of TRIPS to live up to its promise of key political concessions in the multilateral framework, coupled with the exercise of political and economic influences by developed countries, undermines achieving a balanced (and fair) operation of TRIPS. The notable conclusions from the above discussions are:

(1) The WTO as a rule-based institution makes claims of fairness and mutual advantageousness. Its claim of being a mutually advantageous arrangement is confined to the reading of the relevant provisions. The general policy statements and objectives of balance and promotion of public interest under Arts 7 and 8 are very limited compared to the specific provisions contained under TRIPS. This limits the scope for consideration of public interests at different levels of development.
(2) Although developing countries can limit their obligations to the extent provided under TRIPS, the approach of developed countries of insisting upon more extensive IP rights protection militates against achieving the appropriate development balance.
(3) The typical feature of FTAs between developed and developing countries is marked by undermining the flexibilities and further regulating their utilisation. The use of the flexibilities under TRIPS is also undermined by the failure of developed countries to implement their obligations providing support and cooperation in relation to the introduction of innovative technologies and processes into developing countries.
(4) Although some developing countries have shown a willingness to use and implement the flexibilities under TRIPS, they lack adequate institutional capability and supportive international frameworks. Some of the TRIPS flexibilities contain onerous conditions that frustrate their

use. Furthermore, the technical assistance expected under TRIPS is not directed towards the use of flexibilities.

(5) The interpretation of TRIPS by the panels and the AB reveals a commitment to narrow formalism, although there are signs of a gradual development of a jurisprudence that weighs up the complex policy and legal issues at stake. This has led to mixed results. On the one hand, the reliance on plain language of the agreement can undermine the scope of the flexibilities. However, relatively narrow reading of the relevant provisions also assists in delineating the exact scope of the obligations of countries.

(6) The use of the TRIPS Council to monitor the operational performance of enforcement procedures would go beyond the requirements of TRIPS, create an undue burden on public resources for the enforcement of private rights, and might create a barrier to international trade.

Since the adoption of the Agreement, developing countries have sought a rebalancing of the IP agenda by seeking to address questions about the political economy of IP rights standard-setting and their ability to use the flexibilities enshrined in the Agreement. The Doha Declaration reinforced some of the expectations of developing countries that TRIPS be interpreted in a way that permitted them to undertake measures for promoting public health (WT/MIN(01)/DEC/2). Developing countries sought the Declaration because of several instances in which developed countries and their enterprises claimed that measures taken to protect public health were a violation of TRIPS (Abbott 2004, p. 444). In particular, the Declaration helps developing countries to protect their public interest by requiring the conditions on adoption of limited exceptions to IP rights permitted under TRIPS to be interpreted in the light of the objective of promoting balance and by reinstating the freedom of countries to determine the factual circumstances leading to the use of the flexibilities.

The Declaration also paved the way for the amendment of TRIPS inserting Art 31*bis* in order to enable the exporting of pharmaceutical products produced under compulsory licence to countries with limited or no manufacturing capacity. The adoption of the Protocol amending TRIPS in 2005 follows a provisional arrangement under the decision of the General Council on the implementation of para. 6 of the Declaration of 30 August 2003 (see WT/L/540 for the Decision and WT/L/641 for the Protocol). Although the amendment has expanded the scope of flexibilities, its numerous conditions, notification, pre-shipment and labelling requirements and regulations to prevent re-exportation continue to challenge the feasibility of utilising the system.

There are also other decisions that expanded the flexibilities available under TRIPS. The Council extended the transition period for the implementation of TRIPS other than Arts 3, 4, and 5 by LDCs. However, that decision required LDCs not to roll back their existing level of IP rights protection in a manner that results in lesser consistency with TRIPS (IP/C/40). On the other hand, the transition period for LDCs for the implementation of certain obligations with respect to pharmaceutical products is extended until 2016 (IP/C/25). The Council has also adopted mechanisms to monitor the implementation of the technology transfer obligations of the developed countries to LDCs (IP/C/28). Furthermore, the lack of progress to adopt the scope modalities for non-violation and situation complaint and the overall tendency not to enforce such kinds of complaint remain the critical contribution of recent developments in the WTO.

Recognition of the existing gaps and weakness of TRIPS should continue to guide norm-setting in the WTO and other important organisations such as the WIPO. The credibility and the achievement of the objectives of TRIPS depend on the direction taken in addressing some of the outstanding questions of balance. FTAs and WIPO norm-setting are expected to establish higher IP standards than presently exist under TRIPS. This will lead to the exporting of developed world standards without adequate adjustment to accommodate the socio-economic circumstances of the developing countries. TRIPS can play a significant role by addressing the gap between its permissive standards for more extensive protections and restrictive standards for re-examining the balance of interest under domestic law. The next section discusses the key areas under the ongoing processes in the WTO that can fill gaps and promote the development balance in the TRIPS arrangements.

6. KEY OUTSTANDING ISSUES AND REVIEW OF TRIPS TO PROMOTE THE DEVELOPMENT BALANCE OF TRIPS

The review of TRIPS in accordance with Art 71 should address the development dimension of the Agreement as recognised under the Declaration of the Fourth Ministerial Conference of the WTO (WT/MIN(01)/DEC/2). This should include some of the gaps in the Agreement that weakened the multilateral framework and undermined the promotion of balance of interests under domestic law. In particular, the promotion of more extensive protections than provided by TRIPS should not render the Agreement superfluous. As a result:

(1) The levels of development of WTO member states should be taken into account in implementing, reviewing and settling disputes under TRIPS, especially in relation to measures for the promotion and protection of public welfare, enhancing affordability and accessibility of drugs and other essential technological goods and the role of public institutions in enforcement of private rights.

(2) Although members can still promote more extensive protection than the minimum standards established by the agreement they should also be able to expand the limited exceptions to the extent necessary to balance interests. Assessment of mechanisms to address the impact of more extensive protection of IP rights on the international supply of essential and intermediary products and technologies is necessary. Norms for subsidy and quantitative restrictions on exports could guide such a task. According to Art XVI(2) of GATT, the grant of subsidies on primary products should not result in the subsidising state having more than an equitable share of the world export trade in the given primary product. The availability of disproportionately more extensive protection of IP rights compared to other countries could have the effect of according more than an equitable share of the control of the global market of knowledge and technological goods by countries providing such extensive protection. The application of, for example, technological protection measures and digital management rights by copyright holders in one country can allow them to control the legitimate use and access to knowledge over the internet in the rest of the world. A review of TRIPS should address the impacts of according more extensive protection than required, considering the impact on global trade.

(3) The flexibilities that require the cooperation of other members should include enforceable obligations in order to ensure that the balance created by the existence of the flexibilities is not lost by the difficulty of implementing them. The technology transfer obligation of the developed countries with respect to the transition period for LDCs is a particular example. Other optional provisions of TRIPS, such as the requirements for a patent applicant to indicate the best mode for carrying out the inventions under Art 29 of TRIPS would contribute to technology transfer if it were made mandatory.

(4) The review of the Understanding on Rules and Procedures Governing the Settlement of Disputes and the TRIPS provisions on dispute settlement should address the use of unilateral mechanisms to enable determinations of violations of TRIPS and to seek redress outside the dispute settlement mechanism of the WTO. Particular attention should be given to the legal aspect of the use of trade rules

on preferential market access and aid in a manner to seek redress and trigger changes to TRIPS consistent domestic laws of developing countries.

(5) A related issue involves the exclusion of the applicability of non-violation and situation complaints under TRIPS. WTO members have agreed to maintain the moratorium on the use of this kind of complaint until the next meeting of the Ministers in 2007. However, there should be final determination on the applicability of these kinds of complaint procedures, instead of developing modalities and scope as proposed under Art 64(2) of TRIPS.

(6) Finally, the recognition by the developing world of the global production of knowledge can play an important role in addressing the basic imbalances under TRIPS. The legal protection and recognition of the contribution of traditional knowledge, genetic resources and cultural expressions is a long-standing demand of fairness from the developing world (IP/C/W/356). There is an inherent bias against the contributions of the developing world regarding the forms of IP rights protection recognised under TRIPS. In this regard, developing countries proposed an amendment to TRIPS to require the disclosure of the origin and source of genetic resources and traditional knowledge used in the process of invention and submission of evidence of prior informed consent and arrangements for fair and equitable benefit sharing (IP/C/W/474). The proposal is important for promoting equity and fairness under TRIPS.

7. CONCLUSION

The use of TRIPS in a manner that supports the development needs of the developing countries involves a broad spectrum of issues in addition to the questions about the interpretation of the provisions of the agreement. The legal question has to address the important aspect of the political economy of IP rights norm setting in the post-TRIPS world. For many developing countries, TRIPS is no more the point of reference. Even where it is, the use of TRIPS by developed countries outside the dispute settlement mechanism entails political and economical pressure on developing countries. The mere existence of the US Special Section 301 review will have a chilling effect on developing countries' independent policy-making on IP rights. As a result, this chapter has demonstrated the need to address the political economy of the global IP rights norm-setting as an important element of the use of TRIPS for development.

REFERENCES

Abbott, F. (1996), 'Commentary: the International Intellectual Property Order Enters the 21st Century', *Vanderbilt Journal of Transnational Law*, 29(3), 471–479.

Abbott, F. (2004), 'WTO Dispute Settlement Practice Relating to the Agreement on Trade-Related Intellectual Property Rights', in F. Ortino and E. -U. Petersmann (eds), *The WTO Dispute Settlement System 1995–2003 18 Studies in Transnational Economic Law*, The Hague: Kluwer Law International.

Albin, C. (2001), *Justice and Fairness in Internalisation Negotiation*, New York: Cambridge University Press.

Albin, C. (2003), 'Negotiating International Cooperation: Global Public Goods and Fairness', *Review of International Studies*, 29(3), 365–385.

China Electronic Standards Institute (CESI) (2003), 'Review on Technology Barriers Related with Intellectual Property', *September, 2003 Information Technology & Standardization, translation* CST Inc, available at http://www.simmtester.com/page/news/pubnews.asp, last visited on 27 July 2006.

Commission on Intellectual Property Rights (2002), *Integrating Intellectual Property Rights and Development Policy: Report of the Commission on Intellectual Property Rights*, London: Commission on Intellectual Property Rights.

Correa, C. (2002), *Implications of the Doha Declaration on the TRIPS Agreement and Public Health*, Geneva: World Health Organization.

Dinwoodie, G. and R. Dreyfuss (2005), 'TRIPS and the Dynamics of Intellectual Property Lawmaking', *International Law and Justice Working Paper 2005/9*, New York: Institute for International Law and Justice, New York University School of Law.

Drahos, P. (2002), 'Developing Countries and International Intellectual Property Standard-setting', *Commission on Intellectual Property Rights Study Paper 8*, London: Commission on Intellectual Property Rights.

Drahos, P. with J. Braithwaite (2004), 'Who Owns the Knowledge Economy? Political Organising Behind TRIPS', *Corner House Briefing 32*, London: The Corner House.

European Union (2005), 'EU–US Action Strategy for the Enforcement of Intellectual Property Rights', available at http://www.eurunion.org/partner/summit/Summit06212006/2006EUUSSummitIntellProp.pdf, last visited on 22 March 2007.

European Union (2006), 'EU–US Summit Declaration', available at www.eu2006.at/includes/Download_Dokumente/2106EUUSDeclaration.pdf, last visited on 12 June 2007.

G/TBT/M/38 (2006), *Minutes of the Meeting of 15 and 17 March 2006, Committee on Technical Barriers to Trade: Note by the Secretariat*, Geneva: World Trade Organization.

G8 Gleneagles (2005), 'Reducing IPR Piracy and Counterfeiting through more Effective Enforcement: Statement', available at: http://www.fco.gov.uk/Files/kfile/PostG8_Gleneagles_CounterfeitingandPiracy.pdf, last visited on 27 July 2006.

Gathii, J. (2002), 'The Legal Status of the Doha Declaration on TRIPS and Public Health under the Vienna Convention on the Law of Treaties', *Harvard Journal of Law & Technology*, 15(2), 291–317.

GATT Council (1960), 'Restrictive Business Practices: Arrangements for Consultations', Report of Experts, Adopted 2 June 1960, L/1015, BISD 9S/170.

International Telecommunication Union (ITU) (2005), *Guidelines for Implementation of ITU-T Patent Policy*, Geneva: International Telecommunication Union.

IP/C/25 (2002), *Extension of the Transition Period under Art 66.1 of the TRIPS Agreement for Least-Developed Country Members for Certain Obligations With Respect to Pharmaceutical Products*, Geneva: World Trade Organization.

IP/C/28(2003), *Implementation of Art 66.2 of the TRIPS Agreement*, Geneva: World Trade Organization.

IP/C/40 (2005), *Extension of the Transition Period under Art 66.1 for Least-Developed Country Members*, Geneva: World Trade Organization.

IP/C/W/356 (2002), *The Relationship between the TRIPS Agreement and the CBD and the Protection of Traditional Knowledge*, Geneva: World Trade Organization.

IP/C/W/468 (2006), *Communication from the European Union, Enforcement of Intellectual Property Rights*, Geneva: World Trade Organization.

IP/C/W/474 (also circulated as WT/GC/W/564/ and TN/C/W/41/) (2006), *The Outstanding Implementation Issue on the Relationship between the TRIPS Agreement and the Convention on Biological Diversity*, Geneva: World Trade Organization.

Juma, C. and L. Yee-Cheong (2005), 'Applying Knowledge in Development', *UN Millennium Project Task Force on Science, Technology, and Innovation*, London: Earthscan.

Khan, M. and H. Dernis (2006), 'Global Overview of Innovative Activities from the Patent Indicators Perspective', *STI Working Paper 2006/3: Statistical Analysis of Science, Technology and Industry,* OECD DSTI/DOC(2006)3.

Kostecki, M. (2006), 'Intellectual Property and Economic Development: What Technical Assistance to Redress the Balance in Favour of Developing Nations?', *ICTSD Programme on IPRs and Sustainable Development Issue No. 12*, Geneva: ICTSD Programme.

Leifer, A. (2004), 'Harry Potter and the Battle of the International Copyright Law', *The Boothe Prize Essays*, Winter 2004, Stanford University.

Levis, M. (2006), 'Roles, Perspectives and Challenges of the Generic Pharmaceutical Industry in Latin America', in P. Roffe, G. Tansey and D. Vivas-Eugui (eds), *Negotiating Health: Intellectual Property and Access to Medicines*, Geneva: UNCTAD/ICTSD, pp. 133–150.

Lewis-Lettington, R. and P. Munyi (2004), *Willingness and Ability to Use TRIPs Flexibilities: Kenya Case Study*, DFID Health Systems Resource Centre (HSRC), London: Health Systems Resource Centre.

Maskus, K. (2005), 'The Role of Intellectual Property Rights in Encouraging Foreign Direct Investment and Technology Transfer', in C. Fink and K. Maskus (eds), *Intellectual Property and Development*, New York: World Bank.

Menell, P. (2000), 'Intellectual Property: General Theories', in B. Bouckaert and G. De Geest (eds), *Encyclopedia of Law and Economics, Volume II. Civil Law and Economics*, Cheltenham, UK and Northampton, MA, USA: Edward Elgar.

Musungu, S. and C. Oh (2006), *The Use of Flexibilities in TRIPS by Developing Countries: Can they Promote Access to Medicines?*, Geneva: South Centre.

Obenski, S. (2002), 'Retroactive Protection and Shame Diplomacy in the US-Japan Sound Recordings Dispute, or, How Japan Got Berne-d', *Minnesota Intellectual Property Review*, 4(1), 183–208.

Organisation for Economic Co-operation and Development (2003), *Development Dimensions of Intellectual Property Rights: The Relationship between Trade,*

FDI and Licensing, Paris: Organisation for Economic Co-operation and Development.

Okediji, R. (2006), 'The International Copyright System: Limitations, Exceptions and Public Interest Considerations for Developing Countries', *UNCTAD – ICTSD Issue Paper No. 15*, Geneva: UNCTAD.

Roffe, Pedro (2004), 'Bilateral Agreements and a TRIPS-plus World: the Chile-USA Free Trade Agreement', *TRIPS Issue Paper 4*, Quaker International Affairs Programme, Ottawa.

South Centre (2007), 'Development and Intellectual Property under EPA', *Policy Brief 6*, Geneva: South Centre.

United Nations (1948), 'Final Act of the United Nations Conference on Trade and Employment: Havana Charter for an International Trade Organization' (E/Conf. 2/78), available at www.wto.org/english/docs_e/legal_e/havana_e.pdf, last visited on 12 June 2007.

UNCTAD-ICTSD (2005), *Resource Book on TRIPS and Development*, New York: Cambridge University Press.

United States Bipartisan Trade Promotion Authority Act of 2002, H.R.2149, available at http://www.govtrack.us/congress/bill.xpd?bill=h107-2149, last visited 12 June 2007.

United States Trade Representative (USTR) (2005), '2005 Special 301 Report', available at www.ustr.gov, last visited 27 July 2006.

United States Trade Representative (USTR) (2006), '2006 Special 301 Report', available at www.ustr.gov, last visited 27 July 2006.

Vivas-Eugui, D. (2003), 'Regional and Bilateral Agreements and a TRIPS-plus World: The Free Trade Area of the Americas (FTAA)', *TRIPS Issues Papers 1*, Geneva: Quaker United Nations Office and Ottawa: Quaker International Affairs Programme.

WIPO/PR/2006/436 (2006), 'Exceptional Growth from North East Asia in Record Year for International Patent Filings: Press Release', Geneva: World Intellectual Property Organization.

World Intellectual Property Organization (WIPO) (1990), 'Beneficiaries of and Exceptions to National Treatment under Treaties Administered by WIPO', Communication from the World Intellectual Property Organization – MTN.GNG/NG11/W/66, Geneva: World Intellectual Property Organization.

WT/DS28/1 (1996), *Japan – Measures Concerning Sound Recordings*: Request for Consultations by the United States, Geneva: World Trade Organization.

WT/DS50/AB/R (1998), *India – Patent Protection for Pharmaceutical and Agricultural Chemical Products*, Geneva: World Trade Organization.

WT/DS54/R (1998), *Indonesia – Certain Measures Affecting the Automobile Industry*, Geneva: World Trade Organization.

WT/DS114/R (2000), *Canada – Patent Protection of Pharmaceutical Products*, Geneva: World Trade Organization.

WT/DS152/R (1999), *United States – Sections 301–310 of the Trade Act 1974*, Geneva: World Trade Organization.

WT/DS160 (2000), *United States – Section 110(5) of the US Copyright Act*, Geneva: World Trade Organization.

WT/DS170/R (2000) *Canada – Terms of Patent Protection*, Geneva: World Trade Organization.

WT/DS170/AB/R (2000), *Canada – Terms of Patent Protection*, Geneva: World Trade Organization.

WT/DS174/R (and WT/DS290) (2005), *EC – Protection of Trademarks and Geographic Indications for Agricultural Products and Foodstuffs*, Geneva: World Trade Organization.
WT/DS176/R (2001), *United States – Section 211 Omnibus Appropriations Act of 1998*, Geneva: World Trade Organization.
WT/DS176/AB/R (2002), *United States – Section 211 Omnibus Appropriations Act of 1998*, Geneva: World Trade Organization.
WT/DS362/1, IP/D/26 and G/L/819, (2007), *China – Measures Affecting the Protection and Enforcement of Intellectual Property Rights*, Geneva, World Trade Organization.
WT/L/540 (2003), *Implementation of paragraph 6 of the Doha Declaration on the TRIPS Agreement and Public Health*, Geneva: World Trade Organization.
WT/L/641 (2006), *Amendment of the TRIPS Agreement*, Geneva: World Trade Organization.
WT/MIN(01)/DEC/2 (2001), *Declaration on the TRIPS Agreement and Public Health*, Geneva: World Trade Organization.

7. The evolution of the CBD's development agenda that may influence the interpretation and development of TRIPS

Charles Lawson and Jay Sanderson

1. INTRODUCTION

The United Nations' Convention on Biological Diversity (CBD) entered into force for Contracting Parties on 29 December 1993. At the same time, minimum intellectual property standards were being established and codified in the Agreement on Trade-Related Aspects of Intellectual Property Rights (TRIPS) for World Trade Organization (WTO) Member States. After more than ten years, the interaction between the CBD and TRIPS remains unresolved (see IP/C/W/368/Rev.1; IP/C/W/369/Rev.1; IP/C/W/370/Rev.1), and the internationally contested inherent conflicts between TRIPS and the CBD remain. The conflict can be summed up as follows: TRIPS requires that genetic materials be protected by patents or a *sui generis* plant variety regime that privately appropriates genetic resources over which a country has sovereign rights under the CBD (see, for example, IP/C/W/368, p. 2), and that these privileges do not also require the additional measures set out in the CBD, such as prior informed consent, mutually agreed terms and benefit-sharing (see, for example, IP/C/M/28, p. 43; IP/C/W/368, p. 2). Resolving this apparent conflict has, this chapter argues, consequences for both the CBD and TRIPS. This chapter therefore considers the likely interpretive effects of the CBD on TRIPS, with the CBD providing some insight into the failure to negotiate a satisfactory balance between access and benefit-sharing, and providing some indication of developments that are likely to affect the future interpretation and development of TRIPS.

The chapter is structured as follows:

- Part 2 examines the inception of the CBD and TRIPS, setting out the underlying principles of the CBD (sustainable development) and TRIPS (economic growth);

- Part 3 examines, in the form of an historical narrative, the developments in the Conference of the Parties to the CBD (COP) implementing the CBD's third objective of access and benefit-sharing. The analysis shows that despite considerable achievement and consensus on some aspects of access and benefit-sharing, the specific concerns of some developing countries have not been satisfied and that these countries have expanded the CBD debates to the TRIPS forums;
- Part 4 examines the expansion of the concerns expressed by some developing countries into the TRIPS forums. The analysis shows that some of these countries' concerns have been addressed, but that substantial disagreement remains with an uncertain future;
- Part 5 examines the 'flexibility' in TRIPS Arts 7 and 8(1) dealing with the objective and principles of TRIPS. This analysis suggests that the recent developments in the interpretation of these provisions recognise that the minimum intellectual property standards set by TRIPS need to be considered in the context of the developmental stage of implementing countries, and that other policy objectives might be taken into account when implementing TRIPS. The place of trade agreements is examined to illustrate that some developing countries are entrenching TRIPS standards despite this outcome potentially undermining the expressly stated CBD's objectives and the interests of some developing countries; and
- Part 6 sets out the conclusion that the development agenda founded in the CBD has expanded to influence the future of TRIPS. How this will finally affect the interpretation of TRIPS remains uncertain, with the preference for some developed countries to favour TRIPS over the CBD in pursuing their economic and other development objectives. However, the failure to address the underlying concerns expressed in the CBD's objectives means that the future of TRIPS will remain contested and its interpretation and development consequently unsettled, albeit under the direct influence of the CBD.

2. THE INCEPTION OF THE CBD AND TRIPS

The CBD was signed on 5 June 1992 at the conclusion of the United Nations Conference on Environment and Development (for an overview see United Nations Conference on Environment and Development 1992; Grubb et al. 1993). The CBD set out three objectives:

> . . . to be pursued in accordance with its relevant provisions, are [a] the conservation of biological diversity, [b] the sustainable use of its components

> and [c] the fair and equitable sharing of the benefits arising out of the utilization of genetic resources, including by appropriate access to genetic resources and by appropriate transfer of relevant technologies, taking into account all rights over those resources and to technologies, and by appropriate funding (Art 1).

On the face of the CBD, the third objective of benefit-sharing – relating to the uses of genetic resources – marked a fundamental shift in binding international measures to conserve biodiversity;[1] doing so in three ways. First, by recognising the sovereign right of countries over their genetic resources; secondly, by linking access to those resources with the outcomes of scientific research and commercial uses, and access to technology on more favourable and non-commercial terms, including the products and technologies of the private sector derived from those genetic resources; and thirdly, by introducing intellectual property into the economic and policy debates about conserving genetic resources that might benefit future technological, economic and social development (see Organisation for Economic Co-operation and Development 2003, pp. 18–19 and 109; Commission on Intellectual Property Rights 2002, pp. 57–72).

At the time the CBD was being negotiated, there was almost universal consensus that the predominantly poor countries with the majority of the Earth's useful biological diversity (the 'South') should benefit from the exploitation of that diversity by the predominantly rich and technologically advanced countries (the 'North') (see Gillespie 1995, pp. 389–392 and the references therein). However, the specific content of the benefits to be shared from exploiting that accessed diversity and the issue of access to and transfer of technology to exploit those genetic resources remained unresolved. The North contended that intellectual property should be maintained and respected (see, for example, Panjabi 1997). On the other hand, the South contended that its genetic resources were valuable and that the exploitation of these resources was an opportunity to address poverty alleviation and technological development requiring more favourable and non-commercial terms of access to useful technology (see, for example, UNEP/BioDiv2/3, p. 7). In essence, the contentions over the CBD might be reduced to: '[t]he South wants the technology and the North wants the South to have it. But while the South sees itself as a potential partner, the North looks south and sees only paying customers' (Tilford 1998, p. 419).

The outcome of these contentions in the final text of the CBD was to postpone the resolution through agreeable diplomatic language effecting a compromise: 'that patents and other intellectual property rights may have an influence on the implementation of this [CBD]' with an obligation to 'cooperate in this regard subject to national legislation and international law in order to ensure that such rights are supportive of and do not run counter to its objectives' (Art 16(5)). The diplomatic language allowed the technology-rich North countries (principally the United States, the European Union and Japan) to agree to preferential and concessional access to and transfer of technology using undefined terms that would not undermine the concern of the North countries to maintain their existing intellectual property arrangements (see Grubb et al. 1993, p. 29). The outcome was, at best, just an in-principle agreement to exchange genetic resources for benefits that might include access to and transfer of technology.[2]

This compromise also reflected, in part, the unresolved tensions in concurrently negotiating in different forums the intellectual property provisions in the evolving international trade and environment agreements. At the same time the CBD was being negotiated under the auspices of the United Nations Environment Programme, the international trade TRIPS was being negotiated under the auspices of the General Agreement on Tariffs and Trade (GATT, and soon to be WTO). TRIPS attempted to establish new rules and disciplines moving intellectual property into the realm of international trade laws so as to reduce distortions and impediments to international trade while encouraging new inventions relying on the formula 'patents = free trade + investment = economic growth' (see Sell and Prakash 2004, p. 154; Drahos 1995, p. 7). In contrast, the CBD attempted to set a balance between exploitation and conservation by encouraging the biodiversity-rich countries to maintain their resources so they might be sustainably used by the countries with highly developed technology, with the benefits accruing to both the biodiversity-rich and poor countries (see Organisation for Economic Co-operation and Development 2003, pp. 18–19 and 109). According to the generalised South-North divide (see, for a contemporaneous commentary, Palmer 1992) the CBD imposes obligations on the biodiversity-rich South to provide access to its genetic resources (Arts 6–15). In return, the technology-rich North facilitates access to and transfer of technology, know-how and financial support and incentives (Arts 16–21), that promote economic growth directly addressing the development agenda to alleviate poverty (see A/CONF.151/26, annex 1). At its most simple, the CBD established the sovereign country biodiversity holder as the gatekeepers of the genetic resource whilst subjecting those seeking access to enter into mutually agreeable terms and prior informed consent with the resource holder and, in return, a promise to share the benefits resulting from access to those resources (see Lawson and Pickering 2001, pp. 104–106). The challenge for the CBD's COP has been to determine the role of intellectual property in delivering the benefits from the access to the genetic resources in the mutually agreeable terms.

3. THE CBD'S COP DELIBERATIONS

To date, the major areas where intellectual property has been considered by the COP under the CBD are access to genetic resources and benefit-sharing; the protection of traditional knowledge, innovations and practices; access to and transfer of technology; and scientific and technical cooperation (UNEP/CBD/COP/5/23, p. 11). These are not discrete areas and many of the COP's considerations have overlapped, with the various considerations evolving with the implementation of the CBD.

Following the signing of the CBD, the first COP (November–December 1994) adopted a medium-term 'Access to Genetic Resources' programme of work that included the compiling of information and documents about: (1) access to genetic resources and the sharing of its benefits (Art 15) and (2) access to and transfer of technology in exchange for that access (Art 16) (UNEP/CBD/COP/1/17, p. 62). Significantly, the consideration of intellectual property was placed under the 'Access to Genetic Resources' programme rather than the 'Issues Relating to Technology' programme, thereby linking intellectual property considerations to the transfer of technologies that made use of the accessed genetic resources (UNEP/CBD/COP/1/17, p. 62; UNEP/CBD/COP/2/19, p. 28). The effect of this decision was to place a focus on the role of intellectual property in the arrangements for access to genetic resources (thus linking Arts 15 and 16(5)), rather than on the broader debate about restricting intellectual property in making technology available to developing countries as a possible means of alleviating poverty (as set out in Art 16(1) and (2)) (UNEP/CBD/COP/2/17, p. 2; UNEP/CBD/COP/3/38, pp. 97–98; see also UNEP/CBD/COP/3/21).[3] This focusing of attention, however, did not ease tension between the developing South and the developed North over access to and transfer of technology, as reflected in a statement at the time by the Algerian representative on behalf of the G-77 and China (the predominant South countries):

> G-77 and China are deeply concerned that intellectual property rights deny developing countries access to affordable technology and equitable benefits that accrue from the conservation and sustainable use of biodiversity. This is especially dismaying when it is in the fields of agriculture, nutrition and health care, the very fields in which traditional communities, by their sustainable life styles, have preserved resources and knowledge of their use for centuries. If the [CBD] is to have any meaning beyond superficialities, then the removal of these distortions is crucial. G-77 and China can therefore regard the decision on the intellectual property rights as only the first step in a long journey, and urge that a thorough study be undertaken to ensure that intellectual property rights are supportive of and do not run counter to the objectives of the [CBD] . . . we call for an urgent implementation of Art 16(5) on transfer of technology (UNEP/CBD/COP/1/17, p. 23).

At the second COP (November 1995) the 'Access to Genetic Resources' programme was considered (UNEP/CBD/COP/2/19, pp. 26–28). The COP decided to compile the views on possible options for developing national legislative, administrative or policy measures to implement Art 15 (UNEP/CBD/COP/2/19, p. 64). The second COP also sought to analyse the impact of intellectual property on the conservation and sustainable use of biological diversity and the equitable sharing of benefits from their use 'in order to gain a better understanding of the implications of Art 16(5)', including 'inviting Governments and other relevant stakeholders to submit case studies that address the role of intellectual property rights in the technology transfer process, in particular the role of intellectual property rights in the transfer of biotechnology' (UNEP/CBD/COP/2/19, p. 65).

The third COP (November 1996) decided to seek further information about existing mechanisms in relation to access to genetic resources and sharing the benefits (UNEP/CBD/COP/3/38, pp. 95–97). In addition, the third COP sought to extend cooperation with other institutions dealing with intellectual property, notably: inviting the United Nations World Intellectual Property Organization (WIPO) to take into account, in their development programmes, the objectives of the CBD and requesting observer status at the Committee on Trade and Environment (CTE) of the WTO (UNEP/CBD/COP/3/38, pp. 98–101; see also UNEP/CBD/COP/3/22).

After considering the various materials before the meeting (see UNEP/CBD/COP/4/21; UNEP/CBD/COP/4/22; UNEP/CBD/COP/4/23; UNEP/CBD/RG LAC/3/2), the fourth COP (May 1998) decided to convene a Panel of Experts on Access and Benefit-sharing (the Panel):

> . . . to draw upon all relevant sources, including legislative, policy and administrative measures, best practices and case studies on access to genetic resources and benefit-sharing arising from the use of those genetic resources, including the whole range of biotechnology, in the development of a common understanding of basic concepts and to explore all options for access and benefit-sharing on mutually agreed terms including guiding principles, guidelines, and codes of best practice for access and benefit-sharing arrangements (UNEP/CBD/COP/4/27, p. 109).

At the time, the focus was to be on legislative, administrative and policy measures relating to four areas: (1) prior informed consent, (2) references to the country of origin in relevant publications and patent applications, (3) mutually agreed terms including on benefit-sharing and intellectual property rights and technology transfer, and (4) incentive measures to encourage the conclusion of 'contractual partnerships' (UNEP/CBD/COP/4/27, p. 110). The subsequent report of the Panel reached a broad consensus about the 'principles that should govern access and benefit-sharing arrangements' and 'a common understanding of the key concepts such as prior informed consent, mutually agreed terms, and fair and equitable benefit-sharing', together with 'important information and capacity-building needs associated with access and benefit-sharing arrangements' (UNEP/CBD/COP/5/23, pp. 24–25). The key recommendation of the Panel was the need to develop guidelines about prior informed consent and mutually agreed terms (UNEP/CBD/COP/5/23, pp. 24 and 54–55; see also UNEP/CBD/COP/5/8).

At this early stage, the Panel considered that intellectual property might provide an incentive to comply with the CBD's prior informed consent obligations through a requirement to provide evidence of satisfactory consent on applying for intellectual property (presumably this was addressed to patents and plant breeders' rights that require formal registration) (UNEP/CBD/COP/5/8, p. 23). Significantly, the Panel considered that the COP needed to explore intellectual property issues 'in greater depth' recognising that intellectual property was a component of other domestic and international legal instruments (UNEP/CBD/COP/5/8, p. 24). However, in dealing with intellectual property, the Panel acknowledged:

> . . . that intellectual property rights may have an influence on the implementation of access and benefit-sharing arrangements and may have a role in providing incentives for users to seek prior informed consent. The Panel was not able to come to any conclusions about these issues, and therefore suggests that the [COP] consider these matters further (UNEP/CBD/COP/5/8, p. 27).

Usefully the Panel identified a number of issues that required further study, including that intellectual property application procedures require that the applicant submit evidence of prior informed consent, the place of intellectual property in traditional knowledge related to genetic resources, the guiding parameters for contractual arrangements, application of the formal intellectual property threshold standards and the resulting scope, and an assessment of the effect of intellectual property as an incentive to conservation and benefit-sharing (UNEP/CBD/COP/5/8, pp. 23–26).

In parallel with the Panel's work, the fourth COP had also decided to convene an Inter-Sessional Meeting on the Operations of the Convention (ISOC) as 'a preparatory discussion' on access to genetic resources (UNEP/CBD/COP/4/27, p. 132). The ISOC began assessing the relationship between intellectual property and the relevant provisions of the TRIPS and the CBD, *ex situ* collections made before 29 December 1993, and a number of other matters that the Panel should consider (UNEP/CBD/COP/5/4, pp. 28–32). All of this was done without formally making firm conclusions about the place of intellectual property in access and benefit-sharing arrangements.

The fifth COP (May 2000) took note of the Panel report (UNEP/CBD/COP/5/23, p. 25; see also UNEP/CBD/COP/5/21) and the ISOC report

(UNEP/CBD/COP/5/23, p. 21; see also UNEP/CBD/COP/5/21), and then decided, in dealing with access to genetic resources, to establish an Ad Hoc Open-Ended Working Group on Access to Genetic Resources and Benefit-sharing with the mandate to develop guidelines and other approaches to access and benefit-sharing (UNEP/CBD/COP/5/23, pp. 197–198). The consequence of this decision was to convene an Ad Hoc Open-Ended Working Group and a report that recommended the adoption of the then *Draft Bonn Guidelines on Access to Genetic Resources and Fair and Equitable Sharing of the Benefits Arising out of their Utilization* (UNEP/CBD/COP/6/6, p. 14). The key objective of these guidelines was 'to assist Parties in developing an overall access and benefit-sharing strategy . . . and in identifying the steps involved in the process of obtaining access to genetic resources and sharing benefits' (UNEP/CBD/COP/6/6, p. 16). However, key terms remained to be defined, including 'access to genetic resources', 'benefit-sharing', 'commercialization', 'derivatives', 'provider', 'user', 'stakeholder', '*ex situ* collection' and 'voluntary nature' (UNEP/CBD/COP/6/6, pp. 14 and 15).

In addressing the role of intellectual property in implementing access and benefit-sharing arrangements, the Ad Hoc Open-Ended Working Group recommended that the COP 'invite' countries to disclose the country of origin of genetic resources in applications for intellectual property 'as a possible contribution to tracking compliance' with the obligations under the CBD of prior informed consent and the mutually agreed terms to access genetic resources (UNEP/CBD/COP/6/6, p. 36). Further information-gathering about intellectual property and access and benefit-sharing was also recommended and a role was envisioned for WIPO to develop model intellectual property clauses for negotiation of mutually agreed terms in contractual agreements (UNEP/CBD/COP/6/6, pp. 36–38).

The sixth COP (April 2002) adopted the *Bonn Guidelines on Access to Genetic Resources and Fair and Equitable Sharing of the Benefits Arising out of their Utilization* (Bonn Guidelines) (UNEP/CBD/COP/6/20, pp. 60–62 and 253–269) as voluntary guidelines that apply to *all* genetic resources covered by the CBD (except human genetic resources) (cl. 7), in a manner that is 'coherent and mutually supportive of the work of relevant international agreements and institutions' (cl. 8) and 'without prejudice' to the International Treaty on Plant Genetic Resources for Food and Agriculture (cl. 8). The sixth COP 'invited' countries to adopt the Bonn Guidelines 'when developing and drafting legislative, administrative or policy measures on access and benefit-sharing, and contracts and other arrangements under mutually agreed terms for access and benefit-sharing' (UNEP/CBD/COP/6/20, p. 253).

The Bonn Guidelines proposed the establishment of a 'competent national authority' (cl. 12), identified the responsibilities of Contracting

Parties that are the origin of genetic resources and the implementation of mutually agreed terms (cl. 14), and set out the steps in the access and benefit-sharing process (cls 20–48). While the Bonn Guidelines do not appear to favour a specific approach to intellectual property, they contemplate private contracts addressing intellectual property and other matters between the resource holder and the exploiter dealing with the access and benefit-sharing arrangements (UNEP/CBD/COP/6/20, pp. 263 and 274–275). However, the Bonn Guidelines do deal at some length with the various methods by which benefits might be shared, including the identification of those involved in the resource management, scientific and commercial process (UNEP/CBD/COP/6/20, pp. 264–265) and the various kinds of monetary and non-monetary benefits (UNEP/CBD/COP/6/20, pp. 267–269).

The Bonn Guidelines have impacted upon other activities under the CBD, including: the Global Strategy for Plant Conservation (UNEP/CBD/COP/6/20, p. 142), the Action Plan on Capacity-Building for Access and Benefit-sharing (UNEP/CBD/COP/6/20, p. 195), and the Programme of Work on Forest Biological Diversity (UNEP/CBD/COP/6/20, pp. 233 and 235). Significantly, however, the sixth COP clearly identified the Bonn Guidelines as merely a step in the evolution of the CBD's objectives (UNEP/CBD/COP/6/20, pp. 253 and 255): initiating further work in developing other approaches to access and benefit-sharing and capacity building (UNEP/CBD/COP/6/20, pp. 253 and 270–273; see also UNEP/CBD/COP/7/21, p. 298), other measures to implement prior informed consent (UNEP/CBD/COP/6/20, p. 253), and documenting the experience from countries implementing the Bonn Guidelines (UNEP/CBD/COP/6/20, p. 253; see also UNEP/CBD/COP/7/21, pp. 297–298).

The sixth COP also decided to reconvene the Ad Hoc Open-Ended Working Group on Access to Genetic Resources and Benefit-sharing to advise the COP because it recognised that 'a package of measures may be necessary to address the different needs of Parties and stakeholders in the implementation of access and benefit-sharing arrangements' (UNEP/CBD/COP/6/20, p. 271). Importantly, some COP members asserted that the Bonn Guidelines should 'be used through a negotiation process to develop an international legally binding instrument on access to genetic resources and fair and equitable sharing of the benefits arising out of their utilization' (UNEP/CBD/COP/6/20, p. 62). In addressing the role of intellectual property in access and benefit-sharing, the sixth COP made no decisions, but merely invited countries:

> . . . to encourage the disclosure of the country of origin of genetic resources in applications for intellectual property rights, where the subject matter of the application concerns or makes use of genetic resources in its development, as a

possible contribution to tracking compliance with prior informed consent and the mutually agreed terms on which access to those resources was granted (UNEP/CBD/COP/6/20, p. 274).

At the seventh COP (February 2004), further information-gathering was sought about experiences and lessons from implementing the Bonn Guidelines and its key terms (UNEP/CBD/COP/7/21, pp. 297–298), and other approaches to access and benefit-sharing (UNEP/CBD/COP/7/21, p. 298). Significantly, however, the seventh COP responded to the broader concerns of the South about fairly and equitably sharing the benefits from using genetic resources under the CBD that had been expressed at the United Nations World Summit on Sustainable Development (see A/CONF.199/20, p. 35; see also UNEP/CBD/COP/7/6) and at the United Nations General Assembly (see A/RES/57/260, p. 2; see also A/RES/58/212), and decided:

> . . . to mandate the Ad Hoc Open-Ended Working Group on Access and Benefit-sharing with the collaboration of the Ad Hoc Open-Ended Inter-Sessional Working Group on Art 8(j) and Related Provisions, ensuring the participation of indigenous and local communities, non-governmental organizations, industry and scientific and academic institutions, as well as intergovernmental organizations, to elaborate and negotiate an international regime on access to genetic resources and benefit-sharing with the aim of adopting an instrument/instruments to effectively implement the provisions in Art 15 and Art 8(j) of the [CBD] and the three objectives of the [CBD] (UNEP/CBD/COP/7/21, p. 300).

The seventh COP decision, to begin 'to elaborate and negotiate an international regime on access to genetic resources and benefit-sharing' (UNEP/CBD/COP/7/21, p. 300), was significant because it outlined: (1) the express recognition of the broader place of access and benefit-sharing in achieving the objectives of the CBD (UNEP/CBD/COP/7/21, p. 299), (2) the evolving nature of access and benefit-sharing arrangements (UNEP/CBD/COP/7/21, p. 299),[4] and (3) the important place of the CBD's access and benefit-sharing arrangements in addressing 'poverty eradication and environmental sustainability' (UNEP/CBD/COP/7/21, p. 299; see also A/RES/55/2). These deliberations also expanded the scope of the access and benefit-sharing considerations to address the promise of the CBD of 'fair and most favourable terms, including on concessional and preferential terms where mutually agreed, and where necessary in accordance with the financial mechanism' to developing countries (Art 16(2)); in doing so, recognising that both access to and transfer of technology among the Contracting Parties was an essential element for attaining the objectives of the CBD (UNEP/CBD/COP/7/21, p. 14). This was also reflected in the sixth COP decision that 'encouraged' WIPO 'to make rapid progress in the development of model intellectual property clauses which may be considered for inclusion in contractual agreements when mutually agreed terms are under negotiation' (UNEP/CBD/COP/6/20, p. 275).

In response to the sixth COP's request, WIPO made a submission to the seventh COP outlining its work and findings on the disclosure requirements related to genetic resources (UNEP/CBD/COP/7/Inf/17).[5] WIPO's interpretation of the role of intellectual property in implementing the access and benefit-sharing obligations in the CBD were either to disclose the origin (or source) of genetic resources used in, or connected with, an invention as a requirement of a patent application. Alternatively, WIPO recommended the disclosure of the legal context in which relevant genetic resources were accessed, such as by providing evidence that the access complied with a certain procedure or legal standards, such as, for example, specific criteria for adequate prior informed consent (UNEP/CBD/COP/7/Inf/17, p. 9; see also WIPO/GRTKF/IC/6/11). As a consequence of these submissions, the seventh COP decided to implement a work programme addressing technology transfer and technology cooperation. It established an expert group on technology transfer and scientific and technical cooperation (UNEP/CBD/COP/7/21, pp. 366–378). The significance of this work programme (according to a COP resolution) was that:

> The purpose of this programme of work is to develop meaningful and effective action to enhance the implementation of Arts 16 to 19 as well as related provisions of the [CBD] by promoting and facilitating the transfer of and access to technologies from developed to developing countries, including the least developed among them and small island developing States, as well as to countries with economies in transition, as well as among developing countries and other Parties, necessary to ensure implementation of the three objectives of the [CBD], and in support of the target to achieve a significant reduction of the current rate of biodiversity loss at the global, regional and national level by 2010. Implementation of this programme of work shall also contribute to the attainment of the Millennium Development Goals to ensure environmental sustainability and to eradicate extreme poverty and hunger by 2015, and shall fully take into account specific national circumstances and constraints such as remoteness or vulnerability (UNEP/CBD/COP/7/21, p. 369).

The role of intellectual property was addressed in the work programme as part of 'creating enabling environments' that identify and put in place 'institutional, administrative, legislative and policy frameworks conducive to private and public sector technology transfer and cooperation' (UNEP/CBD/COP/7/21, p. 374). This was to include technical studies that explore and analyse the role of intellectual property in technology transfer in the context of the CBD, including the costs and benefits of intellectual property (UNEP/CBD/COP/7/21, p. 374). Significantly, this was also to 'identify potential options to increase synergy and overcome barriers to technology transfer and cooperation' consistent with the United Nations World Summit on Sustainable Development's Plan of Implementation (UNEP/CBD/COP/7/21, p. 374; see also A/CONF.199/20, p. 35). The outcome of this work programme by the eighth COP was to take note of a progress report (see UNEP/CBD/COP/8/19) and establish an Ad Hoc Technical Expert Group on Technology Transfer and Scientific and Technological Cooperation to 'collect, analyse and identify ongoing tools, mechanisms, systems and initiatives to promote the implementation of Arts 16 to 19 as well as to propose strategies for practical implementation of the programme of work on technology transfer and scientific and technical cooperation' (UNEP/CBD/COP/8/31, p. 220).

The precise role of intellectual property in any 'international regime on access to genetic resources and benefit-sharing' proposed by the seventh COP is presently unclear. The 'scope' of this regime was to extend to '[a]ccess to genetic resources and promotion and safeguarding of fair and equitable sharing of the benefits arising out of the utilization of genetic resources in accordance with relevant provisions of the [CBD]' and '[t]raditional knowledge, innovations and practices in accordance with Art 8(j)' (UNEP/CBD/COP/7/21, p. 301). The elements of this regime include measures:

> . . . for benefit-sharing including, inter alia, monetary and non-monetary benefits, and effective technology transfer and cooperation so as to support the generation of social, economic and environmental benefits;
>
> . . . to promote and safeguard the fair and equitable sharing of benefits arising out of the utilization of genetic resources;
>
> . . . to ensure the sharing of benefits arising from the commercial and other utilization of genetic resources and their derivatives and products, in the context of mutually agreed terms; and
>
> . . . to promote access and benefit-sharing arrangements that contribute to the achievement of the Millennium Development Goals, in particular on poverty eradication and environmental sustainability (UNEP/CBD/COP/7/21, p. 302).

At the eighth COP (March 2006), the Ad Hoc Open-ended Working Group on Access to Genetic Resources and Benefit-sharing reported (see UNEP/CBD/COP/8/5; UNEP/CBD/COP/8/6), together with reports from WIPO (UNEP/CBD/COP/8/Inf/7), United Nations Conference on Trade and Development (UNEP/CBD/COP/8/Inf/25), and the WTO (UNEP/CBD/COP/8/Inf/37). The eighth COP then referred a draft text of an international regime on access and benefit-sharing to the Ad Hoc Open-ended Working Group on Access to Genetic Resources and Benefit-sharing for further elaboration and negotiation before 2010 (UNEP/CBD/COP/8/31, pp. 128–136; see also UNEP/CBD/MYPOW/6; UNEP/CBD/COP/6/20, p. 316). However, the positions so far (and the highly bracketed text) suggest agreement is a long way off, and the role and place of intellectual property very uncertain. The key issue of scope remains contentious with the text providing '[t]he international regime applies to, [in accordance with national legislation and other international obligations]' (UNEP/CBD/COP/8/31, p. 130) remaining unresolved and leaving open the possibility that North countries might consider their national legislation and international agreements dealing with intellectual property (such as TRIPS) are outside the scope of the international regime.

As can be seen, the essentially North–South contentions about intellectual property have not been resolved by the CBD's COP. This suggests that the CBD has failed to satisfactorily balance the objective of access for benefit-sharing and the different interests of the South and North countries. Perhaps as a consequence, these unresolved and different interests are now spilling over into other forums and are likely to influence the interpretation of other trade and environment agreements as developing South countries seek to achieve the CBD objectives through these other agreements.

4. EXPANSION OF THE CBD TO THE TRIPS FORUM

The United Nations Development Program has asserted that the 'relevance of TRIPS is highly questionable for large parts of the developing world' and that countries should 'begin dialogues to replace TRIPS . . . with alternative intellectual property paradigms' (United Nations Development Program 2003, pp. 221–222). The United Nations General Assembly has also reiterated that the CBD, rather than TRIPS, 'is the key international instrument for the conservation and sustainable use of biological resources and the fair and equitable sharing of benefits arising from the use of genetic resources' (A/RES/58/212, p. 1). These developments echo the earlier contentions about the benefits of intellectual property and the attempts by developing South countries to gain preferential treatment under the WIPO Paris Convention for the Protection of Industrial Property (Paris Convention 1967) (for an analysis of the WIPO Diplomatic Conference for the Revision of the Paris Convention, see Sell 1998, pp. 107–130), and the response of the developed North shifting intellectual property to a trade forum at GATT through TRIPS (see Das 1994, p. 158; Sell 1998, pp. 132–138). These ongoing tensions are best illustrated in the divergent views about the appropriate balance between the CBD and TRIPS in the WTO forum.

The fourth WTO Ministerial Conference Declaration (the Doha Ministerial Declaration) 'strongly reaffirm[ed] our commitment to the objective of sustainable development' (WT/MIN(01)/DEC/1, p. 1; see also A/RES/57/260, p. 2) and expressly instructed the WTO's Council of TRIPS (TRIPS Council) to examine the relationship between the CBD and TRIPS (WT/MIN(01)/DEC/1, p. 4 (para 19)), and the WTO's Committee on Trade and Environment (CTE) to consider the effects of the relevant provisions of TRIPS (WT/MIN(01)/DEC/1, p. 7 (paras 32–33)). The Doha Ministerial Declaration also provided that Members 'agree that negotiations on outstanding implementations shall be an integral part of the Work Program [of the TRIPS Council]' (WT/MIN(01)/DEC/1, pp. 2–3 (para 12)). Biodiversity issues were not provided a specific negotiating mandate and therefore formed part of the 'other outstanding implementation issues' (WT/MIN(01)/DEC/1, pp. 2–3 (para 12)). For these, the Doha Ministerial Declaration provided that such 'implementation issues shall be addressed as a matter of priority by the relevant WTO bodies, which shall report to the Trade Negotiations Committee . . . by the end of 2002 for appropriate action' (WT/MIN(01)/DEC/1, pp. 2–3 (para 12)). This included the Outstanding Implementation Issues (WT/MIN(01)/DEC/17, p. 8; see also JOB(01)/152/Rev.1) and, in particular, the suggestion that patents 'shall not be granted' when they are inconsistent with the CBD (JOB(01)/152/Rev.1, Tiret 88), as well as a belief that TRIPS should be amended to take into account the provisions of the CBD (and International Treaty on Plant Genetic Resources for Food and Agriculture) (JOB(01)/152/Rev.1, Tiret 95), and that 'all living organisms, including plants, animals and parts of plants and animals, including gene sequences, and biological and other natural processes for the production of plants, animals and their parts, shall not be granted patents' (JOB(01)/152/Rev.1, Tiret 95).

After the Doha Ministerial Declaration, the South agenda in the TRIPS Council appears to have crystallised two objectives. The first involved amending TRIPS to include requirements that patent applicants disclose the 'source and country of origin of the biological resource' (and traditional knowledge) used in the invention, provide 'evidence of prior informed consent through approval of authorities under the relevant national regime' and disclose 'evidence of fair and equitable benefit-sharing under the relevant national regime' (WT/MIN(01)/DEC/1, p. 4 (para. 19); see also IP/C/W/368/Rev.1). The second involved an attempt to re-balance the effects of TRIPS on South countries and resolve difficulties putting TRIPS into effect (WT/MIN(01)/DEC/1, pp. 2–3 (para. 12); see also WT/MIN(01)/DEC/17, pp. 7–8).

In contrast, the North agenda is to maintain existing standards (see, for example, WT/GC/W/193; IP/C/W/383; IP/C/W/400/Rev.1), remove potential exclusions (see, for example, WT/GC/W/115, p. 6), or to negotiate 'TRIPS-plus' bilateral agreements imposing more stringent standards than

TRIPS requires (see Drahos 2001). There appeared, however, to be some willingness on behalf of some North countries to accept some disclosures in patent applications (see, for example, IP/C/W/473; IP/C/W/423).[6] In the CTE, the CBD issue remained deadlocked with three apparent blocks: those favouring amending TRIPS, those seeing no conflict between TRIPS and the CBD, and those considering that the Council of TRIPS was addressing the issue and that it should not be duplicated by the CTE (Secretariat of the World Trade Organization 2004, p. 42). The final resolution of these issues before the TRIPS Council and the CTE is not presently clear (see, for example, WT/L/579, p. 2; JOB(03)/150/Rev.2, pp. 4–5 (paras 21 and 23))[7] although there was an active commitment as part of the Doha Development Round to place the 'the needs and interests of developing and least-developed countries at the heart of the Doha Work Programme' (WT/L/579, p. 1). The existing patent systems appears to be capable of recognising the 'source and country of origin of the biological resource' (and traditional knowledge) and 'evidence of prior informed consent' (see for example, IP/C/W/423; IP/C/W/420). The remaining issues of establishing evidence of fair and equitable benefit-sharing under the relevant national regimes, and re-balancing the effects of TRIPS for South countries, appear to be a long way from resolution, with the familiar South-North divide persisting (IP/C/M/50, pp. 3–19).

However, the fifth WTO Ministerial Council Declaration (the Hong Kong Declaration) provided:

> 39. We reiterate the instruction in the Decision adopted by the General Council on 1 August 2004 to the [Trade Negotiations Committee], negotiating bodies and other WTO bodies concerned to redouble their efforts to find appropriate solutions as a priority to outstanding implementation-related issues. We take note of the work undertaken by the Director-General in his consultative process on all outstanding implementation issues under para 12(b) of the Doha Ministerial Declaration, including . . . those related to the relationship between the TRIPS Agreement and the *Convention on Biological Diversity*. We request the Director-General, without prejudice to the positions of Members, to intensify his consultative process on all outstanding implementation issues under para 12(b) . . .
>
> . . .
>
> 44. We take note of the work undertaken by the Council for TRIPS pursuant to para 19 of the Doha Ministerial Declaration and agree that this work shall continue on the basis of para 19 of the Doha Ministerial Declaration and the progress made in the Council for TRIPS to date . . . (WT/MIN(05)/DEC, pp. 7–8 (paras 39 and 44)).

Despite these commitments in the Hong Kong Ministerial Declaration, the TRIPS Council has merely agreed 'to maintain its present method of work' and 'to keep this method under review to assess whether any change might prove appropriate in the light of developments' (IP/C/M/50, p. 19).

Meanwhile, Members have addressed possible principles for developing an amendment (IP/C/W/473), and possible amending text for TRIPS (IP/C/W/474) directly addressing the Hong Kong Ministerial Declaration. The likely outcome of these developments remains uncertain with the apparent entrenching of South and North blocks (see, for example, IP/C/M/50, pp. 3–19). However, these developments confirm that the CBD issues about access and benefit-sharing are influencing the TRIPS forums, albeit the effect of this influence is not yet certain in the outcomes of TRIPS forums.

Developments in the implementation of TRIPS suggest that there is 'room to manoeuvre' in the text of TRIPS to balance the competing interests of the South and North (see generally UNCTAD-ICTSD 2005). The failure of the CBD to provide a negotiated resolution to South concerns and the increasingly entrenched position of most North countries perhaps signals that future resolution of their different interests will be through disputes over TRIPS. These disputes are likely to arise where the South countries apply an interpretation of TRIPS that favours their development agenda and the North countries object seeking to enforce their interpretation of TRIPS (WT/DS37/1; WT/DS196/1; WT/DS199/1; and so on). However, the negotiation of other trade agreements and policy preferences suggests that this 'room to manoeuvre' may be receding. The following discussion of the objective and principles of TRIPS illustrates this.

5. INTERPRETING TRIPS' OBJECTIVE AND PRINCIPLES

TRIPS sought to establish new rules and disciplines moving intellectual property into the realm of international trade laws:

> . . . to reduce distortions and impediments to international trade, and taking into account the need to promote effective and adequate protection of intellectual property rights, and to ensure that measures and procedures to enforce intellectual property rights do not themselves become barriers to legitimate trade (TRIPS Preamble).

The 'effective and adequate' intellectual property standards recognise the underlying public policy objective and principles of TRIPS:

> 7. Objective – The protection and enforcement of intellectual property rights should contribute to the promotion of technological innovation and to the transfer and dissemination of technology, to the mutual advantage of producers and users of technological knowledge and in a manner conducive to social and economic welfare, and to a balance of rights and obligations (Art 7).

> 8(1). Principle – Members may, in formulating or amending their laws and regulations, adopt measures necessary to protect public health and nutrition, and to promote the public interest in sectors of vital importance to their socio-economic and technological development, provided that such measures are consistent with the provisions of this Agreement (Art 8(1)).

The WTO Member States have not yet reached a consensus on the effect of these provisions, or the interpretation and implementation of TRIPS' obligations (see Vienna Convention on the Law of Treaties Art 31(1); see also WT/DS2/AB/R). As a generalisation, North countries consider intellectual property such as patents, to be a necessary incentive to promote investment in new innovations and, as a consequence, this promotes the objective and principles of Arts 7 and 8 (see, for example, IP/C/M/31, p. 36; IP/C/W/280, p. 2). In contrast, South countries (the developing and least developed states: Arts 65 and 66) consider each provision of TRIPS should be read in light of this objective and these principles and moreover, that TRIPS co-exists with other public policy objectives so that its provisions may be overridden to meet these other policy objectives (see, for example, IP/C/M/31, p. 4; IP/C/W/296, pp. 5–6). Despite these different perspectives, most Members consider TRIPS to be sufficiently 'flexible' to enable Members to implement their TRIPS obligations as well as their public policy objectives. Thus, the majority consensus now appears to be:

> . . . we remain committed to [the] implementation of the TRIPS Agreement based on its proper and flexible interpretation and in accordance with the objectives and principles contained in Arts 7 and 8 . . . Some provisions of the TRIPS Agreement may elicit different interpretations. This 'room to manoeuvre' served the purpose of accommodating different positions held by members at the time of negotiation of the Agreement. We strongly believe that nothing in the TRIPS Agreement reduces the range of options available to governments to promote and protect public health, as well as other overarching public policy objectives (IP/C/W/296, p. 3).

This view is consistent with the WTO's Panel decision in *Canada – Patent Protection of Pharmaceutical Products*. In this dispute, the European Union argued that the phrase in Art 8(1), 'provided that such measures are consistent with the provisions of this [TRIPS] Agreement' meant that any other considerations beyond the patent holder's rights were subordinate to the protection of the minimum intellectual property guaranteed by TRIPS (WT/DS114/R, p. 50). The Panel rejected the European Union argument and accepted adjustments to a patent holder's rights were contemplated according to the objective and principles of Arts 7 and 8(1) (and other relevant provisions of TRIPS) (WT/DS114/R, p. 154). However, the Panel expressed the view that these provisions were to be 'borne in mind' and a re-negotiation of the balance of TRIPS was not appropriate (WT/DS114/R, p. 154). This approach has now been confirmed in the Declaration on the TRIPS Agreement and Public Health (the Health Declaration) in response to Member States 'taking measures to protect public health':

> while maintaining our commitments in the TRIPS Agreement, we recognize that these flexibilities include: (a) In applying the customary rules of interpretation of public international law, each provision of the TRIPS Agreement shall be read in the light of the object and purpose of the Agreement as expressed, in particular, in its objectives and principles (WT/MIN(01)/DEC/2, p. 1).

It remains to be seen how broadly these provisions apply and to what extent the limitations will be imposed, although consensus seems more difficult and unlikely in the context of 'negotiation' as a consequence of the suspension of the Doha Work Programme in July 2006 (see, for example, WT/GC/M/102, pp. 2–3). It is certainly clear, however, after the Health Declaration that some Members consider these provisions 'flexible' enough to allow intellectual property to be curtailed to make pharmaceutical products protected by patents accessible in cases of epidemics (IP/C/W/296, pp. 5–6). For example, some South countries have asserted:

> The objective of the promotion of technological innovation and the transfer and dissemination of technology places the protection and enforcement of [intellectual property] in the context of the interests of society. Such an objective is essential for the promotion of health policies, as it encourages the development of domestic production of pharmaceutical products . . . Where the patent holder fails to meet the objectives of the TRIPS Agreement and of public health policies, however, Members may take measures to ensure transfer and dissemination of technology to provide better access to pharmaceuticals (IP/C/W/296, p. 6).

The Doha Work Programme adopted by the WTO General Council 'rededicates and recommits Members to fulfilling the development dimension of the Doha Development Agenda, which places the needs and interests of developing and least-developed countries at the heart of the Doha Work Programme' (WT/L/579, p. 1). Consistent with this development agenda is the potential in applying the object and principle of TRIPS to develop and implement intellectual property in a way that coincides with promoting the CBD's objectives. However, other competing agreements suggest that some North countries are less committed to this outcome, as the recent free trade agreement between Australia and the United States illustrates.

The likely effect of the Australia–United States Free Trade Agreement (AUSFTA) will be to limit the options available for biological diversity conservation objectives to co-exist with, or take precedence over, the believed benefits of patents in promoting innovation according to the policy settings presently in place (see Lawson and Pickering 2004, pp. 357–361 and 363–366). The following examples of 'most favoured nation' treatment and the failure to re-state the TRIPS object and principles illustrate this contention.[8]

National treatment and most favoured nation are part of an international norm in the trade law of non-discrimination. The AUSFTA's dealing with intellectual property is significant in that it makes provision for 'national treatment', requiring Australia and the United States to extend the same treatment to a national of the other country as it extends to its own (Art 17.1.6), but makes no provision for 'most favoured nation' treatment. The exact application of the national treatment requirement under the AUSFTA remains uncertain as some derogation from the national treatment is allowed for 'judicial and administrative procedures, including requiring a national of the other Party to designate an address for service of process in its territory, or to appoint an agent in its territory', provided that it is 'necessary to secure compliance with laws and regulations that are not inconsistent with this Chapter' and 'not applied in a manner that would constitute a disguised restriction on trade' (Art 17.1.7), or WIPO agreements dealing with 'the acquisition or maintenance of intellectual property rights' (Art 17.1.8). However, two questions remain unclear. First, whether the national treatment exceptions (in the WIPO Paris Convention 1967) were saved by TRIPS (TRIPS Art 2(1)). Secondly, whether Australia and the United States might apply different standards to other nationals thereby avoiding the 'most favoured nation' standards.

A likely effect is that the AUSFTA, by providing for national treatment and not for most favoured nation, will require Australia (and the United States) to accord the same treatment required by the AUSFTA to *all* other WTO members according to the TRIPS' most favoured nation requirement (TRIPS Art 4). In implementing the AUSFTA, the Commonwealth appears to adopt this approach applying the same patent standards to all nationals (see US Free Trade Agreement Implementation Act 2004 (Cth) Sch. 8), suggesting that the AUSFTA probably does establish the minimum patent standards to be met by all applicants.

The consequence of failing to re-state the 'most favoured nation' standards in the AUSFTA may then be to entrench the patent standards articulated in the AUSFTA,[9] thereby losing the significant 'flexibility' in TRIPS to deal with other social and economic policy objectives and principles that exist in TRIPS Arts 7 and 8(1) (see Lawson and Pickering 2004, p. 357). If the TRIPS provisions dealing with other social and economic policy objectives are interpreted to mean that each provision of TRIPS should be read in light of these provisions, and that TRIPS co-exists with other public policy objectives (see IP/C/M/31, p. 4; IP/C/W/296, pp. 5–6), then TRIPS' patent standards might be tailored to meet other policy objectives including the transfer and dissemination of technology, public health and nutrition and socio-economic and technological development (see WT/MIN(01)/DEC/2, p. 1; WT/L/540, pp. 2–5; see also WT/GC/M/82, pp. 6–7). This interpretation was certainly open to Australia (see, for example, Lawson and Pickering 2002).

Thus, leaving the TRIPS' objective and principles provisions out of the AUSFTA probably confirms that Australia prefers to consider patents as a fixed and necessary incentive to promote investment in new inventions and, as a consequence, this promotes the objective and principles of TRIPS (see, for example, IP/C/M/31, p. 36; IP/C/W/280, p. 2). In effect, the AUSFTA is likely to affirm that TRIPS, and the TRIPS-plus measures set out in the AUSFTA, override other regulatory schemes providing paramountcy of AUSFTA's standards over those articulated by TRIPS. The consequence for implementing the CBD in Australia is that intellectual property considerations are likely to override conservation and other CBD considerations, entrenching intellectual property as an end in itself, rather than a policy tool to be tailored to most efficiently and effectively address market failures. An analysis of the competing conservation and patenting policies in Australia starkly shows that in implementing the Bonn Guidelines, Australia has maintained its patent standards even though they may be promoting biodiversity destruction and decline (see Lawson 2006) contrary to the CBD's expressly stated requirement that:

> The Contracting Parties, recognizing that patents and other intellectual property rights may have an influence on the implementation of this Convention, shall cooperate in this regard subject to national legislation and international law in order to ensure that such rights are supportive of and do not run counter to its objectives (Art 16(5)).

While the CBD may be influencing TRIPS forums, it may not, however, have much effect in the North countries.

6. CONCLUSIONS

The development agenda reflected in the imperative to link development and conservation in the CBD has expanded through the implementation of its third objective of providing for access and benefit-sharing. Despite the considerable achievements of the COP in implementing the Bonn Guidelines, there remain unresolved South concerns. For example, the seventh COP decision to begin 'to elaborate and negotiate an international regime on access to genetic resources and benefit-sharing' (UNEP/CBD/COP/7/21, p. 300) reflects the failure of the Bonn Guidelines to adequately address the concerns of all the Contracting Parties. These concerns are also being restated in other forums, such as the General Assembly of the United Nations (A/RES/57/260, p. 2), and extend to TRIPS forums through the TRIPS Council (WT/MIN(01)/DEC/1, p. 4), the CTE (WT/MIN(01)/DEC/1, p. 7) and more recently as part of the Doha Development Agenda (see WT/L/579, p. 1). While the response of some developed North countries has been to favour TRIPS at the expense of the CBD, there appears to be persistence among the developing South countries to press for TRIPS to reflect their particular interests. As a consequence, TRIPS has recently been amended (Art 31*bis*; see also WT/L/641; WT/L/540/Corr.1) and further CBD-related amendments are proposed (see, for example, the draft text for TRIPS Art 29*bis*; see WT/GC/W/564/Rev.1; IP/C/W/473). There is also a continuing focus on TRIPS' objectives and principles (see, for example, WT/MIN(01)/DEC/2, p. 1; IP/C/W/473, p. 2) and the interface between TRIPS and the CBD (see, for example, WT/MIN(01)/DEC/1, pp. 2–3 (para 12); see also IP/C/W/368/Rev.1). The increasing focus on the other commitments in the CBD will also require the 'flexibility' in TRIPS to be addressed (see, for example, UNEP/CBD/COP/8/5, p. 44). These include the express recognition in the CBD that patents and other forms of intellectual property should support the CBD's objectives (Art 16(5)), and that Contracting Parties should adopt incentive measures that promote biodiversity conservation rather than its destruction and decline (Art 11). How each of these developments will finally affect TRIPS remains uncertain, although the failure to address the underlying concerns expressed in the CBD's objectives means that the future interpretation and development of TRIPS will almost certainly be influenced by the CBD.

ACKNOWLEDGEMENTS

This work was supported by an Australian Research Council grant to research 'Developing a Systematic, Inclusive and Just Jurisprudential Account of TRIPS'.

NOTES

1. An earlier non-binding arrangement adopted in the International Undertaking on Plant Genetic Resources for Food and Agriculture (Resolution 8/83, 22nd Session of the FAO Conference 1983) applied the 'common heritage' principles to certain agricultural plant genetic resources. These were later amended to recognise farmers' rights and the

legitimacy of intellectual property over elite plant varieties (Resolutions 4/89 and 5/89, 25th Session of the FAO Conference 1989), and later amended to recognise 'that nations have sovereign rights over their plant genetic resources' (Resolution 3/91, 26th Session of the FAO Conference 1991). For a review of the developments leading to fundamental shift from 'common heritage' to 'state sovereignty' principles governing biological resources see, for example, Aoki 2003, pp. 305–313; Tilford 1998, pp. 387–418.

2. Noting that a number of North countries were careful to declare their position on intellectual property; for example Switzerland declared on ratification that 'transfers of technology and access to biotechnology, as defined in the text of the [CBD] will be carried out in accordance with Art 16 of the said [CBD] and in compliance with the principles and rules of protection of intellectual property, in particular multilateral and bilateral agreements signed or negotiated by the Contracting Parties to this [CBD]': Secretariat of the Convention on Biological Diversity 2003, p. 310.
3. Notably, Australia asserted that '[t]he owners of technologies should be able to earn a commercial return on their investment, thereby encouraging investment and technology transfer. There is a greater incentive for entrepreneurs to invest in developing countries and to license patented environmental technologies where there is a string system of intellectual property rights': UNEP/CBD/COP/3/Inf/4, pp. 3–4.
4. Noting that the Panel of Experts on Access and Benefit-sharing convened by the fourth COP stated that '[c]ontractual arrangements, *for the moment*, are the main mechanism for gaining access to genetic resources and delivering benefits' (emphasis added): UNEP/CBD/COP/5/8, p. 11.
5. This report was provided with the proviso that 'it should not be considered a formal paper expressing a policy position on the part of WIPO, its Secretariat or its Member States': UNEP/CBD/COP/7/Inf/17, p. 1. Notably the Secretariat of the CBD also concluded a Memorandum of Understanding with WIPO and WIPO had extended its focus on international intellectual property issues including the place of the CBD in existing intellectual property arrangements: see UNEP/CBD/COP/7/21, p. 21.
6. Although other North countries consider this might be achieved as effectively by other means, such as contract notifications: see, for example, IP/C/W/393.
7. Noting that the WTO's Cancún Ministerial Conference failed to reach a definitive conclusion, although the Ministerial Conference in Hong Kong was expected to (at least) provide a progress report: see WT/GC/M/83, pp. 4–5.
8. For an overview of other limitations placed on patenting in Australia by the AUSFTA, see Joint Select Committee on Treaties 2004, pp. 70–88. Unfortunately these issues were not explored further in the public inquires by the Joint Select Committee on Treaties or the Senate Select Committee on the Free Trade Agreement between Australia and the United States of America: see Joint Standing Committee on Treaties 2004; Senate Select Committee on the Free Trade Agreement between Australia and the United States of America 2004.
9. Noting that the AUSFTA provides that '[e]ach Party shall, at a minimum, give effect to the [Intellectual Property] Chapter' (Art 17.1.1), '[e]ach Party may only exclude from patentability inventions . . .' (Art 17.9.2), and so on (see Arts 17.9.1, 17.9.4, 17.9.5 and 17.9.7).

REFERENCES

A/CONF.151/26 (1992), *Rio Declaration on Environment and Development*, New York: General Assembly of the United Nations.

A/CONF.199/20 (2002), *Report of the World Summit on Sustainable Development*, New York: United Nations.

Aoki, K. (2003), 'Weeds, Seeds & Deeds: Recent Skirmishes in the Seed Wars', *Cardozo Journal of International and Comparative Law*, 11(2), 247–331.

A/RES/55/2 (2000), *United Nations Millennium Declaration*, 55th Session, New York: General Assembly of the United Nations.
A/RES/57/260 (2003), *Resolution 57/260: Convention on Biological Diversity*, 57th Session, New York: General Assembly of the United Nations.
A/RES/58/212 (2004), *Resolution 58/212: Convention on Biological Diversity*, 58th Session, New York: General Assembly of the United Nations.
Commission on Intellectual Property Rights (2002), *Integrating Intellectual Property Rights and Development Policy*, London: Commission on Intellectual Property Rights.
Das, B-G. (1994), 'Intellectual Property Dispute, GATT, WIPO: Of Playing by the Game Rules and Rules of the Game', *IDEA*, 35(2), 149–181.
Drahos, P. (1995), 'Global Property Rights in Information: The Story of TRIPS at the GATT', *Prometheus*, 13(1), 6–19.
Drahos, P. (2001), 'BITs and BIPs: Bilateralism in Intellectual Property', *Journal of World Intellectual Property*, 4(6), 791–808.
Gillespie, A. (1995), 'Common Property, Private Property and Equity: Clash of Values and the Quest to Preserve Biodiversity', *Environmental and Planning Law Journal*, 12(6), 388–399.
Grubb, M., M. Koch, A. Munson, F. Sullivan and K. Thomson (1993), *The Earth Summit Agreements: A Guide and Assessment*, London: Earthscan Publications Ltd.
IP/C/M/28 (2000), *Minutes of Meeting Held in the Centre William Rappard on 21 and 22 September 2000*, Geneva: Council for Trade-Related Aspects of Intellectual Property Rights.
IP/C/M/31 (2001), *Special Discussion on Intellectual Property and Access to Medicines*, Geneva: Council for Trade-Related Aspects of Intellectual Property Rights.
IP/C/M/50 (2006), *Minutes of Meeting Held in the Centre William Rappard on 14–15 March 2006*, Geneva: Council for Trade-Related Aspects of Intellectual Property Rights.
IP/C/W/280 (2001), *Communication from the European Communities and their Member States*, Geneva: Council for Trade-Related Aspects of Intellectual Property Rights.
IP/C/W/296 (2001), *Submission by the African Group, Barbados, Bolivia, Brazil, Cuba, Dominican Republic, Ecuador, Honduras, India, Indonesia, Jamaica, Pakistan, Paraguay, Philippines, Peru, Sri Lanka, Thailand and Venezuela*, Geneva: Council for Trade-Related Aspects of Intellectual Property Rights.
IP/C/W/368 (2002), *The Relationship Between the TRIPS Agreement and the Convention on Biological Diversity – Summary of Issues Raised and Points Made*, Geneva: Council for Trade-Related Aspects of Intellectual Property Rights.
IP/C/W/368/Rev.1 (2006), *The Relationship Between the TRIPS Agreement and the Convention on Biological Diversity: Summary of Issues Raised and Points Made*, Geneva: Council for Trade-Related Aspects of Intellectual Property Rights.
IP/C/W/369/Rev.1 (2006), Council for Trade-Related Aspects of Intellectual Property Rights, *Review of the Provisions of Art 27.3(b): Summary of Issues Raised and Points Made*, Geneva: Council for Trade-Related Aspects of Intellectual Property Rights.
IP/C/W/370/Rev.1 (2006), *The Protection of Traditional Knowledge and Folklore: Summary of Issues Raised and Points Made*, Geneva: Council for Trade-Related Aspects of Intellectual Property Rights.
IP/C/W/383 (2002), *Communication from the European Communities and their Member States*, Geneva: Council for Trade-Related Aspects of Intellectual Property Rights.

IP/C/W/393 (2003), *Access to Genetic Resources Regime of the United States National Parks – Communication from the United States*, Geneva: Council for Trade-Related Aspects of Intellectual Property Rights.

IP/C/W/400/Rev.1 (2003), *Art 27.3(b), the Relationship between the TRIPS Agreement and the Convention on Biological Diversity, and the Protection of Traditional Knowledge – Communication from Switzerland (Revision)*, Geneva: Council for Trade-Related Aspects of Intellectual Property Rights.

IP/C/W/420 (2004), *The Relationship Between the TRIPS Agreement and the Convention on Biological Diversity (CBD): Checklist of Issues*, Geneva: Council for Trade-Related Aspects of Intellectual Property Rights.

IP/C/W/423 (2004), *Additional Comments by Switzerland on its Proposals Submitted to WIPO Regarding the Declaration of the Source of Genetic Resources and Traditional Knowledge in Patent Applications – Communication from Switzerland*, Geneva: Council for Trade-Related Aspects of Intellectual Property Rights.

IP/C/W/473 (2006), *Amending the TRIPS Agreement to Introduce an Obligation to Disclose the Origin of Genetic Resources and Traditional Knowledge in Patent Applications*, Geneva: Council for Trade-Related Aspects of Intellectual Property Rights.

IP/C/W/474 (2006), *Doha Work Programme – The Outstanding Implementation Issue on the Relationship between the TRIPS Agreement and the Convention on Biological Diversity*, Geneva: Council for Trade-Related Aspects of Intellectual Property Rights.

JOB(01)/152/Rev.1 (2001), *Compilation of Outstanding Implementation Issues Raised by Members*, Revision, Geneva: Ministerial Conference of the World Trade Organization.

JOB(03)/150/Rev.2 (2003), *Preparations for the Fifth Session of the Ministerial Conference Draft Cancún Ministerial Text, Second Revision*, Geneva: Ministerial Conference of the World Trade Organization.

Joint Select Committee on Treaties, *Australia–United States Free Trade Agreement: A Critique of Industrial Property – Patents*, Submission 191, Canberra: Department of the Parliament.

Joint Standing Committee on Treaties (2004), *Australia–United States Free Trade Agreement*, Report 61, Canberra: Senate Printing.

Lawson, C. (2006), 'Exploiting Genetic Resources in Queensland under the *Biodiscovery Act 2004* (Qld): Patents and Biological Diversity Conservation, Destruction and Decline', *European Intellectual Property Review*, 28(8), 418–428.

Lawson, C. and C. Pickering (2001), 'The Conflict for Patented Genetic Materials Under the *Convention on Biological Diversity* and the *Agreement on Trade Related Aspects of Intellectual Property Rights*', *Australian Intellectual Property Journal*, 12(2), 104–115.

Lawson, C. and C. Pickering (2002), 'Successfully Controlling Access Under the *Environment Protection and Biodiversity Conservation Act 1999* and its Regulations Requires a Proper Assessment of the Impact of the *Patents Act 1990*', *Australian Intellectual Property Journal*, 13(3), 109–120.

Lawson, C. and C. Pickering (2004), '"TRIPS-Plus" Patent Privileges – An Intellectual Property "Cargo Cult" in Australia', *Prometheus*, 22(4), 355–377.

Organisation for Economic Co-operation and Development (2003), *Harnessing Markets for Biodiversity: Towards Conservation and Sustainable Use*, Paris, France: Organisation for Economic Co-operation and Development.

Palmer, G. (1992), 'The Earth Summit: What Went Wrong at Rio?', *Washington University Law Quarterly*, 70(4), 1005–1028.

Panjabi, R. (1997), *The Earth Summit at Rio: Politics, Economics and the Environment*, Boston: Northeastern University Press.

Secretariat of the Convention on Biological Diversity (2003), *Handbook of the Convention on Biological Diversity*, 2nd edn, London: Earthscan Publications Ltd.

Secretariat of the World Trade Organization (2004), *Trade and Environment at the WTO*, Geneva: World Trade Organization.

Sell, S. (1998), *Power and Ideas: North-South Politics of Intellectual Property and Antitrust*, Albany: State University of New York Press.

Sell, S. and A. Prakash (2004), 'Using Ideas Strategically: The Contest between Business and NGO Networks in Intellectual Property Rights', *International Studies Quarterly*, 48(1), 143–175.

Senate Select Committee on the Free Trade Agreement between Australia and the United States of America (2004), *Final Report on the Free Trade Agreement between Australia and the United States of America*, Canberra: Senate Printing.

Tilford, D. (1998), 'Saving the Blueprints: The International Legal Regime for Plant Resources', *Case Western Reserve Journal of International Law*, 30(2–3), 373–446.

UNCTAD-ICTSD (2005), *Resource Book on TRIPS and Development*, Cambridge: Cambridge University Press.

UNEP/BioDiv2/3 (1990), *Report of the Ad Hoc Working Group on the Work of the Second Session in Preparation for a Legal Instrument on Biological Diversity*, New York: United Nations Environment Program.

UNEP/CBD/COP/1/17 (1995), *Report of the First Meeting of the Conference of the Parties to the Convention on Biological Diversity*, Montreal: Conference of the Parties to the Convention on Biological Diversity.

UNEP/CBD/COP/2/17 (1995), *Intellectual Property Rights and Transfer of Technologies which Make Use of Genetic Resources*, Montreal: Conference of the Parties to the Convention on Biological Diversity.

UNEP/CBD/COP/2/19 (1995), *Report of the Second Meeting of the Conference of the Parties to the Convention on Biological Diversity*, Montreal: Conference of the Parties to the Convention on Biological Diversity.

UNEP/CBD/COP/3/21 (1996), *Promoting and Facilitating Access to, and Transfer and Development of Technology*, Montreal: Conference of the Parties to the Convention on Biological Diversity.

UNEP/CBD/COP/3/22 (1996), *The Impact of Intellectual Property Rights Systems on the Conservation and Sustainable Use of Biological Diversity and on the Equitable Sharing of Benefits from its Use (A Preliminary Study)*, Montreal: Conference of the Parties to the Convention on Biological Diversity.

UNEP/CBD/COP/3/38 (1997), *Report of the Third Meeting of the Conference of the Parties to the Convention on Biological Diversity*, Montreal: Conference of the Parties to the Convention on Biological Diversity.

UNEP/CBD/COP/3/Inf/4 (1996), *Submissions Received by the Executive Secretary Concerning Ways and Means to Promote and Facilitate Access to and Transfer and Development of Technology*, Montreal: Conference of the Parties to the Convention on Biological Diversity.

UNEP/CBD/COP/4/21 (1998), *Measures to Promote and Advance the Distribution of Benefits from Biotechnology in Accordance with Art 19*, Montreal: Conference of the Parties to the Convention on Biological Diversity.

UNEP/CBD/COP/4/22 (1998), *Addressing the Fair and Equitable Sharing of the Benefits Arising out of Genetic Resources: Options for Assistance to Developing Country Parties to the Convention on Biological Diversity*, Montreal: Conference of the Parties to the Convention on Biological Diversity.

UNEP/CBD/COP/4/23 (1998), *Review of National, Regional and Sectoral Measures and Guidelines for the Implementation of Art 15*, Montreal: Conference of the Parties to the Convention on Biological Diversity.

UNEP/CBD/COP/4/27 (1998), *Report of the Fourth Meeting of the Conference of the Parties to the Convention on Biological Diversity*, Montreal: Conference of the Parties to the Convention on Biological Diversity.

UNEP/CBD/COP/5/4 (1999), *Report of the Inter-Sessional Meeting on the Operations of the Convention*, Montreal: Conference of the Parties to the Convention on Biological Diversity.

UNEP/CBD/COP/5/8 (1999), *Report of the Panel of Experts on Access and Benefit-Sharing*, Montreal: Conference of the Parties to the Convention on Biological Diversity.

UNEP/CBD/COP/5/21 (2000), *Access to Genetic Resources*, Montreal: Conference of the Parties to the Convention on Biological Diversity.

UNEP/CBD/COP/5/23 (1998), *Report of the Fifth Meeting of the Conference of the Parties to the Convention on Biological Diversity*, Montreal: Conference of the Parties to the Convention on Biological Diversity.

UNEP/CBD/COP/6/6 (2001), *Report of the Ad Hoc Open-Ended Working Group on Access and Benefit-Sharing*, Montreal: Conference of the Parties to the Convention on Biological Diversity.

UNEP/CBD/COP/6/20 (2002), *Report of the Sixth Meeting of the Conference of the Parties to the Convention on Biological Diversity*, Montreal: Conference of the Parties to the Convention on Biological Diversity.

UNEP/CBD/COP/7/6 (2003), *Report of the Ad Hoc Open-Ended Working Group on Access and Benefit-Sharing on the Work of its Second Meeting*, Montreal: Conference of the Parties to the Convention on Biological Diversity.

UNEP/CBD/COP/7/21 (2004), *Report of the Seventh Meeting of the Conference of the Parties to the Convention on Biological Diversity*, Montreal: Conference of the Parties to the Convention on Biological Diversity.

UNEP/CBD/COP/7/Inf/17 (2003), *Technical Study on Disclosure Requirements Related to Genetic Resources and Traditional Knowledge*, Montreal: Conference of the Parties to the Convention on Biological Diversity.

UNEP/CBD/COP/8/5 (2006), *Report of the Ad Hoc Open-Ended Working Group on Access and Benefit Sharing on the Work of its Third Meeting*, Montreal: Conference of the Parties to the Convention on Biological Diversity.

UNEP/CBD/COP/8/6 (2006), *Report of the Ad Hoc Open-Ended Working Group on Access and Benefit Sharing on the Work of its Fourth Meeting*, Montreal: Conference of the Parties to the Convention on Biological Diversity.

UNEP/CBD/COP/8/19 (2006), *Technology Transfer and Scientific and Technical Cooperation: Progress Report on Implementation*, Montreal: Conference of the Parties to the Convention on Biological Diversity.

UNEP/CBD/COP/8/31 (2006), *Report of the Eighth Meeting of the Conference of the Parties to the Convention on Biological Diversity*, Montreal: Conference of the Parties to the Convention on Biological Diversity.

UNEP/CBD/COP/8/Inf/7 (2006), *Interrelation of Access to Genetic Resources and Disclosure Requirements in Applications for Intellectual Property Rights*,

Montreal: Conference of the Parties to the Convention on Biological Diversity.

UNEP/CBD/COP/8/Inf/25 (2006), *Analysis of Options for Implementing Disclosure of Origin Requirements in Intellectual Property Applications*, Montreal: Conference of the Parties to the Convention on Biological Diversity.

UNEP/CBD/COP/8/Inf/37 (2006), *The Relationship between the TRIPS Agreement and the Convention on Biological Diversity: Summary of Issues Raised and Points Made*, Montreal: Conference of the Parties to the Convention on Biological Diversity.

UNEP/CBD/MYPOW/6 (2003), *International Regime on Access and Benefit-sharing: Proposals*, Montreal: Open-ended Inter-Sessional Meeting on the Multi-Year Programme of Work of the Conference of the Parties up to 2010.

UNEP/CBD/RG LAC/3/2 (1998), *Report of the Latin American and the Caribbean Regional Preparatory Meeting*, Montreal: Regional Meetings on Biological Diversity.

United Nations Conference on Environment and Development (1992), *Agenda 21*, New York: United Nations Conference on Environment and Development.

United Nations Development Program (2003), *Making Global Trade Work for People*, London: Earthscan Publications Ltd.

WIPO/GRTKF/IC/6/11 (2004), *Certain Decisions of the Seventh Meeting of the Conference of the Parties to the Convention on Biological Diversity Concerning Access to Genetic Resources and Benefit-Sharing*, Geneva: Intergovernmental Committee on Intellectual Property and Genetic Resources, Traditional Knowledge and Folklore.

WT/DS2/AB/R (1996), United *States – Standards for Reformulated and Conventional Gasoline*, Geneva: World Trade Organization.

WT/DS37/1 (1996), *Portugal – Patent Protection under the Industrial Property Act*, Geneva: World Trade Organization.

WT/DS114/R (2000), *Canada – Patent Protection of Pharmaceutical Products*, Geneva: World Trade Organization.

WT/DS196/1 (2000), *Argentina – Certain Measures on The Protection of Patents and Test Data*, Geneva: World Trade Organization.

WT/DS199/1 (2000), *Brazil – Measures Affecting Patent Protection*, Geneva: World Trade Organization.

WT/GC/M/82 (2003), *Minutes of Meeting on 2 September 2003*, Geneva: General Council of the World Trade Organization.

WT/GC/M/83 (2003), *Minutes of Meeting Held in the Centre William Rappard on 21 October 2003*, Geneva: General Council of the World Trade Organization.

WT/GC/M/102 (2006), *Minutes of Meeting Held in the Centre William Rappard on 19 July 2006*, Geneva: General Council of the World Trade Organization.

WT/GC/W/193 (1999), *Preparations for the 1999 Ministerial Conference – EC Approach to Trade-Related Aspects of Intellectual Property in the New Round*, Geneva: General Council of the World Trade Organization.

WT/GC/W/115 (1998), General Council of the World Trade Organization, *Preparations for the 1999 Ministerial Conference – General Council Discussion on Mandated Negotiations and the Built-In Agenda 23 November 1998 – Communication from the United States*, Geneva: General Council of the World Trade Organization.

WT/GC/W/564/Rev.1 (2006), *Doha Work Programme – The Outstanding Implementation Issue on the Relationship Between the TRIPS Agreement and the*

Convention on Biological Diversity (2006), Geneva: General Council (Trade Negotiations Committee).

WT/L/540 (2003), *Implementation of Paragraph 6 of the Doha Declaration on the TRIPS Agreement and Public Health*, Geneva: General Council of the World Trade Organization.

WT/L/540/Corr.1 (2005), *Implementation of Paragraph 6 of the Doha Declaration on the TRIPS Agreement and Public Health*, Geneva: General Council of the World Trade Organization.

WT/L/579 (2004), *Doha Work Programme: Decision Adopted by the General Council on 1 August 2004*, Geneva: General Council of the World Trade Organization.

WT/L/641 (2005), *Amendment of the TRIPS Agreement*, Geneva: General Council of the World Trade Organization.

WT/MIN(01)/DEC/1 (2001), *Ministerial Declaration*, Geneva: Ministerial Conference of the World Trade Organization.

WT/MIN(01)/DEC/2 (2001), *Declaration on the TRIPS Agreement and Public Health*, Geneva: Ministerial Conference of the World Trade Organization.

WT/MIN(01)/DEC/17 (2001), *Ministerial Declaration*, Geneva: Ministerial Conference of the World Trade Organization.

WT/MIN(05)/DEC (2005), *Ministerial Declaration*, Geneva: Ministerial Conference of the World Trade Organization.

8. TRIPS-plus treaty terms: Dealing with coercion

Justin Malbon

1. INTRODUCTION

A number of chapters in this book criticise bilateral Free Trade Agreements (FTA) between a strong state and a weak state containing TRIPS-plus terms.[1] The general criticism made is that the TRIPS-plus terms are unfair or exploitative and serve the self-interest of a strong state at the expense of the interests of a weak state.

This chapter is interested in how it might be decided within a legal framework whether TRIPS-plus terms are unfair or exploitative. An implication underlying the criticisms is that TRIPS-plus terms are obtained through coercion or undue influence, or unfair exploitation of the strong party's dominant position.

Under present law, a treaty is void if procured by the threat or use of force in violation of the principles of international law embodied in the Charter of the United Nations. Arguably, a treaty is also void if procured by the threat or use of economic duress. It seems highly unlikely that the TRIPS-plus FTAs referred to in this book were attained by the threat of force. It might be possible to claim they were attained by actual or threatened economic duress. Even on a generous interpretation of the law the threatened or actual duress needs to be reasonably blatant. There probably needs to be a threat of the imposition of economic sanctions if the weak nation does not agree to the treaty terms. Again, it seems unlikely that the TRIPS-plus FTAs have been obtained through economic duress defined in this way.

Given that the present state of the law probably does not provide the legal basis for satisfying the critics of TRIPS-plus terms, this chapter will consider whether extending the law beyond its current parameters can meet their concerns about abuse of dominant party position. The chapter will leapfrog into an imagined future state of the law in which treaty terms are challengeable on the basis that they unjustifiably give a party an excessive advantage. The imagined law will also enable a party to seek to have treaty terms suspended, amended or set aside in circumstances of hardship. Although the imagined law extends beyond existing law, it is not as outlandish as may first appear as it is consistent with the overarching international law obligations of good faith. The imagined law also builds upon current rules and principles of contract law, which pay increasing attention to matters of substantive fairness.

Domestic law is not uncommonly referred to for reforming the international law. In the case of treaty law it is useful to refer to domestic contract law principles. Treaties have been likened to contracts in the sense that they are entered into upon the basis of party autonomy (in the case of international law this has parallels with notions of state sovereignty) for the purpose of the parties obtaining mutually beneficial outcomes (or maximising their joint welfare).

This chapter will propose a plausible set of rules regarding treaties based upon contract law to deal with circumstances in which a party abuses its dominant position by extracting unfair treaty terms. It will also suggest a means for dealing with situations in which the prevailing circumstances unpredictably change causing hardship to a party.

The question arises in the present context as to which domestic contract law should be borrowed from to gain inspiration for reforming treaty law. Fortunately, we can side-step the somewhat xenophobic undertones of this question by referring to two sets of internationally devised contract laws or principles: the Convention on the International Sale of Goods (CISG) and the UNIDROIT Principles of International Commercial Contracts. The CISG says very little about oppressive contract terms, whilst the UNIDROIT Principles contain a number of provisions on the topic. Of present interest is Art 3.10, which deals with contracts and contract terms that result in a gross disparity between the obligations of the parties that gives one party an unjustifiable advantage; and Chapter 6, Section 2 of the UNIDROIT Principles, which deals with hardship.

This chapter will borrow from Art 3.10 to construct an imagined amendment to the Vienna Convention on the Law of Treaties that will deal with treaties and treaty terms which, at the time a treaty was entered into, resulted in gross disparity of the party's treaty obligations leading to one party gaining an unjustifiable advantage. Chapter 6, Section 2 of the UNIDROIT Principles will be borrowed from to suggest ways of dealing with circumstances of hardship arising after the treaty was entered into. It will be assumed for present purposes that parties could challenge treaties with TRIPS-related subject matter (including TRIPS-plus terms) before the WTO's Disputes Settlements Body.

This chapter will proceed to speculate as to how such a treaty law would affect the behaviour of parties to TRIPS-plus FTAs, or parties negotiating

TRIPS-plus terms. It will be speculated that it is unlikely (although possible) that a nation would challenge the TRIPS-plus terms of an FTA under the imagined reformed position. Even if nations rarely or never challenge treaty terms under the imagined law, it will be claimed that the reformed position will alter the existing normative regime at the margins thereby placing greater emphasis on issues of substantive fairness than presently exists. This shift would not be insignificant as treaty law has a long antecedence of toleration of bullying and coercive behaviour by strong states. Arguably, the TRIPS Agreement itself resulted from oppressive conduct by strong states. Further tilting the normative regime so that it places greater emphasis on substantive fairness is arguably a good thing, even if it is not a complete answer to the concerns of critics regarding TRIPS-plus terms.

2. FORWARD-BASE REGULATORY MODEL

As mentioned, this chapter will leapfrog from the present to an imagined future state of the international law. That leap requires explanation. In order to skip the usual debates about whether there should be reform of international relations and the attendant law that ought to deal with this apparent abuse of party position, this chapter will postulate a set of reforms to offer the analyst a different (imaginary) future place in time for assessing initially conceived proposals for reform. The objective of proposing an idealised set of reforms – or a 'forward-base regulatory model' as it will be described in this chapter – is to shift focus from a present day perspective, which is locked into an 'ought to' debate, to a future in which the idealised reform scheme exists. Although the aim is to skip the 'ought to' debate, the strictures of this methodology will be relaxed somewhat in order to justify the policy considerations upon which the model is based. Although this is not strictly necessary (and risks sliding into an 'ought to' debate) it is done to explain the plausibility of the reformed position and offer insights into the problematics of the unreformed position.

The forward-base regulatory model proposed here is positioned at a 'forward-base' in the sense that the posited law does not exist at present, but theoretically could exist at some future point in time. It is regulatory, in the sense that the model is about the regulation of behaviour using recognisably legal mechanisms. Finally, it is an idealised model built upon specified and plausible assumptions. Building the model has the advantages of:

- clarifying what reform advocates are actually seeking when they criticise the present state of the law;

- offering a different perspective from which to consider alternate reform measures, or consider whether reform is necessary in the first place;
- exposing assumptions and limitations about the existing system; and
- allowing assessments to be made as to how various players might respond to a particular reformed set of laws.

The purpose of offering an idealised set of international regulations, therefore, is to allow an additional way of reflecting upon alternative regulatory reform proposals and theories than generally exists. It also opens another space, and another position, for applying methodologies that attempt to either predict or gain additional insights into the way people and organisations respond to regulatory change (see, for example, Lempert et al. 2003). The methodologies can, for example, include game theory and adaptive agent modelling (see, for example, Banks and Duggan 2006; Mahoney and Sanchirico 2003). These methodologies will not be attempted in this chapter. They do, however, offer ways of analysing reform proposals and offering some (albeit limited) capacity for predicting likely party responses to reform measures.

Proponents claim that game theory and dynamic game theory offer a means for assessing how parties might interact with each other to advance their perceived self-interest. They also claim the theories have the capacity to predict party behaviour, and in other contexts, predict market behaviour. Critics claim, however, that these methodologies tend only to work well in analysing two or three agents, and they are concerned with equilibrium outcomes rather than any process (Moss 2002, p. 7267). These methodologies and concomitant theories are, therefore, unlikely to cope with the complexity of international relations overlayed with assessments of how judges and tribunals will respond to a hypothesised set of legal regulations.

An interesting development involves the use of multiagent models for building theories about complex organisational behaviour and strategies. These have been used to analyse decisions, and policies influencing the performance, effectiveness, flexibility and survivability of complex social systems (Carley 2002, p. 7257). According to Carley:

> Multiagent models used in a 'what-if' fashion are improving our understanding of how different technologies, decisions, and policies influence the performance, effectiveness, flexibility, and survivability of complex social systems (Carley 2002, p. 7257).

She adds that the key point is that 'these models enable the analyst to look at complex systems and reason about such scenarios in a more systematic fashion than many other forms of theorizing' (Carley 2002, p. 7262). There are a number of computer programs available to assist analysis for the multiagent models. Given the enormous complexity of human organisational behaviour, and the bounded rationality and emotional responses of the actors the multiagent models seek to analyse, the capacity for the analyst to predict organisational behaviour remains somewhat limited. Their greater value, like other theories and methodologies, often lies in their capacity to lay bare hidden assumptions and potential limitations in existing ways of doing things (Carley 2002, p. 7267). Similarly, the forward-base regulatory model proposed here is unlikely to predict accurately how states and tribunals might respond to the hypothetical regulations, but it does offer new perspectives for making additional hypothesises about likely party behaviour, as well as exposing assumptions and limitations about the existing system.

Claims about likely party responses to the modelled rules will therefore be tentative and generalised. Generalised predictions can often be more accurate, but potentially less useful (although possibly sufficiently useful), than more precise predictions. By way of analogy, I can make the very general but reliable prediction that next year in Cape Town the average temperatures during summer will be higher than the average temperatures during winter. This is likely to be a highly accurate although not altogether useful prediction, as it is so widely known. However if I make the more precise prediction that the maximum temperature in Cape Town on 1 September next year will be 20°C, chances are it will be wrong. The complexities of weather systems are so great and susceptible to so many variable influences that precise prediction of maximum temperatures and prevailing weather conditions beyond a few days into the future is impossible. Much the same can be said of human behaviour in complex institutional settings. Predicting to any level of detail how states might perform under a particular (hypothesised) regulatory regime is extremely fraught. The way key-diplomats and negotiators perceive their self-interest, read the prevailing political climate, develop relationships and alliances with other diplomats and negotiators and so on, all add an increasing array of variables that can dramatically change the outcomes of any modelling that attempts to predict future behaviour. Generalised claims about future responses to a hypothetical reform scenario are therefore likely to be more reliable than specific claims.

The model applied here is itself deliberately generalised and simplified to attain greater utility. The model seeks to gain insights into the behaviour of 'strong states' and 'weak states' in negotiating TRIPS-plus terms. The term 'weak state' is highly generalised, and contestable. China, for example, might be thought of as a weak state as it is classified as a developing country because of its low household incomes and its consumption is quite low in rural and inland areas. On the other hand, it might be thought of as a strong state because it is the fourth largest economy in the world in terms of gross domestic product at 2006 exchange rates, and the second largest when adjustments are made for the differences in the domestic purchasing power of national currencies.[2] It might therefore be considered to be negotiating as a strong state even where the other party is the US. In some contexts a developed country might be considered to be a relatively weak state. Australia, for example, is a developed country with a diverse economy. It is also a small economy on world rankings and remains heavily dependent upon its primary industries. The US economy, on the other hand, dwarfs the Australian economy.

Although highly generalised and contestable, the terms strong state and weak state are useful for making broad theoretical claims and for gaining generalised insights into party behaviour. The forward-base regulatory model theorises that:

- strong states (particularly the United States) are using their dominant market position to extract contentious TRIPS-plus terms from weak parties;
- the weak states would not have agreed to the contentious terms if they were dealing with a state with equal bargaining power; and
- the present law is insufficiently robust to deal with a party abusing its dominant position to extract 'unfair' treaty terms.

Given these theoretical assumptions, this chapter proposes a reformed position based upon commercial contract law principles, which are at the same time consistent with the overarching obligation under international law that parties deal with each other on the basis of good faith.

This analysis will not be run as an 'ought to' debate (although such a debate lies in the shadows of this analysis), but rather as an 'as if' analysis of how parties might respond to the reformed position. The first two propositions mentioned above are dealt with at some length in other chapters in this book and will therefore not be discussed at any great length in this chapter.[3] Taking the third proposition first (that the law is insufficiently robust), it is necessary to examine the state of the existing law.

3. PRESENT STATE OF THE LAW

Treaty law and contract law have long been built upon the foundational assumption of party autonomy, or sovereignty. It follows from this that parties are free to enter into mutually beneficial bargains or compacts. The law of both contracts and treaties provides remedies for behaviour that militates against the contract or treaty being the result of a free and consensual agreement of the parties. Militating behaviour includes fraud, threats of violence and other behaviour by one party that oppresses the will of the other. Consistent with giving effect to party autonomy and the concomitant freedom of the parties to negotiate mutually agreed terms, both contract law and treaty law (in theory at least) treat the legal rights of the parties to the agreement as being equal. That is, the law applies equally to both parties; it does not provide more legal rights to one party at the expense of the other. A limited exception applies to rebalance party rights where one party exploits its dominant position by extracting unfair terms from the other under the contract. This exception is discussed below.

As mentioned, the ideal, regarding the status of international states, is that they enter into treaties as equals, and each has equal rights at law. The reality is somewhat more contentious. Marshall CJ of the United States Supreme Court expressed the ideal of state equality some time ago in his usual lofty way:

> No principle of general law is more universally acknowledged than the perfect equality of nations. Russia and Geneva have equal rights. It results from this equality that no one can rightfully impose a rule on another (*The Antelope* 1825, p. 122).

His sentiments are now echoed in Art 2, Chapter 1 of the Charter of the United Nations, which states that Members shall act in accordance with a number of principles, including that the '[o]rganization is based on the principle of the sovereign equality of all its Members'. The principle of state equality is also voiced in the preamble to the Vienna Convention on the Law of Treaties, which states that the Convention has in mind 'the principles of international law embodied in the Charter of the United Nations, such as the principles of the equal rights and self-determination of peoples, of the sovereign equality and independence of all States, of non-interference in the domestic affairs of States, of the prohibition of the threat or use of force and of universal respect for, and observance of, human rights and fundamental freedoms for all'. Consistent with the principle of state equality, the Preamble also observes that 'the principles of free consent and of good faith and the *pacta sunt servanda* rule are universally recognized'.

All this speaks to the idea (and the ideal) that nation-states deal with each other on the basis of mutual respect rather than on the basis of strong-arm tactics and bullying. The reality, at least prior to the Charter of the United Nations, was somewhat different. Kaufmann claimed in 1911 that:

> The right to equality, in the sense of inherent equality of power and rights, is nonsense, and in the sense of formal equality of capacity for rights is nothing else but a tautological expression for the conception of International Personality (Kaufmann 1911, p. 195).

After citing a number of examples of 'political inequalities' in international society, McNair concluded in 1927 that:

> The truth is that in two important and relevant respects international law lags behind the private law of most civilized States and international treaties differ from private contracts. The first is that international law does not recognize the fact that one party to a treaty was induced by duress or coercion or undue influence to make it, as a ground for treating it as invalid. The second is that only in the most rudimentary degree does international law recognize that a treaty which conflicts with morality or with policy is void and need not be performed (McNair 1927, p. 139).

In any event, he concluded, '[n]o one can regard the position of duress in international law as satisfactory or as consistent with a civilized society' (McNair 1927, p. 140). McNair cited a number of examples of treaties obtained by duress, including the system of capitulations resulting in China and Turkey agreeing to surrender the right to try certain classes of foreigners for crimes committed in their territories; the Peace Treaties of 1919 which required Germany, Austria, Hungary and Bulgaria to forfeit the privileges and immunities of sovereignty; and the impairing of Panama's freedom of action (McNair 1927, p. 140). He was not to know it at the time, but the inherent unfairness of these treaties was to contribute to international instability in the lead up to World War II, in some cases to a spectacular degree (McNair 1927, p. 139).

The United Nations International Law Commission, which drafted the Vienna Convention on the Law of Treaties, noted that prior to the advent of the Covenant of the League of Nations a treaty's validity was unaffected by the fact it had been brought about by the threat of the use of force. The Commission stated that this doctrine:

> . . . was simply a reflection of the general attitude of international law during that era towards the legality of the use of force for the settlement of international disputes. With the Covenant and the Pact of Paris there began to develop a strong body of opinion which held that such treaties should no longer be recognized as legally valid (United Nations International Law Commission 1966, p. 246).

In 1970 the United Nations General Assembly adopted the Declaration of Principles of International Law Concerning Friendly Relations, which stated in part that:

> No State may use or encourage the use of economic, political or any other type of measures to coerce another State in order to obtain from it the subordination of the exercise of its sovereign rights and to secure from it advantages of any kind.

At around this time the United Nations International Law Commission concluded its work on the Vienna Convention on the Law of Treaties, which included a number of provisions dealing with treaties obtained by fraud and coercion. The Convention codifies the grounds on which a treaty may be impeached.[4] Art 51 provides that the expression of a State's consent to be bound to a treaty which has been procured by the coercion of its representative through acts or threats shall be without any legal effect. Of interest for present purposes is Art 52, which provides:

> *Coercion of a State by the threat or use of force*
> A treaty is void if its conclusion has been procured by the threat or use of force in violation of the principles of international law embodied in the Charter of the United Nations.

There was a deal of controversy amongst the members of the United Nations International Law Commission engaged in drafting the Convention about this provision. Delegates from developing nations wanted it to expressly mention economic duress as a basis for voiding a treaty, whilst developed nations sought to narrow the grounds for voidance (see, for example, Bowett 1972; Briggs 1967; Nahlik 1971). According to the Commission's Commentary on the provision:

> Some members of the Commission expressed the view that any other forms of pressure, such as a threat to strangle the economy of a country, ought to be stated in the article as falling within the concept of coercion. The Commission, however, decided to define coercion in terms of a 'threat or use of force in violation of the principles of the Charter', and considered that the precise scope of the acts covered by this definition should be left to be determined in practice by interpretation of the relevant provisions of the Charter (United Nations International Law Commission 1966, p. 246).[5]

In the end a compromise was reached in which economic coercion was not expressly mentioned, but the following declaration was annexed to the Final Act of the Conference on the Law of Treaties:

> *Declaration on the prohibition of military, political or economic coercion in the conclusion of treaties*
> Having adopted the Declaration on the prohibition of military, political or economic coercion in the conclusion of treaties as part of the Final Act of the Conference:

1. Requests the Secretary-General of the United Nations to bring the Declaration to the attention of all Member States and other States participating in the Conference, and of the principal organs of the United Nations;
2. Requests Member States to give the Declaration the widest possible publicity and dissemination (UN Doc A/CONF 39/26).

The declaration notably describes Art 52 as a declaration on the prohibition of military, political or *economic* coercion in the conclusion of treaties. In any event, Art 52 refers to 'the principles of international law embodied in the Charter of the United Nations', which in turn references Art 2(4) of the United Nations Universal Declaration of Human Rights, which prohibits the use of force. The term 'force' in this context has its ambiguities (Schachter 1991, p. 111), and sometimes is used in a wide sense to 'embrace all types of coercion: economic, political and psychological as well as physical' (Schachter 1991, p. 111). Opposition to economic coercion against states also appears in the United Nations Charter of Economic Rights and Duties of States.[6] Arguably, the impugned behaviour includes intentionally interfering with the trading patterns of a state (Barrie 1988, p. 314).[7] A number of commentators state that economic coercion can only be employed in support of self-defence or to redress an international wrong (Barrie 1988, p. 314; Thomas and Thomas 1972, pp. 90–91; Farer 1985, p. 411).

A broader and perhaps more fundamental question is what precisely do we mean by coercion? Farer observes that most people instinctively divide threats into two categories: threats not to give a benefit or to withdraw a previously given benefit (Farer 1985, p. 405). In the international community these include threats to refuse to provide or to withdraw economic aid and to deny most favoured nation status. Indeed, he says, threats, 'more or less subtle, have always been an important feature of the intercourse of states, even among allies' (Farer 1985, p. 406). Farrer goes so far as to say that:

> The nub of the matter is that the word 'coercion' has no normative significance; there is nothing illegal about coercion. Coercion is normal in all human relationships, including those between lovers. It's part of life. So is cooperation. Indeed, every human relationship is some mixture of coercion and cooperation. So to say that a particular relationship is coercive is to say nothing at all about its legitimacy (Farer 1985, p. 406).

His claim that coercion has no normative significance goes too far as it empties the term of any real meaning. His point is significant, however, to the extent that to have a meaning in a legal context the term 'coercion' must be given clear definition.

Despite the threat or use of force being a ground for voiding a treaty, various forms of duress continue to exist in more or less subtle forms today. This leads to a present situation where, in Harris's assessment:

> Much of the unfairness in international law results from severe power inequalities among the various nations and the power-based regime that undergirds global governance. The remedy for treaties negotiated unfairly is quite often more treaties or, alternatively, hollow talk of promoting national sovereignty. Neither of these solutions directly attacks the problem. Indeed, there is lack of political will among nations to address the structural defects and power asymmetries in the international system (Harris 2006, p. 684).

Given it was not so long ago that overt threats of force and other forms of duress were tolerated, it is easy to imagine that old mind-sets die hard. Dominant states no doubt find irresistible the urge to place pressure on states to extract favourable treaty terms. It is, after all, the way international relations have been conducted for centuries. It is unsurprising then that coercive conduct, although more subtlety conducted nowadays, remains the norm.

As we have seen then, over the course of the 20th century international law shifted from a position where bullying and coercive tactics were generally tolerated (and even considered acceptable) to one where this is no longer the case, at least as far as overt threats or use of force are concerned. It is possible that economic coercion is unacceptable under present international law, although it is probable that the coercion must amount to a real threat or use of economic sanctions or some other form of substantial economic harm to constitute a breach.

Over the course of the 20th century, domestic contract law has grown increasingly intolerant of oppressive conduct, and paid increasing attention to issues of substantive fairness regarding the conduct of contractual relations.[8] At the same time, international law has also become increasingly concerned with matters of substantive fairness, including with regard to the conduct of treaty relations, although it lags well behind domestic law by failing to match these concerns with sufficiently developed legal principles and sufficiently robust means for their enforcement (see DiMatteo 1997, p. 149 referring to Nassar 1995, p. 234). Under domestic law, the norm of fairness provides an umbrella for a number of doctrines including the civil law's notion of just contract and the common law doctrine of unconscionability. Any apparent divergence between the civil and common law on this issue ultimately is a difference of semantics (DiMatteo 1997, p. 149). These domestic law developments in contract law can usefully inform developments in treaty law, although analogising contract law with treaty law is an exercise that should be undertaken with due caution.

4. BORROWING FROM THE DOMESTIC LAW OF CONTRACT

Analogising treaties with contracts has its limits. Caution needs to be exercised to ensure the analogising is not taken too far, and the purpose for the analogising needs always to be borne in mind.

There are clear differences between the nature and role of treaties and contracts. They differ to the extent that treaties perform functions that in national systems would be carried out by statutes, whereas contacts are legal transactions that create rights and duties only for the contracting parties, who are usually few in number (Malanczuk 1997, p. 37). Treaties can appear to have effects analogous to legislation because they are a source of rules that apply to a very large number of people, although it must be said that there are also problems with analogising treaties with national legislation (Malanczuk 1997, p. 37).[9] McNair, who drew heavily upon contract law as a resource for treaty law, noted a number of distinctions between the two. States use treaties 'not only to agree on the rules which will govern a particular private relationship, but also to convey, to create an organization or association, and to legislate' (Hutchinson 1989, p. 375). In addition, 'the way in which States conduct their relations and enforce their rights has no obvious parallel in municipal law', for example when engaging in war and concluding a war with peace treaties. Allott cautions against conceiving the relationship of the sources of customary international law and treaty law 'either in terms of a lazy analogy with contract law or by a one-to-one correspondence with their relationship in a national legal system' (Allott 1999, para. 37(3)). Rather, he conceives the treaty and the law as creating a unique 'micro-legal system within the general legal system from which they derive their legal effect, and within the society from which they derive their social effect' (Allott 1999, para. 35).

The distinction between national and international legal systems can nevertheless be overdrawn. Kelsen says there is no absolute borderline between communities constituted by national and by international law. He notes that national law can rise from international law, as is the case when a State is established by an international treaty (Kelsen 1944, p. 211). Contract law offers a rich experience of dealing with inter-party disputes which can inform the development of treaty law. When reviewing the republication in 1986 of Lord McNair's classic work *The Law of Treaties* Hutchinson noted that McNair's view was that:

> . . . the devices and notions of municipal law represent a resource on which to draw for the purpose of analysing international legal practice and expounding the rules which it exemplifies. Developed after a long and detailed study by

> municipal legislators, judges and jurists, and tested through extensive application, they probably represent the most justified and workable solutions to international legal problems, just as they have provided satisfactory solutions to legal problems arising at the national level (Hutchinson 1989, p. 375).[10]

McNair employed municipal law analogies believing the law of contract is 'potentially the most fruitful source of ideas for explaining and analysing treaty law' (Hutchinson 1989, p. 375). The value of analogising contract law with treaty law was recognised by the WTO Appellate Body in *Japan – Taxes on Alcoholic Beverages*, when it said that:

> The WTO Agreement is a treaty – the international equivalent of a contract. It is self-evident that in an exercise of their sovereignty, and in pursuit of their own respective national interests, the Members of the WTO have made a bargain. In exchange for the benefits they expect to derive as Members of the WTO, they have agreed to exercise their sovereignty according to the commitments they have made in the WTO Agreement (WT/DS8/AB/R).[11]

Drawing from contract law, then, it is possible to envisage ways in which the Vienna Convention on the Law of Treaties could be expanded so as to deal with oppressive conduct in the negotiation of treaties. The question becomes, which is the most appropriate domestic contract law from which to draw? Fortunately, there are two internationally devised contract law instruments that can be referred to: the Convention on the International Sale of Goods (CISG) devised by the United Nations Commission on International Trade Law; and the UNIDROIT Principles of International Commercial Contracts (UNIDROIT Principles).[12]

5. INTERNATIONAL CONTRACT LAW

The CISG says very little about coercive or oppressive conduct. The UNIDROIT Principles, on the other hand, offer ground that is more fertile for present purposes. The UNIDROIT Principles are non-binding and therefore rely on their persuasive value for adoption. They have been used as the basis for reforming the domestic law of contract in a number of countries (Bonell 2004, p. 7). In addition, they can be, and are, chosen as the law governing contract by parties to contracts for the international sale of goods or services. Also, arbitrators to international commercial disputes will often apply the UNIDROIT Principles to a contract that states that the law applying to the contract are the 'general principles of law', 'principles of international law', '*lex mercatoria*' or the like, or where the contract makes no choice of law at all (Bonell 2004, p. 13). That is to say, the Principles are taken to represent 'a particularly authoritative expression of similar supra-national or transnational principles and rules of law' (Bonell 2004, p. 13). This is probably unsurprising given that the 2004 Principles, which built on an earlier version of the Principles, was drafted by a Working Party comprised of 17 members who offered a wide representation of the major legal systems and regions of the world, and who hold the highest professional qualifications (Bonell 2004, p. 5; see also Bonell 2005).

A number of the UNIDROIT Principles' provisions deal with oppression by one party of the will of the other. Art 3.9 states that a party may avoid the contract 'when it has been led to conclude the contract by the other party's unjustified threat which, having regard to the circumstances, is so imminent and serious as to leave the first party no reasonable alternative'. Art 3.9 adds that, in particular, 'a threat is unjustified if the act or omission with which a party has been threatened is wrongful in itself, or it is wrongful to use it as a means to obtain the conclusion of the contract'. Art 3.10 deals with gross disparity. Specifically it states that:

(1) A party may avoid the contract or an individual term of it if, at the time of the conclusion of the contract, the contract or term unjustifiably gave the other party an excessive advantage. Regard is to be had, among other factors, to:
   (a) the fact that the other party has taken unfair advantage of the first party's dependence, economic distress or urgent needs, or of its improvidence, ignorance, inexperience or lack of bargaining skill; and
   (b) the nature and purpose of the contract.
(2) Upon the request of the party entitled to avoidance, a court may adapt the contract or term in order to make it accord with reasonable commercial standards of fair dealing.
(3) A court may also adapt the contract or term upon the request of the party receiving notice of avoidance, provided that that party informs the other party of its request promptly after receiving such notice and before the other party has reasonably acted in reliance on it. The provisions of Art 3.13(2) apply accordingly.

Bonell says that this was one of the most difficult provisions of the UNIDROIT Principles to draft (Bonell 2004, p. 165). Delegates to the UNDROIT Study Group sessions for the drafting of the Principles were divided over whether the proposed principles for dealing with gross disparity went far enough and whether it should appear in the Principles at all. Opponents argued that the proposal ventured beyond dealing with incidences of defects of consent and into the content of the contract itself (Bonell 2004, p. 167). Some argued that it was doubtful in the context of international trade that such a provision was appropriate as it would be extremely rare, between merchants, for them to agree to grossly unfair terms (Bonell 2004, p. 167). In the end a compromise was reached in which a party can only resort to Art 3.10 if it can establish that (a) there is gross disparity between the obligations of the parties, giving one party an excessive advantage; and (b) the excessive advantage must be unjustifiable. That is, it must have been obtained by exploiting a bargaining handicap of the other party or otherwise be lacking justification (Bonell 2004, p. 168). Consequently:

> From this perspective the provision is in line with the tendency, which is more and more prevalent within domestic laws, to consider procedural and substantive unfairness as two distinct but in most cases interrelated matters (Bonell 2004, p. 168).

According to the official UNIDROIT Commentary to its Principles the excessive advantage gained by a party must have existed at the time of the conclusion of the contract (UNIDROIT Commentary to its Principles). If an excessive advantage occurs after the conclusion of the contract, then the hardship provisions may assist the prejudiced party. The term 'excessive advantage' under Art 3.10(1) requires more than even a 'considerable disparity in the value and the price or some other element which upsets the equilibrium of performance and counter-performance' of the contract. What is required, according to the UNIDROIT Commentary is 'that the disequilibrium is in the circumstances so great as to shock the conscience of a reasonable person'. Thus, not only must the advantage be excessive, it must be unjustifiable.

The Commentary gives as an example of unjustifiable advantage a party selling an outdated automobile assembly line for a price that corresponds to the price of a modern assembly line. The contract may be avoided even if the seller made no representations about the efficiency of the assembly line. Other factors that may need to be taken into account when deciding whether a party has gained an unjustifiable advantage, according to the Commentary, include the ethics prevailing in the business or trade. This factor can be taken into account in determining whether there has been a breach of good faith.

With minimal redrafting of Art 3.10 of the UNIDROIT Principles to place it within the Vienna Convention on the Law of Treaties it is possible to envisage the provision reading as follows:

> (1) A party to a treaty may avoid the treaty or an individual term of it if, at the time of the conclusion of the treaty, the treaty or term unjustifiably gave the other party an excessive advantage. Regard is to be had, among other factors, to:
> (a) the fact that the other party has taken unfair advantage of the first party's dependence, economic distress or urgent needs, or of its improvidence, ignorance, inexperience or lack of bargaining skill; and
> (b) the nature and purpose of the treaty.

(2) Upon the request of the party entitled to avoidance, a duly appointed tribunal may adapt the treaty or term in order to make it accord with international law standards of fair dealing.
(3) A duly appointed tribunal may also adapt the treaty or term upon the request of the party receiving notice of avoidance, provided that that party informs the other party of its request promptly after receiving such notice and before the other party has reasonably acted in reliance on it. The provisions of Art 3.13(2) apply accordingly.[13]

Translating the requirements for establishing gross disparity under Art 3.10 to an imagined equivalent set of requirements under the Vienna Convention would require a weak state to establish that the strong state had taken unfair advantage of the weak state's dependence, economic distress or urgent needs. To establish this, evidence of dependence could be adduced regarding the extent to which the weak state is dependent on the strong state for foreign aid, for favourable economic and security treatment, and so forth.

All nations, of course, are to a greater or lesser extent mutually dependent upon each other for trade and investment. Dependence in this context must mean more than the usual degree of international economic, diplomatic and defence relations. It would therefore need to amount to an overwhelming dependence, such that the nation would suffer severe economic and social consequences if the strong party withdrew any privileges and favoured status to the weak party. Another factor that could be taken into account is whether the weak party is suffering economic distress. This might require evidence that the strong party gained an unjustified advantage under the treaty by exploiting a bargaining handicap by taking advantage of the weak state's poor economic status. The advantage gained would need to be such that the disequilibrium is in the circumstances so great as to 'shock the conscience' of the international community, or to constitute a breach of 'the principles of free consent and of good faith', as per the preamble of the United Nations Charter.

Chapter 6, Section 2 UNIDROIT Principles provides for remedial action if there are circumstances of hardship. The mere fact that the performance of the contract has become more onerous for one of the parties is itself insufficient grounds for establishing hardship (Art 6.2.1). Hardship arises if 'the occurrence of events fundamentally alters the equilibrium of the contract either because the cost of a party's performance has increased or because the value of the performance a party receives has diminished', and:

(a) the events occur or become known to the disadvantaged party after the conclusion of the contract;
(b) the events could not reasonably have been taken into account by the disadvantaged party at the time of the conclusion of the contract;

(c) the events are beyond the control of the disadvantaged party; and
(d) the risk of the events was not assumed by the disadvantaged party (Art 6.2.2).

Hardship entitles the disadvantaged party to request renegotiation of the contract (Art 6.2.3). If this fails, either party may request a court to terminate the contract on a date and terms to be fixed, or that the court adapt the contract with a view to restoring its equilibrium.

UNIDROIT appears to have intended that the hardship provisions reflect the domestic contract law concept of frustration of purpose (UNIDROIT Commentary to its Principles, p. 183). The change in circumstances must result in a fundamental alteration of the equilibrium of the contract. Whether there is a fundamental alteration will depend on the circumstances of each case (UNIDROIT Commentary to its Principles, p. 184). An illustration of an unforeseeable fundamental alteration of circumstances offered by the UNIDROIT Commentary is where one month after the conclusion of a contract a political crisis occurs leading to a massive devaluation of 80 per cent of a party's currency (UNIDROIT Commentary to its Principles, p. 186).

The UNIDROIT hardship provisions have some parallels with the doctrine of *rebus sic stantibus* under customary international law, which permits a party to terminate, withdraw from or suspend its obligations under a treaty if there is a fundamental change of circumstances from those that existed at the time of the conclusion of the treaty that was not foreseen by the parties. As an example, the United States terminated an international agreement on shipping load restrictions because of the outbreak of World War II (see Nelson 2006, p. 19). Art 62 of the Vienna Convention on the Law of Treaties limits the grounds for termination or withdrawal to those changed circumstances (a) that constituted an essential basis of the consent of the parties to be bound by the treaty, and (b) where the effect of the change is radically to transform the extent of obligations still to be performed by the parties. According to Jennings and Watts, *rebus sic stantibus* 'when kept within proper limits, embodies a general principle of law as expressed in the doctrines of frustration, or supervening impossibility of performance, or the like, and known to the law of many countries' (Jennings and Watts 1996, p. 1306).

The UNIDROIT test is whether 'the occurrence of events fundamentally alters the equilibrium of the contract', whilst Art 62 of the Vienna Convention refers to circumstances in which 'the effect of the change is radically to transform the extent of obligations still to be performed under the treaty'. There is probably little practical difference between these two tests, although UNIDROIT's test places emphasis on attaining party balance whilst Art 62 merely speaks of a transformation of the obligations of the parties. UNIDROIT is also clearer about the options available if hardship occurs, and requires the parties to attempt renegotiation of the terms as a first step. Modifying the Vienna Convention to take on board these aspects of the UNIDROIT Principles has a number of attractions, particularly the way in which it focuses attention on the substantive fairness issue of party balance.

6. GOOD FAITH UNDER TREATY LAW

The law proposed by the forward-base regulatory model in this chapter might not involve so great an imaginative leap as might first be thought if it accepted that the UNIDROIT Principles provision dealing with gross disparity is simply an elaboration of the overarching obligation upon the parties to deal with each other on the basis of good faith. Good faith is an obligation known under both domestic contract law and international treaty law.

The International Court of Justice proclaimed in the *Nuclear Tests* case that '[o]ne of the basic principles governing the creation and performance of legal obligations, whatever their source, is the principle of good faith' (*Australia v France* 1974, p. 268). In terms of treaties, Art 26 of the Vienna Convention on the Law of Treaties provides that '[e]very treaty in force is binding upon the parties to it and must be performed by them in good faith'.[14] In addition, Art 31 of the Vienna Convention provides that, '[a] treaty shall be interpreted in good faith in accordance with the ordinary meaning to be given to the terms of the treaty in their context and in the light of its object and purpose'. Moreover, according to the WTO Appellate Body in *US–Gasoline* the 'general rule of interpretation' contained in Art 31 of the Vienna Convention had attained the status of customary or general international law (WT/DS2/AB/R, p. 17).

An overarching obligation of good faith plays an important role for contracts in civil law countries. Section 242 of the German Civil Code *Bürgerliches Gesetzbuch* (BGB) provides, for instance, that a debtor is bound to perform according to the requirements of good faith, ordinary usage being taken into consideration (Ebke and Steinhauer 1997, p. 171). Although the section refers to the debtor, interpreters place attention on the debtor's obligation to perform and the creditor's right of performance. This is achieved by utilising section 157 of the Code which states contracts must be interpreted according to the requirements of good faith (Ebke and Steinhauer 1997, p. 171; see also Teubner 1998, pp. 25–27). The usual remedy applied in Germany for breach of contract is specific performance rather than damages. Damages are usually only payable if performance is impossible. In addition, the German Law on General Business Conditions, or *AGB-Gesetz* (AGBG) provides that a contract provision is void if it 'work[s] to the disadvantage of [a party] in a way irreconcilable with good faith' (see von Teichman 1983, p. 217; DiMatteo 1997, p. 147). A German court can interpret a clause that was not freely negotiated in a literal and restrictive way and can consider surrounding oral evidence that leads to a more equitable reading of a harsh contract term. In providing a remedy that may result in an equitable reformation or rescission of the contract a court will first attempt to adapt the contract to the new circumstances by re-writing it according to the parties' intentions and interests, and if this fails, declare the contract void (von Teichman 1983, p. 218).

Common law countries have generally shied away from imposing an overarching obligation of good faith. Despite that, most of the good faith obligations as understood in civil law countries exist in some form or another in common law countries, even if not under the good faith banner. The common law, for instance, can set aside a contract if there is inequality or inadequacy of consideration. In *Wolford v Powers* the court held that if the consideration 'is so grossly inadequate as to shock the conscience, courts will interfere' (*Wolford v Powers* 1882, p. 301; see also *Williams v Walker-Thomas Furniture Co* 1965; DiMatteo 1997, p. 150), and in *Girard Trust Bank v Castle Apartments Inc* (1977) the court stated that if the 'value is more than twice the sale price, there is such gross inadequacy as will shock the conscience of the Court and justify setting the sale aside' (p. 1145 quoting *Central National Bank v Industrial Trust Co* 1947). Perhaps not coincidently, the UNIDROIT commentary on Art 3.10 states, as we have seen, that an 'excessive advantage' exists if the disequilibrium of the performance and counter-performance of the contract is so great as to shock the conscience of a reasonable person.

Under international law, good faith can be said to be both a generalised expression of one of the main conditions for the functioning of any legal order (see Virally 1983, pp. 131–133), and a term containing a number of more specific obligations that apply to parties to treaties. Aspects of the overarching obligation at international law find expression in more particular obligations such as *pacta sunt servanda* (pacts must be respected). According to Virally, a function of good faith is 'that it furnishes a measure – or pattern – for determining the extent of the legal obligations assumed by states or other subjects of international law' (Virally 1983, p. 132). This is why, in his view, good faith is not only the basis, but also an integral part of *pacta sunt servanda*. Under treaty law, good faith requires, amongst other things, that parties refrain from acts calculated to frustrate the object of the treaty (see *Certain German Interests in Polish Upper Silesia*

1926, p. 30; see also United Nations International Law Commission 1966, p. 211). It prohibits the abusive exercise of a party's rights, which means that if a party's assertion of a right impinges on the field covered by a treaty obligation, it must be exercised bona fide, which is to say, reasonably (WT/DS58/AB/R, para. 158). Nor can a party benefit from its own inconsistencies (*The Arbitral Award made by the King of Spain* 1960, pp. 213 and 214; *The Temple of Preah Vihear* 1962, pp. 23–32; see also United Nations International Law Commission 1966, p. 239).

It is possible, then, that the requirement that a strong party not use its position to unjustifiably gain an excessive advantage under treaty terms from a weak party is a particularisation of the overarching good faith obligation. Such a particularisation places emphasis on matters of substantive justice, which is of increasing interest to both domestic and international legal systems. The claim that international law stretches as far as this, however, is far from uncontroversial. Jennings and Watts state categorically in *Oppenheim's International Law* that the 'invalidity of "unequal treaties" has found no general acceptance'.[15] Recall, however, that under Art 3.10 of UNIDROIT mere inequality of bargaining positions or contract terms is not enough, the terms must also be unjust. Jennings and Watts' statement is consistent with Art 3.10 on the first proposition, and may possibly be silent on the second.

7. THE VIEW FROM HERE

It can be plausibly argued, then, that under customary international law states are subject to an overarching obligation of good faith in their dealings with each other. This general obligation finds particularised form in various ways, including the obligation not to extract treaty terms by means of coercion. The precise meaning of coercion under Art 52 of the Vienna Convention on the Law of Treaties is not definite, but can conceivably include economic coercion. It might also plausibly be argued that the good faith obligation extends to the requirement that a party will not use its position of dominance to extract unfair treaty terms. If this obligation does indeed exist, we may seek guidance from domestic contract law to gain a sense of when a treaty term would be judged to be unfair. In all likelihood it would be a term that so far departed from normative conduct that it would shock the mind of a reasonable observer. In addition, the overarching obligation of good faith can plausibly be argued to include the capacity to alter terms in circumstances of undue hardship.

Even if this is not the present state of the international law, this chapter leap-frogs over the question whether the above-described possible state of the law is in fact the law or not, or even whether it 'ought to' be the law. Under the forward-based regulatory position an imagined future state of the law is posited in which the above-described law is in fact the law.

The question arises as to what impact the modelled law would likely have on party behaviour? Taking the TRIPS-plus provisions in the United States FTAs with Morocco, Chile, Peru, the parties to the Central American FTA, or even the United States with Singapore and Australia for that matter, would a challenge to these provisions be likely to be successful? (see Table 8.1). On a superficial examination, at least, it appears unlikely. The TRIPS-plus provisions, even if they are taken to be as one-sided as the critics claim, do not appear to reach a point where they amount to terms causing so great a disequilibrium as to shock the conscience of the international community. Although the matter is of course arguable. Interestingly, some of the preambles to the intellectual property chapters in the FTAs go to some lengths to suggest the intellectual property terms will advance the interests of both parties. The Preamble to the chapter dealing with intellectual property in the United States – Chile FTA, for example, hints at technology transfer gains for Chile:

> *Emphasizing* that the protection and enforcement of intellectual property rights is a fundamental principle of this Chapter that helps promote technological innovation as well as the transfer and dissemination of technology to the mutual advantage of technology producers and users, and that encourages the development of social and economic well-being.

It would be interesting to know whether Chile does in fact receive any substantial technological transfer gains as hinted at by the FTA.

Would there be any point then in, say, amending the Vienna Convention on the Law of Treaties to introduce provisions dealing with gross disparity and hardship? Such provisions would not constitute a radical realignment of the law, as they are consistent with the duty of good faith and place additional emphasis on matters of substantive fairness. As a practical matter, however, it would appear unlikely that the provisions would ever be invoked, except in the most extreme of circumstances.

The emphasis upon issues of substantive fairness under the modelled provisions could serve to tilt the normative environment sufficiently to encourage states to pay greater heed to issues of fairness, and to discourage the sometimes subtle and sometimes unsubtle exercise by strong states of coercive conduct to achieve unduly favourable intellectual property terms in treaties. Recall that international relations have traditionally been transacted in an environment of legal tolerance of treaties obtained by coercion. The normative legal settings therefore require further realignment to counterbalance the long history of toleration of coercion so as to better meet the aspirations of the declarations found in the Charter of the United Nations, the Vienna Convention on the Law of Treaties and the United Nations Charter of Economic Rights and Duties of States.

8. CONCLUSION

From our forward-based vantage point we can see that the reformed position posited in this chapter does respond to the issue of treaties gained by the oppression of the will of states by promoting improvements to the international normative environment, at least at the margins. As we can also see from this vantage point, the reformed position offers some response (albeit at the margins) to an issue that the law tends to frame as one addressing issues of fairness and substantive justice. There are a number of insights that can be drawn from this analysis. First, legal responses to claimed unfairness of TRIPS-plus terms, even in an idealised form which incorporated the domestic contract law's increasing concern with issues of substantive fairness, are unlikely to address anything but the most extreme

Table 8.1 Free Trade Agreements concluded by the United States

Country	Year of United States signing
Australia	2004
Bahrain	2006
Canada (NAFTA)	1994
Chile	2003
Columbia	2006
Costa Rica (Central American FTA)	2005
Dominican Republic (Central American FTA)	2005
El Salvador (Central American FTA)	2005
Guatemala (Central American FTA)	2005
Honduras (Central American FTA)	2005
Israel	1985; 1996; 2004
Jordan	2000
Korea	2006
Malaysia	2006
Mexico (NAFTA)	1994
Morocco	2005
Nicaragua	2005
Oman	2006
Peru	Not yet signed
Singapore	2003

cases of abuse of dominant state position. Secondly, delving into the way in which treaty law presently deals with coercion it becomes apparent that it inadequately deals with substantive justice, and lags behind domestic contract law in this regard. Thirdly, international law and international relations remains unduly tolerant of coercive conduct, broadly understood. In short, it remains unduly complacent about the abuse of dominant party position, which most likely harms the long-term stability of the existing international relations regime. Given this, it can be said the TRIPS-plus critics raise legitimate concerns about substantive fairness.

NOTES

1. Chapters 3, 5, 6 and 7.
2. Remarks by the Chairman of the US Federal Reserve Board, B.S. Bernanke, 'The Chinese Economy: Progress and challenges' speech delivered at the Chinese Academy of Social Sciences, Beijing, China on 15 December 2006, www.federalreserve.gov/BoardDocs/Speeches/2006/20061215/default.htm.
3. Chapters 3, 5, 6 and 7. See also, Helfer 2004; Panagariya 2002.
4. Art 42.1 states that the 'validity of a treaty or of the consent of a State to be bound by a treaty may be impeached only through the application of the present Convention'. Art 42.2 states that a treaty may only be terminated, denounced or suspended, and a party may only withdraw from a treaty, if permitted by the provisions of the treaty or of the Convention.
5. The commentary relating to Art 52 appears as commentary relating to its draft form, (which then existed as Art 49). The only difference between the draft form as Art 49 and the final version as Art 52 is the addition after the words 'of the principles' of the words 'of international law embodied in'.
6. GA Res. 3281(xxix), UN GAOR, 29th Sess., Supp. No. 31 (1974) 50. Art 1 provides that: '[e]very State has the sovereign and inalienable right to choose its economic system as well as its political, social and cultural systems in accordance with the will of its people, without outside interference, coercion or threat in any form whatsoever'.
7. *Contra*, Farer is of the view that Art 2(4) is 'concerned with violence, with military force, not with economic coercion': Farer 1985, p. 410; and he defines economic coercion as efforts 'to project influence across frontiers by denying or conditioning access to a country's resources, raw materials, semi- or finished products, capital, technology, services or consumers' (p. 408).
8. In terms of the common law, see Atiyah 1985, p. 3 where he said the 'modern growth of statutory interventions in contract law . . . [is] designed to ensure substantive fairness in the exchange'.
9. See also Marshall CJ in *Foster v Neilson* 27 US (2Pet) 253, 314 where he said '[a] treaty is in its nature a contract between two nations, not a legislative act'.
10. Hutchinson 1989 added that: '[t]he explanatory power of this methodology ultimately stems from the fact that States and their legal advisers often do recruit principles from national legal systems in order to develop rules of international law, especially in those fields where State practice is either sparse or ambiguous' (at p. 375).
11. See also Caruso who makes the claim that 'for better or worse, traditional private-law discourse facilitates the emergence of new forms of institutional sovereignty in the age of globalization': Caruso 2006, p. 6.
12. UNIDROIT is an independent intergovernmental organisation established in 1926 as an auxiliary organ of the League of Nations. After the collapse of the League it was re-

established by a multilateral agreement. It is based in Rome and has 61 member nations. See http://www.unidroit.org.
13. This provision would be read subject to Art 75 of the Vienna Convention, which provides that the provisions of the Convention are without prejudice to any obligation in relation to a treaty which may arise from an aggressor state in consequence of measures taken in conformity with the Charter of the United Nations with reference to that state's aggression.
14. This strongly implies the element of reasonableness. See Jennings and Watts 1996, p. 1272 (note 7).
15. Although see *contra* Jennings and Watts 1996, p. 1292.
16. I am only aware of one matter in which Art 3.10 of UNIDROIT Principles was invoked, but unsuccessfully; International Chamber of Commerce Arbitral Award No. 9029, 3 March, 1998: in International Chamber of Commerce Arbitration Bulletin 10/2.

REFERENCES

Allott, P. (1999), 'The Concept of International Law', *European Journal of International Law*, 10(1), 31–50.
The Antelope, 23 US 66 (1825).
Case Concerning The Arbitral Award Made By The King Of Spain On 23 December 1906, International Court of Justice Reports, 18 November 1960.
Atiyah, P. (1985), 'Contract and Fair Exchange', *University of Toronto Law Journal*, 35(1), 1–24.
Australia v France (Nuclear Tests), International Court of Justice Reports, 20 December 1974.
Banks, J. and J. Duggan (2006), 'A General Bargaining Model of Legislative Policy-making', *Quarterly Journal of Political Science*, 1(1), 49–85.
Barrie, G. (1988), 'The Action Violates International Law and Policy', *American Journal of International Law*, 82(2), 311–314.
Bonell, M. (2004), *UNIDROIT Principles 2004*, Sydney: Federation Press.
Bonell, M. (2005), *An International Restatement of Contract Law: The UNIDROIT Principles of International Commercial Contracts*, 3rd edn, New York: Transnational Publishers.
Bowett, D. (1972), 'Economic Coercion and Reprisals by States', *Virginia Law Journal of International Law*, 13, 1–12.
Briggs, H. (1967), 'Procedures for Establishing the Invalidity or Termination of Treaties Under the International Law Commission's 1966 Draft Articles on the Law of Treaties', *American Journal of International Law*, 61(2), 976–989.
Carley, K. (2002), 'Computational Organization Science: A New Frontier', *Proceedings of the National Academy of Science USA*, 99 (Suppl. 3), 7257–7262.
Caruso, D. (2006), 'Private Law and State-Making in the Age of Globalization', *New York University Journal of International Law and Politics*, 39(1), 1–74.
Central National Bank v Industrial Trust Co, 51 A.2d 854 (Del. Super. Ct. 1947).
Certain German Interests in Polish Upper Silesia case, *PCI* (1926) Series A, No. 7.
DiMatteo, L. (1997), 'The CISG and the Presumption of Enforceability: Unintended Contractual Liability in International Business Dealings', *Yale Journal of International Law*, 22(1), 111–170.
Ebke, W. and B. Steinhauer (1997), 'The Doctrine of Good Faith in German

Contract Law', in J. Beatson and D. Friedman (eds), *Good Faith and Fault in Contract Law*, Oxford: Clarendon Press.
Farer, T. (1985), 'Political and Economic Coercion in Contemporary International Law', *American Journal of International Law*, 79(2), 405–413.
Foster v Neilson, 27 US (2Pet) 253.
GA Res. 3281(xxix), UN GAOR, 29th Sess., Supp. No. 31 (1974) 50, *United Nations Charter of Economic Rights and Duties of States*.
Girard Trust Bank v Castle Apartments Inc, 379 A.2d 1144 (Del. Super. Ct. 1977).
Harris, D. (2006), 'Carrying a Good Joke Too Far: TRIPS and Treaties of Adhesion', *University of Pennsylvania Journal of International Economic Law*, 27(3), 681–755.
Helfer, L. (2004), 'Regime Shifting: The TRIPs Agreement and New Dynamics of International Intellectual Property Lawmaking', *Yale Journal of International Law*, 29(1), 1–83.
Hutchinson, D. (1989), 'Review: McNair and the Law of Treaties Revisited', *Oxford Journal of Legal Studies*, 9(3), 374–382.
International Chamber of Commerce Arbitral Award No. 9029, 3 March 1998, in ICC International Court of Arbitration Bulletin 10/2.
International Institute for the Unification of Private Law (2004), *UNIDROIT Principles of International Commercial Contracts*, available at www.unidroit.org/english/principles/contracts/main.htm, visited 22 May 2007.
International Law Commission, *Draft Articles on the Law of Treaties with Commentaries* adopted by the International Law Commission at its eighteenth session, *Yearbook of the International Law Commission, 1966*, vol. II, http://untreaty.un.org/ilc/texts/instruments/english/commentaries/1_1_1966.pdf, visited 22 May 2007.
Jennings, R. and A. Watts (1996), *Oppenheim's International Law*, 9th edn, Vol 1, London: Longman.
Kaufmann, E. (1911), *Das Wesen des Völkerrechts und die Clausula*, rebus sic stantibus, Tübingen: Mohr.
Kelsen, H. (1944), 'The Principle of Sovereign Equality of States as a Basis for International Organization', *Yale Law Journal*, 53(2), 207–220.
Lempert, R., S. Bankes and S. Popper (2003), *Shaping the Next One Hundred Years: New Methods for Quantitative, Long-term Policy Analysis*, Santa Monica: Rand Corporation.
Mahoney, P. and C. Sanchirico (2003), 'Norms, Repeated Games, and the Role of Law', *California Law Review*, 91(5), 1281–1329.
Moss, S. (2002), 'Policy Analysis from First Principles', *Proceedings of the National Academy of Science USA*, 99 (Suppl. 3), 7267–7274.
Nahlik, S. (1971), 'The Grounds of Invalidity and Termination of Treaties', *American Journal of International Law*, 65(4), 736–756.
Nassar, N. (1995), *Sanctity of Contracts Revisited: A Study in the Theory and Practice of International Commercial Transactions*, Dordrecht: Martinus Nijhoff Publishers.
Malanczuk, P. (1997), *Akehurst's Modern Introduction to International Law*, 7th edn, London: Routledge.
McNair, A. (1927), 'Equality in International Law', *Michigan Law Review*, 26(2), 131–152.
Nelson, J. (2006), 'The Application of the International Law of State Succession to the United States: A Reassessment of the Treaty between the Republic of Texas and the Cherokee Indians', *Duke Journal of Comparative and International Law*, 17(1), 1–47.

Panagariya, A. (2002), 'Developing Countries at Doha: A Political Economy Analysis', *The World Economy*, 25(9), 1205–1233.
Schachter, O. (1991), *International Law in Theory and Practice*, Dordrecht: Martinus Nijhoff Publishers.
Teubner, G. (1998), 'Legal Irritants: Good Faith in British Law or How Unifying Law Ends Up in New Divergences', *Modern Law Review*, 61(1), 11–32.
The Temple of Preah Vihear, International Court of Justice Reports, 26 May 1961.
Thomas, A. and A. Thomas (1972), *The Concept of Aggression in International Law*, Dallas: Southern Methodist University Press.
UN Doc A/CONF 39/26, Declaration on the Prohibition of Military, Political and Economic Coercion in the Conclusion of Treaties, annexed to the Final Act of the Vienna Conference on the Law of Treaties.
UNIDROIT, *Commentary to its Principles*, http://unidroit.org/english/principles/contracts/principles 2004/integralversionprinciples 2004-e.pdf.
Virally, M. (1983), 'Review Essay; Good Faith in Public International Law', *American Journal of International Law*, 77(1), 130–134.
von Teichman, C. (1983), 'Germany, Federal Republic', in D. Campbell (ed.), *Legal Aspects of Doing Business in Western Europe*, St Paul: Kluwer.
Williams v Walker-Thomas Furniture Co, 350 F.2d 445 (DC Cir. 1965).
Wolford v Powers (1882) 85 Ind.
WT/DS2/AB/R (1996), *United States – Standards for Reformulated and Conventional Gasoline*, Geneva: World Trade Organization.
WT/DS8/AB/R (1996), *Japan – Taxes on Alcoholic Beverages*, Geneva: World Trade Organization.
WT/DS58/AB/R (1998), *US – Import Prohibition of Certain Shrimp and Shrimp Products*, Geneva: World Trade Organization.

Index